GW01403052

Ray Ilan

Breaking LGBTQ Barriers in Sykarin – Unfiltered

Kiara Chowdhury

ISBN: 9781779697790
Imprint: Telephasic Workshop
Copyright © 2024 Kiara Chowdhury.
All Rights Reserved.

Contents

1.1 The Dawn of Ray Ilan

In the small town of Sykarin, where the sun rises with a hint of nostalgia and the scent of possibility, a legend began to take shape. Ray Ilan, a name that would soon resonate through the halls of activism, was born into a world that often felt constricting, a world where conformity ruled and individuality was seen as a threat. This section delves into the formative years of Ray Ilan, exploring the complexities of his upbringing, the discovery of his true identity, and the initial sparks that ignited his passion for LGBTQ activism.

1.1.1 Ray Ilan's Upbringing in Sykarin

Ray Ilan's childhood in Sykarin was marked by the juxtaposition of picturesque landscapes and societal limitations. Nestled between rolling hills and vibrant meadows, the town presented an idyllic facade. However, beneath this surface lay a rigid adherence to traditional norms, where deviation from the norm was met with skepticism and, at times, hostility. Ray was raised in a modest household, where love was abundant but understanding was often overshadowed by the weight of societal expectations.

The dynamics within Ray's family played a crucial role in shaping his identity. His parents, though well-meaning, struggled to comprehend the complexities of their son's emerging identity. In a society that often equated masculinity with stoicism and femininity with weakness, Ray found himself at odds with the very essence of his being. This internal conflict manifested in a longing for acceptance, a desire to break free from the chains of expectation that bound him.

1.1.2 Discovering His True Identity and Facing Societal Expectations

The journey of self-discovery is rarely linear, and for Ray, it was no different. As he navigated the tumultuous waters of adolescence, he began to grapple with the realization that he did not fit neatly into the boxes society had constructed. The moment of clarity came during a seemingly innocuous school assembly, where a guest speaker—a local LGBTQ activist—shared their story of struggle and triumph. Ray felt an undeniable connection, as if the speaker's words resonated with the very core of his being.

This awakening was not without its challenges. Ray faced the harsh realities of a world that often marginalized those who dared to be different. The whispers in the hallways, the judgmental glances, and the isolation he experienced were constant reminders of the societal barriers he would have to confront. Yet, it was within this crucible of adversity that Ray's resolve began to forge.

1.1.3 Ray's First Encounter with LGBTQ Activism

Ray's first foray into LGBTQ activism occurred during his sophomore year of high school, when he attended a local pride event. The vibrant colors, the palpable energy, and the overwhelming sense of community enveloped him like a warm embrace. For the first time, Ray felt seen and understood. The event was not just a celebration of identity; it was a powerful statement against the oppressive forces that sought to silence voices like his.

Inspired by the courage displayed by others, Ray began to engage with local activist groups. He attended meetings, participated in discussions, and slowly began to find his voice. The camaraderie he experienced with fellow activists was transformative, reinforcing the notion that he was not alone in his struggle. It was during these formative encounters that Ray realized the power of collective action and the importance of standing up for oneself and others.

1.1.4 The Catalyst That Ignited Ray's Passion for Breaking Barriers

The true catalyst for Ray's activism came in the form of a personal tragedy. A close friend, who had also been navigating their own journey of self-acceptance, faced severe bullying and ultimately took their own life. This heartbreaking event shattered Ray's world, igniting a fire within him that could not be extinguished. The pain of loss transformed into a fierce determination to advocate for change, to ensure that no one else would have to endure such suffering in silence.

In the aftermath, Ray channeled his grief into action. He organized vigils, spoke at schools, and began to craft a message that resonated with both LGBTQ individuals and allies. His ability to articulate the struggles faced by the community, coupled with his personal narrative, became a powerful tool for advocacy. Ray's journey was no longer just about self-discovery; it was about creating a legacy of hope and resilience for those who would come after him.

1.1.5 Ray's Journey of Self-Discovery and Acceptance

As Ray continued to immerse himself in activism, he embarked on a profound journey of self-discovery and acceptance. He began to embrace his identity fully, shedding the layers of shame and fear that had once held him captive. This transformation was not instantaneous; it required vulnerability and courage. Ray learned that acceptance begins within, and that true empowerment comes from embracing one's authentic self.

Through workshops, support groups, and personal reflection, Ray honed his understanding of his identity. He explored the intersections of race, gender, and sexuality, recognizing the complexities that shaped his experience. This introspective journey allowed Ray to not only accept himself but also to become a beacon of hope for others grappling with similar struggles.

1.1.6 The Impact of Ray's Upbringing on His Activism

The impact of Ray's upbringing on his activism cannot be overstated. The challenges he faced in Sykarin instilled in him a deep sense of empathy and a commitment to inclusivity. Ray understood that the fight for LGBTQ rights was not just about one identity; it was about dismantling the systems of oppression that affected marginalized communities as a whole.

Ray's experiences in Sykarin shaped his approach to activism, emphasizing the importance of community, education, and dialogue. He recognized that breaking barriers required not only challenging societal norms but also fostering understanding among diverse groups. Ray's upbringing, marked by both struggle and resilience, became the foundation upon which he built his activism—a testament to the power of transformation and the relentless pursuit of justice.

In conclusion, the dawn of Ray Ilan was not just the beginning of an individual's journey; it marked the inception of a movement. Through the lens of his experiences in Sykarin, Ray emerged as a force for change, ready to challenge the status quo and redefine what it means to be an LGBTQ activist. This chapter sets the stage for the remarkable evolution of Ray Ilan, a journey that would transcend personal struggles and ignite a revolution in the fight for equality.

1.1 The Dawn of Ray Ilan

The story of Ray Ilan begins in the small town of Sykarin, a place where tradition and conformity often overshadowed individuality. In this seemingly quiet town, the seeds of a revolution were being sown, and they would soon sprout into a vibrant movement led by none other than Ray Ilan himself.

1.1.1 Ray Ilan's Upbringing in the Small Town of Sykarin

Born into a family that valued conventional norms, Ray's early life was characterized by a struggle between societal expectations and his emerging identity. The picturesque streets of Sykarin, lined with quaint houses and small businesses, belied the turbulent journey that lay ahead for young Ray. He was a dreamer in a world that often discouraged dreams that deviated from the norm.

1.1.2 Discovering His True Identity and Facing Societal Expectations

As Ray grew, so did his awareness of his differences. He often felt like a puzzle piece that didn't quite fit into the established picture of masculinity that surrounded him. The realization of his identity as a member of the LGBTQ community was both liberating and daunting. It was a journey fraught with emotional turmoil, as Ray grappled with the fear of rejection from his family and friends.

$$\text{Identity} = \text{Self-Acceptance} + \text{Courage} - \text{Fear} \tag{1}$$

This equation encapsulates Ray's internal struggle. The path to self-acceptance required immense courage, often overshadowed by the fear of societal rejection.

1.1.3 Ray's First Encounter with LGBTQ Activism

Ray's first brush with activism came unexpectedly during a local pride parade. The colorful banners and the palpable sense of community ignited a fire within him. He witnessed individuals expressing themselves freely, celebrating their identities without fear. It was a stark contrast to the subdued existence he had known in Sykarin. This moment marked the beginning of Ray's transformation from a passive observer to an active participant in the fight for LGBTQ rights.

1.1.4 The Catalyst that Ignited Ray's Passion for Breaking Barriers

The catalyst for Ray's activism was a tragic incident that shook the foundations of Sykarin. A young LGBTQ individual faced harassment that escalated into violence, leaving the community reeling. This event served as a wake-up call for Ray, compelling him to take a stand. He realized that silence was complicity and that he could no longer remain on the sidelines.

1.1.5 Ray's Journey of Self-Discovery and Acceptance

Ray's journey of self-discovery was not linear; it was filled with ups and downs. He sought solace in literature, devouring books that explored themes of identity, love, and acceptance. Authors like James Baldwin and Audre Lorde became his guiding lights, inspiring him to embrace his truth unapologetically.

$$\text{Self-Discovery} = \text{Exploration} + \text{Reflection} + \text{Community} \tag{2}$$

This equation illustrates the multifaceted nature of self-discovery. Exploration of the world around him, deep reflection on his experiences, and the support of a burgeoning community were essential components of Ray's growth.

1.1.6 The Impact of Ray's Upbringing on His Activism

Ray's upbringing, with its strict adherence to tradition, profoundly shaped his approach to activism. It instilled in him a fierce determination to challenge the status quo. His experiences of feeling like an outsider fueled his passion for creating inclusive spaces where everyone could feel safe and accepted.

The juxtaposition of his conservative background and his progressive ideals made Ray a unique voice in the Sykarin LGBTQ community. He understood the struggles faced by those who felt marginalized and used his platform to amplify their voices.

In conclusion, the dawn of Ray Ilan was marked by a series of transformative experiences that shaped him into an unstoppable force for change. His journey from a small-town boy grappling with his identity to a passionate activist ready to break barriers was just beginning. The stage was set for Ray to rise, and Sykarin would never be the same again.

ERROR. thisXsection() returned an empty string with textbook depth = 3.

ERROR. thisXsection() returned an empty string with textbook depth = 3.

ERROR. thisXsection() returned an empty string with textbook depth = 3.

Discovering his true identity and facing societal expectations

In the small town of Sykarin, where the sun rises over the horizon with an unyielding brightness, young Ray Ilan found himself at a crossroads—one that would define his existence and reshape the very fabric of his community. The journey to self-discovery is often fraught with challenges, but for Ray, it was a battle against the expectations imposed by society, family, and the internalized norms of masculinity that loomed like a shadow over his burgeoning identity.

From an early age, Ray was acutely aware of the dichotomy between his authentic self and the persona he was expected to embody. This conflict is not uncommon among LGBTQ individuals, who often grapple with the societal scripts that dictate how one should behave based on their gender and sexual orientation. The theory of gender performativity, proposed by Judith Butler, suggests that gender is not an inherent trait but rather a series of performances shaped by societal expectations. Ray's experiences echoed this theory as he navigated the complex landscape of identity formation.

$$G = P(T) + S(E) \tag{3}$$

Where:

- G = Gender Identity

- $P(T)$ = Performance of Traits

- $S(E)$ = Societal Expectations

Ray's struggle began in the confines of his home, where traditional values dictated a rigid understanding of masculinity. His father, a man of few words but many expectations, envisioned a future for Ray filled with athletic achievements and conventional success. Yet, as Ray's interests began to diverge from these expectations—favoring dance and art over football and hunting—he felt the weight of disappointment pressing down on him. The societal expectation that boys should be tough and emotionless clashed violently with Ray's innate sensitivity and creativity.

In school, the pressure intensified. The environment was a microcosm of societal norms, where heteronormative ideals were upheld through both overt and subtle means. Bullying became a constant companion for Ray, a harsh reminder of the price of nonconformity. This phenomenon aligns with the concept of homophobia as a tool for enforcing conformity within social groups. Studies show that individuals who deviate from established norms often face ostracism, which can lead to detrimental effects on mental health.

$$M = \frac{D}{R} \tag{4}$$

Where:

- M = Mental Health Impact

- D = Degree of Nonconformity

- R = Resilience Factors

For Ray, the degree of nonconformity he experienced was high, leading to significant mental health challenges, including anxiety and depression. The resilience factors—support from a few close friends and a passion for creative expression—became his lifeline. It was through art that Ray began to articulate his feelings and experiences, channeling his pain into vibrant colors and bold strokes on canvas.

The turning point in Ray's journey came during a particularly challenging year in high school. He stumbled upon a local LGBTQ youth group, a sanctuary for individuals like him who were also grappling with their identities. Here, he

discovered the power of community and the importance of shared experiences. The group provided a space where vulnerability was met with understanding, and where discussions about identity, sexuality, and societal expectations became a source of strength rather than shame.

As Ray began to embrace his identity, he also encountered the concept of intersectionality, as coined by Kimberlé Crenshaw. This theory emphasizes that individuals experience overlapping social identities—such as race, gender, and sexual orientation—that create unique modes of discrimination and privilege. For Ray, being a queer person of color in a predominantly conservative town complicated his journey. He recognized that his struggle was not isolated; it was part of a larger narrative that encompassed the experiences of many others.

Ray's journey of self-discovery was not linear. There were setbacks, moments of doubt, and instances where the societal expectations threatened to pull him back into the shadows. However, each challenge fortified his resolve. He began to understand that authenticity was not merely a personal endeavor but a revolutionary act. By living his truth, he was dismantling the very barriers that sought to confine him.

In embracing his identity, Ray also became acutely aware of the responsibility that came with it. He realized that societal change was not just about personal acceptance; it was about challenging the status quo. The catalyst for his activism was ignited by the realization that his journey could inspire others to break free from the chains of societal expectations. This realization marked the beginning of his transformation from a young man seeking acceptance to a fierce advocate for LGBTQ rights in Sykarin.

Thus, Ray's path to discovering his true identity was not merely a personal quest; it was a profound confrontation with societal expectations that would ultimately empower him to become a beacon of hope for others navigating similar struggles. His story is a testament to the resilience of the human spirit and the transformative power of self-acceptance in the face of adversity.

Ray's first encounter with LGBTQ activism

Ray Ilan's first encounter with LGBTQ activism was not a moment of grandiosity; rather, it was a subtle yet profound awakening that would shape his identity and purpose. Growing up in the small town of Sykarin, Ray was often surrounded by a culture steeped in traditional values and societal norms that left little room for deviation from the expected. The first flicker of activism ignited during a local community event—a seemingly innocuous gathering at the town hall where discussions about community issues were held.

The Catalyst of Awareness

At this event, Ray overheard a group of individuals discussing the challenges faced by LGBTQ people in Sykarin. Their voices were filled with passion and frustration, speaking about discrimination, lack of representation, and the urgent need for change. This was Ray's first exposure to the realities of LGBTQ life beyond his own experiences. The stories shared resonated deeply with him, awakening a sense of solidarity that he had not fully recognized before. It was a moment that could be described using the theory of Social Identity, which posits that individuals derive part of their self-concept from their perceived membership in social groups. Ray realized that he was not alone; he was part of a larger community that was fighting for recognition and rights.

The Turning Point

The turning point came when Ray met a local LGBTQ activist named Jamie, who was charismatic and fearless. Jamie introduced Ray to the concept of activism as a means of empowerment. They explained how activism was not just about protests and loud voices but also about education, awareness, and building a community. This was a pivotal moment for Ray, as he began to understand that activism could take many forms, including art, dialogue, and personal storytelling.

Ray was introduced to the idea of intersectionality, a term coined by Kimberlé Crenshaw, which emphasizes how different aspects of a person's social and political identities might combine to create unique modes of discrimination and privilege. Ray realized that his own experiences of marginalization were intertwined with broader societal issues, including race, class, and gender. This understanding would later influence his approach to activism, as he sought to create inclusive spaces that recognized the diversity within the LGBTQ community.

The First Steps into Activism

Motivated by Jamie's encouragement, Ray took his first steps into activism by attending local LGBTQ meetings and forums. These gatherings were often held in the backrooms of coffee shops, where small groups of passionate individuals shared their experiences and strategized on how to effect change. It was here that Ray learned about the importance of grassroots organizing and the power of collective action. The discussions often revolved around pressing issues such as the need for anti-discrimination laws, healthcare access for LGBTQ individuals, and the representation of LGBTQ stories in local media.

Ray's initial involvement was modest; he started by volunteering for events and helping with outreach initiatives. However, his commitment grew as he witnessed the impact of their efforts. For instance, during a local pride event, Ray helped distribute flyers that informed attendees about their rights and available resources. The joy and gratitude expressed by those who received the information fueled his desire to be more involved.

Challenges Faced

Despite the enthusiasm, Ray quickly learned that activism was not without its challenges. The backlash from conservative factions within Sykarin was palpable. Activists often faced threats and hostility, and discussions about LGBTQ rights were met with resistance. Ray experienced this firsthand during a town hall meeting where he spoke about the need for LGBTQ-inclusive policies. The backlash was immediate, with some community members shouting him down and others dismissing his concerns as irrelevant. This experience highlighted the harsh realities of activism and the emotional toll it could take on individuals fighting for their rights.

The Role of Community

Yet, it was within this adversity that Ray found strength. The support of the LGBTQ community became a lifeline for him. He learned the importance of allyship and the necessity of building coalitions with other marginalized groups. The activism he witnessed was not just about LGBTQ rights; it was intertwined with broader social justice movements. Ray began to understand that true activism required a multifaceted approach, addressing issues of race, class, and gender alongside LGBTQ rights.

In conclusion, Ray's first encounter with LGBTQ activism was a transformative experience that set the stage for his future endeavors. It was a journey marked by discovery, resilience, and the realization that activism is not just a solitary endeavor but a collective movement. This foundational experience laid the groundwork for Ray's evolution into a formidable force in the LGBTQ community, igniting a passion that would drive him to break barriers and challenge societal norms for years to come.

The catalyst that ignited Ray's passion for breaking barriers

In the small town of Sykarin, where conformity often overshadowed individuality, Ray Ilan's journey towards activism was ignited by a series of pivotal moments that crystallized his understanding of identity and societal expectations. The catalyst for

Ray's passion was not just a singular event but rather a confluence of experiences that challenged his perception of self and the world around him.

The first significant moment occurred during Ray's high school years, a period characterized by the intense struggle of adolescence. Ray discovered a hidden talent for public speaking, which he initially used to articulate his thoughts on various subjects, including the importance of acceptance and understanding. However, it was during a school debate on the topic of LGBTQ rights that Ray truly felt the fire of activism ignite within him. The heated arguments presented by his peers, often steeped in ignorance and prejudice, struck a chord deep within him. This debate was not merely an academic exercise; it was a reflection of the societal barriers that LGBTQ individuals faced daily.

To illustrate this, consider the framework of **Social Identity Theory**, which posits that an individual's self-concept is derived from perceived membership in social groups. Ray realized that his identity as a member of the LGBTQ community was not only personal but also political. The realization that societal norms were often at odds with the authenticity he yearned for became a driving force in his life. The equation governing this dynamic can be represented as:

$$\text{Self-Identity} = f(\text{Social Group Membership, Societal Norms})$$

where f represents the function that describes the interaction between self-identity and external societal pressures.

The second catalyst was the influence of a local LGBTQ organization that held a community event in Sykarin. Ray attended out of curiosity, but what he encountered was a vibrant space filled with individuals who embraced their identities unapologetically. The event showcased stories of resilience and triumph against adversity, and it was here that Ray met several activists who became his mentors. They shared their journeys, revealing the hardships they faced and the strategies they employed to challenge societal norms. This exposure to lived experiences was transformative, as Ray began to understand the importance of community and solidarity in the fight for equality.

Ray's mentors often spoke of the **Altruism Theory**, which suggests that individuals are motivated to help others out of a selfless concern for the well-being of others. This resonated deeply with Ray, as he recognized that his struggles were not isolated but part of a larger narrative that needed to be told. The equation representing this motivation can be articulated as:

$$\text{Motivation to Act} = \text{Empathy} \times \text{Perceived Injustice}$$

This equation illustrates that Ray's growing empathy for the struggles of others, coupled with his recognition of injustice, catalyzed his desire to act.

The third catalyst was a particularly poignant incident that took place in his community. A close friend of Ray's, who had recently come out, faced severe backlash from their family and peers. This friend's experience of rejection and bullying was a visceral reminder of the harsh realities that LGBTQ individuals often endure. Witnessing this injustice firsthand ignited a fierce determination within Ray to not only support his friend but to advocate for broader change. This incident crystallized Ray's understanding of the urgent need for advocacy and support systems for marginalized communities.

In this context, Ray began to explore the concept of **Intersectionality**, as coined by Kimberlé Crenshaw, which emphasizes the interconnected nature of social categorizations and how they create overlapping systems of discrimination or disadvantage. Ray recognized that his friend's experience was compounded by various factors, including socioeconomic status and race, which further marginalized their voice. This understanding deepened Ray's commitment to breaking barriers, not just for himself but for all who faced discrimination.

Ray's journey towards activism was thus fueled by a combination of personal experiences, exposure to community narratives, and the stark realities faced by those around him. Each catalyst acted as a building block, reinforcing his resolve to challenge societal norms and advocate for LGBTQ rights. This passion would eventually lead him to become a formidable force in the fight for equality in Sykarin, breaking barriers not only for himself but for countless others who dared to dream of a more inclusive world.

In conclusion, the ignition of Ray's passion for activism can be encapsulated by the synthesis of personal identity, community experiences, and the recognition of systemic injustices. As he continued to navigate the complexities of his identity, these catalysts propelled him into a life dedicated to dismantling the barriers that sought to confine him and others like him. The journey had just begun, but the fire within Ray was unmistakable, setting the stage for a revolution that would resonate far beyond the borders of Sykarin.

Ray's journey of self-discovery and acceptance

Ray Ilan's journey of self-discovery and acceptance was not merely a personal odyssey; it was a profound exploration of identity shaped by the societal expectations of Sykarin. Growing up in a small town, Ray faced the dual challenge of understanding his own identity while navigating the rigid norms imposed by his community. This section delves into the complexities of his journey, framed through the lens of psychological theories and real-world examples.

At the core of Ray's journey was the concept of **identity formation**, as articulated by Erik Erikson in his psychosocial development theory. Erikson posits that individuals undergo a series of stages throughout their lives, with each stage presenting a unique conflict that contributes to their identity. For Ray, the pivotal stage of *identity vs. role confusion* emerged during his adolescence. This period was characterized by an intense struggle to reconcile his emerging sexual identity with the expectations of his family and peers.

The societal expectations in Sykarin were steeped in traditional norms, often marginalizing those who deviated from the heterosexual narrative. Ray's initial realization of his sexual orientation was met with confusion and fear. He grappled with the fear of rejection and the potential loss of familial and social support. This internal conflict is well-documented in literature surrounding LGBTQ identity formation, which suggests that individuals often experience a phase of *internalized homophobia*, where societal stigma leads to self-doubt and shame.

As Ray navigated these tumultuous waters, he found solace in the works of LGBTQ activists and authors who articulated similar struggles. Figures such as James Baldwin and Audre Lorde became beacons of hope, providing Ray with the language and framework to understand his own experiences. Inspired by their narratives, Ray began to embrace his identity more fully, recognizing that self-acceptance was a crucial step in his journey.

A significant turning point in Ray's journey occurred during his first LGBTQ pride event in a nearby city. The vibrant celebration of diversity and acceptance starkly contrasted with the oppressive atmosphere of Sykarin. This event served as a catalyst for Ray, igniting a passion for activism and community engagement. He realized that acceptance was not solely an internal process but also a collective one, where solidarity and support from others played a vital role.

In psychological terms, this experience aligns with the concept of **social identity theory**, proposed by Henri Tajfel. This theory posits that an individual's self-concept is derived from their perceived membership in social groups. For Ray, participating in the pride event allowed him to redefine his identity within a supportive community, fostering a sense of belonging that had previously eluded him.

Despite this newfound sense of belonging, Ray's journey was not without its challenges. Upon returning to Sykarin, he faced backlash from some community members who viewed his activism as a threat to traditional values. This external pressure led to moments of doubt and fear, prompting Ray to question whether he could truly be accepted in a society that often rejected those who were different.

To combat these feelings, Ray engaged in what psychologists refer to as **cognitive restructuring**, a technique used in cognitive-behavioral therapy to challenge and change unhelpful thoughts. Ray began to reframe his internal dialogue, viewing challenges as opportunities for growth rather than insurmountable obstacles. This shift in perspective was instrumental in fortifying his resolve to embrace his identity openly.

In addition to cognitive strategies, Ray sought out mentorship within the LGBTQ community. He connected with established activists who provided guidance and support, helping him navigate the complexities of activism and identity. This mentorship not only reinforced Ray's sense of self but also highlighted the importance of community in the journey of self-acceptance.

Ray's journey culminated in a public declaration of his identity during a local town hall meeting, where he shared his experiences and advocated for LGBTQ rights. This moment was a significant milestone, representing not only his personal acceptance but also a challenge to the societal norms that had long dictated the narrative in Sykarin. His speech resonated with many, inspiring others to embrace their identities and fostering a sense of empowerment within the community.

Ultimately, Ray's journey of self-discovery and acceptance was a multifaceted process, marked by personal struggles, community engagement, and a commitment to advocacy. His experiences reflect the broader challenges faced by LGBTQ individuals in similar environments, underscoring the importance of acceptance, both from within and from the community at large. Through resilience and determination, Ray not only embraced his identity but also became a powerful force for change in Sykarin, breaking down barriers and paving the way for future generations.

In summary, Ray Ilan's journey serves as a testament to the transformative power of self-acceptance and the critical role of community support in navigating the complexities of identity. His story is a reminder that while the path to acceptance may be fraught with challenges, it is also rich with opportunities for growth and connection.

The impact of Ray's upbringing on his activism

Ray Ilan's journey as a pioneering LGBTQ activist in Sykarin is deeply intertwined with his upbringing. Growing up in a small town, Ray was constantly surrounded by the conservative values and societal expectations that often stifled individuality and self-expression. This environment played a crucial role in shaping Ray's identity and igniting his passion for activism.

The Influence of a Conservative Environment

From an early age, Ray experienced the weight of societal norms that dictated how individuals should behave based on their gender and sexual orientation. The rigid expectations imposed by his community created a dichotomy between Ray's true self and the persona he felt compelled to present to the world. This internal conflict is a common theme in LGBTQ narratives, where individuals often grapple with their identities in the face of societal rejection.

The psychological impact of this upbringing can be analyzed through the lens of *Erik Erikson's psychosocial development theory*, which posits that individuals navigate various stages of development, each characterized by a specific conflict. Ray's struggle for identity during adolescence aligns with Erikson's stage of *Identity vs. Role Confusion*, where he faced challenges in forming a coherent sense of self amidst societal pressure.

$$\text{Identity Crisis} = \text{Self-Concept} - \text{Societal Expectations} \tag{5}$$

Ray's upbringing in Sykarin served as a catalyst for his activism. The feelings of isolation and confusion he experienced motivated him to seek community and support among others who faced similar struggles. This need for connection led Ray to his first encounter with LGBTQ activism, where he discovered a space that celebrated diversity and acceptance.

Catalysts for Activism

The turning point in Ray's life came when he witnessed the struggles of a close friend who faced discrimination for their sexual orientation. This event acted as a wake-up call, highlighting the urgent need for change within his community. Ray's response to this injustice was not only personal but also political, as he began to understand the systemic nature of oppression faced by LGBTQ individuals.

Ray's experiences can be framed within *social identity theory*, which emphasizes the importance of group membership in shaping individual identity. By aligning himself with the LGBTQ community, Ray found a sense of belonging that empowered him to challenge societal norms.

$$\text{Social Identity} = \text{Personal Identity} + \text{Group Membership} \tag{6}$$

This newfound identity fueled Ray's determination to break barriers and advocate for change. His upbringing, marked by adversity, provided him with a unique perspective on the challenges faced by marginalized groups. Ray's activism was not merely about self-advocacy; it was about amplifying the voices of those who were often silenced.

The Role of Resilience

Ray's upbringing instilled in him a sense of resilience that became a hallmark of his activism. The challenges he faced in his formative years taught him the importance of perseverance and the power of community support. This resilience is reflected in his approach to activism, where he often employed unconventional methods to raise awareness and challenge stereotypes.

For instance, Ray organized local events that combined art, music, and education to create safe spaces for LGBTQ individuals. These events served as both a platform for expression and a means of fostering community. By drawing on his personal experiences, Ray was able to connect with others on a deeper level, transforming his pain into a source of strength.

Legacy of Upbringing in Activism

The impact of Ray's upbringing on his activism is evident in his holistic approach to LGBTQ rights. He recognized that the struggles faced by individuals were not isolated incidents but rather part of a larger societal issue. Ray's commitment to intersectionality—understanding how various forms of discrimination overlap—was influenced by his own experiences of marginalization.

As Ray continued to rise as a local LGBTQ activist icon, he remained grounded in the lessons learned from his upbringing. His journey of self-discovery and acceptance became a beacon of hope for others navigating similar challenges. Ray's activism was not just about breaking barriers for himself; it was about dismantling the very structures that perpetuated inequality.

In conclusion, Ray Ilan's upbringing in Sykarin was a fundamental factor in shaping his identity and activism. The struggles he faced in a conservative environment fueled his passion for change, leading him to become an unstoppable force in the fight for LGBTQ rights. His resilience, coupled with a commitment to community and intersectionality, laid the foundation for a transformative legacy that continues to inspire future generations of activists.

Becoming an Unstoppable Force

Ray's first steps into the LGBTQ community

In the small, unassuming town of Sykarin, where the horizon stretched wide but the minds of its inhabitants often remained narrow, Ray Ilan took his first steps into the vibrant yet tumultuous world of the LGBTQ community. This journey was not merely a personal exploration; it was a radical awakening that would challenge the very fabric of societal norms.

Ray's first encounter with the LGBTQ community occurred at a local pride event, a modest gathering that felt like a pulse of life in a town otherwise dominated by conformity. The air was thick with anticipation and the scent of colorful balloons, but more importantly, it was infused with a sense of belonging that Ray had long craved. This event was not just a celebration; it was a declaration of existence, a bold statement that love transcends boundaries, and a vivid reminder of the struggles faced by those who dare to be themselves.

$$\text{Belonging} = \text{Identity} + \text{Community} \tag{7}$$

This equation encapsulates the essence of Ray's experience. His identity, once a source of internal conflict, began to merge seamlessly with the community around him. The LGBTQ community in Sykarin, though small, was a tapestry of diverse identities, each thread contributing to the rich narrative of resistance against oppression. Ray found solace in the stories shared, the laughter exchanged, and the tears shed. He realized that he was not alone; others had walked similar paths, facing the same societal expectations and prejudices.

However, Ray's entry into this community was not without its challenges. The societal backdrop of Sykarin was steeped in traditional values, and the LGBTQ community often found itself at odds with the prevailing norms. Discrimination, stigma, and ignorance were rampant, creating an environment where acceptance was a luxury few could afford. Ray encountered individuals who had been ostracized by their families, bullied in schools, and marginalized in their workplaces. These stories were not just anecdotes; they were stark reminders of the harsh realities faced by many.

To navigate these complexities, Ray adopted a multifaceted approach to activism. He understood that to foster change, he needed to build bridges between the LGBTQ community and the broader population of Sykarin. This meant engaging in dialogue, educating allies, and challenging misconceptions. Ray often recalled the words of Harvey Milk, who famously said, "You gotta give them hope."

This became a guiding principle for Ray as he sought to inspire hope in the hearts of those around him.

One of Ray's first initiatives was to organize workshops aimed at educating the public about LGBTQ issues. He collaborated with local schools, community centers, and even places of worship, aiming to dismantle the walls of ignorance that separated the LGBTQ community from the rest of Sykarin. The workshops addressed topics such as gender identity, sexual orientation, and the importance of empathy in fostering understanding.

$$\text{Awareness} \rightarrow \text{Empathy} \rightarrow \text{Acceptance} \tag{8}$$

The progression illustrated in this equation became evident as participants began to engage in meaningful conversations. Ray witnessed firsthand the transformation in attitudes as misconceptions were dispelled and empathy flourished. However, the path was fraught with resistance; some individuals were entrenched in their beliefs, unwilling to budge from their prejudices. Ray learned that change was often slow, requiring persistence, resilience, and an unwavering commitment to the cause.

Ray's early involvement in the LGBTQ community also ignited a passion for the arts as a medium for expression and activism. He recognized that art had the power to transcend barriers and convey messages that words alone could not. With this in mind, Ray collaborated with local artists to create murals that depicted the struggles and triumphs of the LGBTQ community. These vibrant pieces became a source of pride for many, serving as a visual representation of the community's resilience.

$$\text{Art} = \text{Expression} + \text{Activism} \tag{9}$$

Through these artistic endeavors, Ray found a voice not only for himself but for those who felt voiceless. He understood that representation mattered; seeing oneself reflected in art could validate experiences and foster a sense of belonging. Ray's murals became landmarks in Sykarin, sparking conversations and encouraging individuals to confront their biases.

As Ray continued to immerse himself in the LGBTQ community, he also faced personal challenges. The weight of societal expectations and the fear of rejection loomed large. He grappled with the duality of his existence—navigating a world that often felt hostile while yearning for acceptance and love. In these moments of vulnerability, Ray turned to his newfound friends within the community, finding solace in their shared experiences. Together, they formed a support network that became a lifeline for many.

Ultimately, Ray's first steps into the LGBTQ community were transformative, setting the stage for a lifelong commitment to activism. He emerged not only as a participant but as a leader, ready to challenge the status quo and advocate for change. His journey was just beginning, but the foundation had been laid—a foundation built on the principles of love, acceptance, and the unwavering belief that everyone deserves to live authentically.

In conclusion, Ray's initial foray into the LGBTQ community was a microcosm of the larger struggles faced by many individuals. It highlighted the importance of community, education, and the power of art as tools for activism. As Ray continued to break barriers, he carried with him the lessons learned during these formative experiences, shaping his identity as a fierce advocate for LGBTQ rights in Sykarin and beyond.

Challenges faced by LGBTQ individuals in Sykarin

In the small town of Sykarin, LGBTQ individuals encounter a myriad of challenges that stem from deeply ingrained societal norms and prejudices. These challenges manifest in various forms, affecting the mental health, social dynamics, and overall well-being of the LGBTQ community.

Social Stigma and Discrimination

One of the most significant challenges faced by LGBTQ individuals in Sykarin is social stigma. This stigma is often rooted in traditional beliefs and cultural norms that view non-heteronormative identities as deviant or abnormal. According to [?], social stigma can lead to internalized homophobia, where individuals may feel shame about their sexual orientation or gender identity, resulting in a diminished self-esteem and a reluctance to engage with the community.

Discrimination in everyday life is prevalent, as LGBTQ individuals may face hostility or exclusion in various settings, including workplaces, schools, and public spaces. For instance, a study by [?] highlights that individuals who identify as LGBTQ are more likely to experience harassment or violence compared to their heterosexual counterparts. In Sykarin, this discrimination can manifest in overt acts of aggression or subtle forms of exclusion, creating an environment where LGBTQ individuals feel unsafe or unwelcome.

Limited Access to Resources

Access to resources, including healthcare, mental health services, and legal protection, is another significant challenge for LGBTQ individuals in Sykarin. The lack of inclusive healthcare services can lead to inadequate support for LGBTQ individuals, particularly concerning sexual health and mental health. Research by [?] indicates that LGBTQ individuals often face barriers in accessing healthcare due to discrimination or lack of understanding from healthcare providers.

Moreover, the absence of legal protections against discrimination in employment and housing exacerbates the vulnerability of LGBTQ individuals. In Sykarin, the legal framework does not adequately safeguard against discrimination based on sexual orientation or gender identity, leaving LGBTQ individuals with little recourse in instances of unfair treatment. This legal invisibility can lead to economic instability and increased reliance on informal support networks.

Mental Health Implications

The compounded effects of social stigma, discrimination, and limited access to resources contribute to significant mental health challenges within the LGBTQ community in Sykarin. According to [?], minority stress theory posits that the chronic stress experienced by marginalized groups, such as LGBTQ individuals, can lead to higher rates of anxiety, depression, and suicidal ideation.

In Sykarin, the lack of acceptance and support can exacerbate feelings of isolation among LGBTQ individuals. Many may feel compelled to hide their identities, leading to a disconnection from their true selves and a sense of loneliness. This internal struggle can manifest in various ways, including substance abuse, self-harm, or even suicidal thoughts.

Cultural and Familial Pressures

Cultural and familial expectations often pose additional challenges for LGBTQ individuals in Sykarin. Many families in this region adhere to traditional values that prioritize heteronormative relationships, leading to potential rejection or ostracism of LGBTQ family members. This familial pressure can create an environment where individuals feel compelled to conform to societal expectations, often at the expense of their authentic selves.

An example of this can be seen in the experiences of LGBTQ youth, who may face immense pressure to conform to their family's expectations regarding relationships and gender roles. According to [?], parental acceptance is crucial for the mental health and well-being of LGBTQ youth. In Sykarin, the fear of rejection can prevent individuals from coming out, leading to prolonged periods of secrecy and self-denial.

Conclusion

In conclusion, the challenges faced by LGBTQ individuals in Sykarin are multifaceted, encompassing social stigma, limited access to resources, mental health implications, and cultural pressures. These barriers not only hinder the personal growth of individuals but also impede the overall progress of the LGBTQ community in the region. Addressing these challenges requires a concerted effort from both LGBTQ activists and allies to foster a more inclusive and accepting environment, ultimately paving the way for a brighter future where diversity is celebrated rather than stigmatized.

Ray's determination to make a difference

Ray Ilan's journey into the heart of LGBTQ activism was not merely a decision; it was a calling. This determination stemmed from a deep-seated understanding of the struggles faced by LGBTQ individuals in Sykarin, a small town where traditional norms often stifled diversity and self-expression. Ray's commitment to making a difference can be analyzed through various lenses, including personal motivation, societal challenges, and the theoretical frameworks that underpin activism.

Personal Motivation

At the core of Ray's determination was a personal narrative marked by adversity. Growing up in Sykarin, Ray witnessed firsthand the pain of isolation and discrimination that many in the LGBTQ community faced. This experience ignited a fire within him—a desire to not only advocate for himself but for others who felt voiceless. Ray often reflected on his childhood, stating:

> "I knew I was different, but I also knew I wasn't alone. I wanted to be the voice for those who felt they had none."

This sentiment encapsulated the essence of his activism. Ray's personal journey of self-acceptance and the desire to uplift others became the bedrock of his commitment to change.

Societal Challenges

Ray's determination was further fueled by the societal challenges that permeated Sykarin. The town was characterized by rigid gender roles and a conservative outlook that often marginalized LGBTQ individuals. Reports indicated that over

70% of LGBTQ youth in Sykarin experienced bullying or discrimination in schools, leading to severe mental health issues, including depression and anxiety [1].

To combat these issues, Ray recognized the necessity of confronting systemic barriers. He understood that activism required more than just passion; it needed a strategic approach. This realization led him to engage with local organizations, participate in community discussions, and ultimately form alliances with like-minded individuals who shared his vision for a more inclusive society.

Theoretical Frameworks

Ray's activism can be framed through several theoretical lenses, including Social Identity Theory and Intersectionality. Social Identity Theory posits that individuals derive a sense of self from their group memberships, which, in Ray's case, included his identity as a gay man and an advocate for LGBTQ rights [2]. This dual identity empowered Ray to channel his experiences into activism, as he sought to create spaces where others could embrace their identities without fear.

Intersectionality, a concept introduced by Kimberlé Crenshaw, further informed Ray's approach. He understood that the LGBTQ community is not monolithic; it encompasses a diverse range of identities influenced by race, class, and gender [3]. By acknowledging these intersections, Ray was able to tailor his activism to address the unique challenges faced by various subgroups within the LGBTQ community. For instance, he organized events specifically aimed at supporting LGBTQ people of color, recognizing that their experiences often differed from those of white LGBTQ individuals.

Examples of Activism

Ray's determination to make a difference manifested in numerous initiatives. One of his early projects was the establishment of the Sykarin Pride Coalition, a grassroots organization aimed at promoting LGBTQ visibility and rights. Under Ray's leadership, the coalition organized the first Pride parade in Sykarin, which drew over a thousand participants from various backgrounds. This event not only celebrated LGBTQ identities but also served as a platform for raising awareness about local issues, such as discrimination in housing and employment.

Furthermore, Ray spearheaded educational workshops in schools, focusing on LGBTQ history and rights. He collaborated with educators to develop curricula that included LGBTQ perspectives, challenging the traditional narratives that often excluded these voices. According to a survey conducted post-workshop, 85%

of students reported an increased understanding of LGBTQ issues, illustrating the tangible impact of Ray's efforts on the younger generation.

Conclusion

Ray Ilan's determination to make a difference was rooted in a combination of personal experience, societal challenges, and a theoretical understanding of activism. His journey exemplifies how individual narratives can inspire collective action and foster change. By confronting discrimination and advocating for inclusivity, Ray not only transformed his community but also set a precedent for future generations of LGBTQ activists. As he often stated:

> "Change begins with us, and it starts with the courage to stand up and speak out."

This unwavering commitment to making a difference continues to resonate, inspiring others to join the fight for equality and justice in Sykarin and beyond.

Bibliography

[1] Smith, J. (2022). *The State of LGBTQ Youth in Sykarin: A Report.* Sykarin Youth Advocacy Group.

[2] Tajfel, H. (1979). *Individuals and Groups in Social Psychology.* In: H. Tajfel (Ed.), Differentiation Between Social Groups: Studies in the Social Psychology of Intergroup Relations. Academic Press.

[3] Crenshaw, K. (1989). Demarginalizing the Intersection of Race and Sex: A Black Feminist Critique of Antidiscrimination Doctrine, Feminist Theory and Antiracist Politics. *University of Chicago Legal Forum,* 1989(1), 139-167.

The birth of Ray's signature rebellious style

Ray Ilan's journey into the world of LGBTQ activism was not just about advocating for rights; it was also about self-expression and redefining societal norms through personal style. In the conservative town of Sykarin, where conformity reigned supreme, Ray's emergence as a fashion icon was both a political statement and a personal rebellion. This section explores how Ray's signature rebellious style was born, the theories behind it, the societal problems it addressed, and its impact on the community.

Theoretical Foundations of Rebellion in Fashion

Fashion has long been a medium for self-expression, particularly within marginalized communities. According to the theory of *symbolic interactionism*, individuals create meaning through social interactions, and their attire plays a crucial role in this process [?]. Ray's style was a direct response to the rigid gender norms and expectations imposed by society. By embracing bold colors, eclectic patterns, and non-traditional silhouettes, Ray challenged the binary perception of gender and sexuality.

Societal Problems Addressed by Ray's Style

Ray's fashion choices were not merely aesthetic; they were laden with meaning. In Sykarin, LGBTQ individuals often faced discrimination and isolation. Ray's style served as a form of protest against the stigma surrounding queer identities. By dressing unapologetically, Ray communicated a powerful message: that self-acceptance and authenticity are paramount, regardless of societal expectations. This aligns with Judith Butler's concept of *gender performativity*, which posits that gender is not an innate quality but rather a performance shaped by societal norms [?].

Examples of Ray's Signature Style

Ray's signature look often included a mix of vintage and contemporary pieces, creating a visual narrative that was distinctly his own. For instance, he frequently paired oversized graphic tees with tailored blazers, combining elements of streetwear with high fashion. Accessories played a crucial role in Ray's style; he was known for his collection of statement jewelry and bold footwear, which he used to express his individuality.

One iconic outfit featured a bright pink leather jacket adorned with patches symbolizing LGBTQ rights, paired with distressed jeans and combat boots. This ensemble not only showcased Ray's fashion sense but also served as a conversation starter about LGBTQ issues in Sykarin. The jacket, in particular, became a symbol of resistance, representing the fight against oppression and the celebration of diversity.

The Impact of Ray's Rebellious Style on the Community

Ray's bold fashion choices inspired others in the LGBTQ community to embrace their identities and express themselves freely. As he became more visible, his style resonated with many who felt marginalized. Local LGBTQ youth began to adopt similar styles, creating a sense of solidarity and community. This phenomenon can be understood through the lens of *cultural appropriation* and *cultural exchange*, where marginalized groups reclaim elements of mainstream culture to assert their identities [?].

Ray's influence extended beyond personal style; it prompted discussions about the importance of representation in fashion. Local designers began to incorporate LGBTQ themes into their collections, fostering an environment where diversity was celebrated. Fashion shows featuring LGBTQ models became a platform for activism, highlighting the intersection of style and social justice.

Conclusion

The birth of Ray Ilan's signature rebellious style was not just about fashion; it was a powerful statement against conformity and a celebration of individuality. By challenging societal norms and embracing his authentic self, Ray inspired a movement within Sykarin that encouraged others to break free from the constraints of traditional gender roles. His style became a symbol of resistance, fostering a sense of community and empowerment among LGBTQ individuals. As Ray's influence grew, so did the understanding that fashion could be a catalyst for change, paving the way for future generations to express themselves without fear.

Ray's rise as a local LGBTQ activist icon

Ray Ilan's transformation into a local LGBTQ activist icon in Sykarin did not happen overnight. It was the culmination of his relentless pursuit of equality and justice, fueled by personal experiences and a deep-seated desire to challenge societal norms. This section explores the factors that contributed to Ray's rise, the challenges he faced, and the impact of his activism on the local LGBTQ community.

The Spark of Activism

Ray's initial foray into activism began with a series of small, yet impactful, community events. These gatherings served as safe spaces for individuals to share their experiences and struggles. Ray understood that the first step to becoming an activist was to create a sense of belonging among LGBTQ individuals in Sykarin. He organized open mic nights and discussion panels where community members could express their feelings without fear of judgment. This grassroots approach not only empowered participants but also helped Ray establish a network of allies who shared his vision for a more inclusive society.

Utilizing Social Media

In the digital age, social media became a powerful tool for Ray. Recognizing its potential, he leveraged platforms like Instagram, Twitter, and Facebook to amplify his message. His posts, often infused with humor and candidness, resonated with a wide audience. The hashtag #RayIlanRevolution quickly gained traction, serving as a rallying cry for those seeking change. Ray's ability to connect with people online allowed him to mobilize support for various initiatives, from pride marches to educational campaigns in local schools.

Challenging Stereotypes

One of the significant barriers Ray faced was the entrenched stereotypes surrounding LGBTQ individuals in Sykarin. Many viewed the community through a narrow lens, perpetuating harmful misconceptions. Ray took it upon himself to challenge these stereotypes head-on. He organized workshops that addressed common myths about LGBTQ individuals, providing factual information to dispel fears and prejudices. By engaging with local media, Ray ensured that the narrative surrounding LGBTQ issues was not solely defined by sensationalism but grounded in real stories and experiences.

The Power of Representation

Ray's rise as an icon was also marked by his commitment to representation. He understood that visibility was crucial in changing perceptions and fostering acceptance. By actively participating in local events and speaking engagements, Ray became a familiar face in Sykarin. He shared his journey of self-discovery and the challenges he faced, allowing others to see the human side of activism. This authenticity resonated deeply with the community, inspiring many to embrace their identities and advocate for their rights.

Building Coalitions

Ray recognized that true change required collaboration. He sought to build coalitions with other marginalized groups, understanding that intersectionality was vital in the fight for equality. By partnering with women's rights organizations, racial justice groups, and disability advocates, Ray created a united front against discrimination. These alliances not only strengthened the LGBTQ movement in Sykarin but also highlighted the interconnectedness of various social justice issues.

Local Media Coverage

As Ray's activism gained momentum, local media began to take notice. Coverage of his events and initiatives increased, further solidifying his status as an activist icon. Articles highlighting his work appeared in local newspapers, and he was invited to speak on radio shows. This media attention played a crucial role in legitimizing his efforts and attracting new supporters. Ray's ability to articulate the struggles of the LGBTQ community in Sykarin made him a sought-after voice in discussions about equality and human rights.

The Impact of Ray's Activism

Ray's rise as a local LGBTQ activist icon had a profound impact on the community. His efforts led to the establishment of the Sykarin LGBTQ Alliance, a nonprofit organization dedicated to advocating for LGBTQ rights and providing resources for individuals in need. The alliance became a cornerstone of the community, offering support groups, legal assistance, and educational programs.

Moreover, Ray's activism inspired a new generation of LGBTQ leaders in Sykarin. Many young individuals, emboldened by his example, stepped forward to advocate for their rights and the rights of others. Ray's influence extended beyond his immediate community, as he became a mentor for aspiring activists, encouraging them to harness their voices and fight for change.

Conclusion

In conclusion, Ray Ilan's rise as a local LGBTQ activist icon in Sykarin was the result of his unwavering dedication to equality and justice. Through grassroots organizing, effective use of social media, challenging stereotypes, and building coalitions, Ray not only transformed his own life but also the lives of countless others in his community. His legacy continues to inspire future generations, reminding them that activism is not just a fight for rights but a celebration of identity and humanity.

Ray's unique methods of raising awareness

Ray Ilan's approach to raising awareness for LGBTQ issues in Sykarin was as bold and unapologetic as the man himself. He understood that traditional methods of activism often fell short in capturing the attention of a society steeped in conservatism and prejudice. Thus, he devised a series of innovative strategies that not only educated but also entertained, engaging a broader audience in the fight for equality.

Creative Public Demonstrations

One of Ray's most effective methods was his use of creative public demonstrations. Rather than the typical protests, Ray organized vibrant flash mobs that combined dance, music, and theatrical performances. These events not only drew large crowds but also attracted media attention, allowing the message of LGBTQ rights to permeate the cultural zeitgeist of Sykarin.

For instance, during one memorable flash mob event titled "Dance for Diversity," participants donned colorful costumes and performed a choreographed routine in the town square. The performance culminated in a powerful spoken word piece that highlighted the struggles faced by LGBTQ individuals. This method of combining art with activism proved to be a game changer, as it transformed a mundane protest into a celebratory expression of identity and resilience.

Utilizing Social Media Platforms

In the digital age, Ray recognized the potential of social media as a powerful tool for advocacy. He leveraged platforms like Instagram, TikTok, and Twitter to share personal stories, highlight local LGBTQ events, and educate followers about issues affecting the community. His unique style, characterized by a blend of humor and authenticity, resonated with many, leading to a significant increase in engagement.

Ray's social media campaigns often featured hashtags that encouraged individuals to share their own stories. For example, the hashtag #SykarinPride became a viral sensation, with users posting about their experiences and struggles. This grassroots movement fostered a sense of belonging and solidarity within the LGBTQ community, while simultaneously raising awareness among allies and the broader public.

Innovative Workshops and Educational Programs

Understanding that education is a cornerstone of awareness, Ray initiated a series of workshops aimed at both LGBTQ individuals and the general public. These workshops tackled various topics, including the history of LGBTQ rights, the importance of intersectionality, and strategies for allyship.

One particularly impactful workshop was titled "Breaking the Binary," which focused on gender inclusivity and the spectrum of gender identities. Participants engaged in interactive activities that challenged traditional notions of gender, fostering an environment of acceptance and understanding. By equipping attendees with knowledge and tools, Ray empowered them to become advocates in their own right.

Collaborations with Local Artists and Influencers

Ray also understood the power of collaboration. He partnered with local artists, musicians, and influencers to amplify the message of LGBTQ rights. These collaborations often resulted in powerful visual art installations and performances that sparked conversations around LGBTQ issues.

For example, Ray collaborated with a local muralist to create a large-scale mural in the heart of Sykarin that depicted prominent LGBTQ figures and symbols of pride. This mural not only beautified the community but also served as a constant reminder of the ongoing struggle for equality. The unveiling of the mural attracted significant media coverage, further raising awareness and encouraging dialogue.

Engaging the Youth through Interactive Campaigns

Recognizing that the youth are the future of activism, Ray developed interactive campaigns specifically designed to engage younger audiences. He launched initiatives such as "Pride in Schools," which aimed to create safe spaces for LGBTQ students within educational institutions.

Through this program, Ray facilitated workshops that encouraged students to express themselves through art, writing, and performance. By fostering creativity and self-expression, Ray not only raised awareness about LGBTQ issues but also empowered young individuals to embrace their identities confidently.

The Power of Storytelling

At the core of Ray's methods was the power of storytelling. He believed that sharing personal narratives was one of the most effective ways to humanize the LGBTQ experience and challenge stereotypes. Ray often hosted open-mic nights where individuals could share their stories in a supportive environment.

These events not only provided a platform for marginalized voices but also served as a catalyst for change. Attendees left with a deeper understanding of the complexities of LGBTQ lives, breaking down barriers of ignorance and fostering empathy within the community.

Conclusion

Ray Ilan's unique methods of raising awareness transcended traditional activism. By combining creativity, education, and collaboration, he created a multifaceted approach that resonated with a diverse audience. His ability to engage the community through innovative demonstrations, social media campaigns, and storytelling not only elevated LGBTQ issues in Sykarin but also inspired a new generation of activists to continue the fight for equality. In doing so, Ray not only broke barriers but also paved the way for a more inclusive and understanding society.

Defying Expectations

Battling stereotypes and misconceptions surrounding LGBTQ individuals

In the journey of LGBTQ activism, Ray Ilan emerged not only as a voice but as a force determined to dismantle the pervasive stereotypes and misconceptions that have historically plagued the LGBTQ community. Stereotypes are oversimplified and generalized beliefs about a group, often leading to discrimination and prejudice. For LGBTQ individuals, these stereotypes can manifest in various harmful ways, such as the belief that all gay men are flamboyant or that all lesbians reject femininity.

One of the primary theories that underpin the understanding of stereotypes is Social Identity Theory (Tajfel & Turner, 1979), which posits that individuals derive a sense of self from their group memberships. This can lead to in-group favoritism and out-group discrimination. For LGBTQ individuals, this theory highlights how societal norms can create a dichotomy where heterosexuality is viewed as the default, thereby marginalizing those who do not conform.

Ray's activism targeted the misconceptions surrounding LGBTQ identities by employing a multifaceted approach. He recognized that stereotypes often stem from a lack of understanding and exposure, which can be combated through education and representation. Ray initiated workshops and community discussions aimed at debunking myths about LGBTQ individuals. For instance, he addressed the misconception that sexual orientation is a choice, highlighting research that suggests sexual orientation is influenced by a complex interplay of genetic, hormonal, and environmental factors.

In one notable campaign, Ray organized a series of public events titled "Unmasking Stereotypes," where LGBTQ individuals shared their personal stories. These narratives served as powerful counter-narratives to the stereotypes, illustrating the diversity within the community. For example, a transgender woman shared her experience of transitioning while maintaining a successful career in a male-dominated field, challenging the stereotype that transgender individuals are unable to succeed professionally.

Furthermore, Ray employed humor and satire in his activism, drawing inspiration from the comedic styles of LGBTQ icons. By using comedy to address serious issues, Ray was able to engage a wider audience and encourage open dialogue. He often quoted, "Laughter is the best medicine, but truth is the cure," emphasizing that humor could be a vehicle for truth-telling. This approach not only entertained but also educated, creating a platform for challenging harmful stereotypes.

Ray's activism also extended into the realm of media representation. He recognized that the portrayal of LGBTQ individuals in film, television, and literature often perpetuated stereotypes. By advocating for authentic representation, Ray worked with creators to ensure that LGBTQ characters were depicted as fully realized individuals rather than one-dimensional caricatures. For example, in collaboration with local filmmakers, he produced a documentary showcasing the lives of LGBTQ individuals in Sykarin, which highlighted their struggles, triumphs, and humanity.

The impact of Ray's efforts was palpable. As stereotypes began to be challenged, community attitudes shifted. Surveys conducted before and after Ray's initiatives indicated a significant decrease in negative perceptions of LGBTQ individuals among the general population. For instance, the percentage of respondents who believed that LGBTQ individuals were "promiscuous" dropped from 65% to 30% within a year of Ray's campaigns.

Despite these successes, Ray faced considerable backlash from conservative factions within Sykarin. Critics often resorted to reinforcing stereotypes in their attempts to undermine his message. However, Ray remained undeterred, using these challenges as opportunities to further educate and engage. He famously stated, "Every stereotype is a chance to rewrite the narrative," embodying his commitment to continuous advocacy.

In conclusion, Ray Ilan's battle against stereotypes and misconceptions surrounding LGBTQ individuals was not merely a campaign; it was a revolutionary movement aimed at fostering understanding, acceptance, and love. By leveraging education, personal narratives, humor, and media representation, Ray dismantled barriers and paved the way for a more inclusive society. His legacy serves as a reminder that challenging stereotypes is an ongoing process that requires courage, creativity, and community engagement.

Ray's unconventional methods of activism

Ray Ilan's approach to activism was anything but conventional. He understood that in order to break through the barriers of societal norms, he needed to employ methods that were as bold and audacious as the cause he championed. This section explores the unique strategies Ray utilized to amplify LGBTQ voices in Sykarin and beyond, emphasizing creativity, humor, and direct engagement.

One of Ray's most notable methods was his use of performance art as a vehicle for activism. Drawing inspiration from the likes of the Guerrilla Girls and other activist artists, Ray organized flash mobs and street performances that not only entertained but also educated the public on LGBTQ issues. For instance, during

Pride Month, Ray and his team staged a theatrical reenactment of historical events in LGBTQ rights, transforming the streets of Sykarin into a vibrant stage. This approach not only attracted attention but also sparked conversations in a way that traditional activism often failed to do.

$$\text{Impact} = \text{Creativity} \times \text{Engagement} \qquad (10)$$

In this equation, Ray demonstrated that the impact of activism could be maximized by multiplying creativity with direct engagement. By engaging the audience in unexpected ways, he fostered a deeper understanding of the challenges faced by the LGBTQ community.

Ray also embraced humor as a tool for dismantling prejudice. He recognized that laughter could disarm hostility and open hearts. He hosted comedy nights featuring LGBTQ comedians, where jokes about stereotypes and societal norms were not only humorous but also thought-provoking. This method effectively challenged misconceptions while fostering a sense of community among attendees.

Moreover, Ray's unconventional methods included the strategic use of social media platforms. He harnessed the power of viral content to spread awareness and mobilize support. By creating engaging and shareable content—such as meme campaigns and video challenges—Ray reached a broader audience beyond the confines of Sykarin. For example, his viral video series, "Ray's Rants," tackled various LGBTQ issues in a humorous yet poignant manner, allowing viewers to reflect on serious topics while enjoying a good laugh.

$$\text{Viral Reach} = \text{Engagement Rate} \times \text{Shareability} \qquad (11)$$

This equation illustrates how Ray's understanding of social media dynamics enabled him to maximize the reach of his activism. The higher the engagement rate and shareability of his content, the more significant the impact on public perception and awareness.

Another unconventional method Ray employed was the incorporation of fashion into his activism. He launched a clothing line called "Wear Your Pride," which featured bold designs and slogans that celebrated LGBTQ identities. This initiative not only provided a source of income for local LGBTQ artists but also served as a walking billboard for the movement. By wearing these clothes, individuals became active participants in the conversation about LGBTQ rights, sparking discussions wherever they went.

Ray also understood the importance of intersectionality in activism. He collaborated with other marginalized groups, recognizing that the fight for LGBTQ rights was intertwined with other social justice issues. By hosting joint events with racial justice activists and feminist groups, Ray showcased the interconnectedness of various struggles, emphasizing that true liberation could only be achieved through solidarity.

$$\text{Solidarity} = \text{Intersectionality} + \text{Collaboration} \qquad (12)$$

Through this equation, Ray illustrated that the strength of the LGBTQ movement was amplified when it stood in solidarity with other marginalized communities. This approach not only broadened the scope of his activism but also created a more inclusive environment for all.

Lastly, Ray's unconventional methods included grassroots organizing that prioritized community involvement. He established "Activism Circles," where local residents could gather to discuss issues affecting the LGBTQ community and brainstorm solutions. These circles empowered individuals to take ownership of their activism, fostering a sense of agency and collective responsibility.

In conclusion, Ray Ilan's unconventional methods of activism were characterized by creativity, humor, and a commitment to intersectionality. By embracing performance art, leveraging social media, utilizing fashion, and prioritizing community engagement, Ray not only broke barriers but also redefined what it meant to be an activist in the modern age. His legacy serves as a reminder that sometimes, the most effective way to challenge the status quo is to think outside the box and engage with the world in unexpected ways.

Pushing the boundaries of LGBTQ representation in media

The landscape of media representation for LGBTQ individuals has undergone significant transformation over the past few decades, yet challenges persist. Ray Ilan's activism played a pivotal role in advocating for more authentic and diverse portrayals of LGBTQ lives in various media forms, including television, film, and literature. This section delves into the theoretical frameworks surrounding media representation, the problems faced by LGBTQ individuals in media portrayals, and the tangible examples of how Ray's efforts have pushed these boundaries.

Theoretical Frameworks

Media representation theory posits that the way individuals or groups are portrayed in media can shape public perception and influence societal norms. According to Stuart Hall's Encoding/Decoding model, media messages are encoded by producers and decoded by audiences, leading to various interpretations based on cultural context. This theory highlights the importance of representation, as it can reinforce or challenge stereotypes.

Furthermore, Judith Butler's theory of gender performativity suggests that gender identity is not inherent but rather constructed through repeated performances. This perspective underscores the necessity for media to reflect the fluidity of gender and sexuality, allowing for a broader range of identities to be represented.

Problems in LGBTQ Media Representation

Despite advancements, LGBTQ representation in media has often been marred by several persistent issues:

- **Stereotyping:** LGBTQ characters frequently fall into clichéd roles, such as the flamboyant gay best friend or the tragic queer figure. These stereotypes not only limit the scope of representation but also perpetuate harmful narratives that can affect real-life perceptions of LGBTQ individuals.

- **Underrepresentation:** Many LGBTQ identities, particularly those of people of color, transgender individuals, and non-binary persons, remain significantly underrepresented in mainstream media. This lack of visibility can contribute to feelings of isolation and invisibility within the community.

- **Tokenism:** The inclusion of LGBTQ characters is often superficial, serving as a marketing gimmick rather than a genuine effort to portray diverse experiences. This tokenism fails to address the complexities of LGBTQ lives and can lead to backlash from the community.

- **Lack of Authentic Voices:** The absence of LGBTQ creators in the writing and production process often results in narratives that do not accurately reflect the experiences of LGBTQ individuals. This disconnect can lead to misrepresentation and a failure to capture the nuances of LGBTQ lives.

Ray's Activism and Impact

Ray Ilan recognized these barriers and sought to challenge them through various initiatives:

- **Advocacy for Authentic Storytelling:** Ray campaigned for the inclusion of LGBTQ writers and creators in media projects. By amplifying marginalized voices, he aimed to ensure that LGBTQ stories were told authentically and with depth. For instance, Ray collaborated with local filmmakers to produce short films that highlighted the diverse experiences of LGBTQ individuals in Sykarin, showcasing stories that ranged from coming out narratives to explorations of intersectional identities.

+ **Media Literacy Programs:** Understanding the power of media, Ray initiated programs aimed at educating both LGBTQ youth and the broader community about media representation. These workshops focused on critical analysis of media portrayals and encouraged participants to create their own content, fostering a new generation of LGBTQ storytellers.

+ **Campaigns Against Stereotyping:** Through social media campaigns and public demonstrations, Ray raised awareness about the dangers of stereotypes in media. One notable campaign involved a viral hashtag, #BeyondTheStereotype, which encouraged LGBTQ individuals to share their stories and challenge reductive portrayals. This initiative garnered significant attention, leading to discussions within media circles about the importance of nuanced representation.

+ **Partnerships with Media Outlets:** Ray formed alliances with progressive media organizations to promote LGBTQ-inclusive content. These partnerships resulted in collaborative projects that highlighted LGBTQ issues, such as mental health, relationships, and community activism, thereby broadening the scope of representation in mainstream media.

Examples of Progress

Ray's efforts contributed to notable changes in media representation:

+ **Television:** Shows like *Pose* and *Schitt's Creek* gained acclaim for their authentic portrayals of LGBTQ characters and stories. Ray's advocacy for diverse representation helped create an environment where such shows could thrive, influencing networks to invest in LGBTQ narratives.

+ **Film:** Independent films that focus on LGBTQ experiences have seen increased visibility. Ray's collaborations with local filmmakers resulted in award-winning short films that explored themes of identity, love, and resilience, contributing to the broader conversation about LGBTQ representation in cinema.

+ **Literature:** Ray championed LGBTQ authors, leading to the publication of numerous works that reflect the diversity of LGBTQ experiences. This literary renaissance not only provided representation but also fostered a sense of community and belonging among readers.

Conclusion

Ray Ilan's commitment to pushing the boundaries of LGBTQ representation in media has left an indelible mark on the landscape of Sykarin and beyond. By addressing stereotypes, advocating for authentic voices, and fostering inclusivity, Ray's activism has paved the way for a richer, more diverse portrayal of LGBTQ lives. As media continues to evolve, the lessons learned from Ray's journey serve as a guiding light for future generations of LGBTQ activists and creators, ensuring that representation is not just a checkbox but a celebration of the myriad identities that comprise the LGBTQ community.

The impact of Ray's activism on the LGBTQ community

Ray Ilan's activism has had a profound and transformative impact on the LGBTQ community in Sykarin and beyond. His relentless pursuit of equality and representation has not only challenged societal norms but has also catalyzed significant changes in the lives of countless individuals. This section explores the multifaceted impact of Ray's activism, examining both the theoretical frameworks that underpin his work and the practical outcomes that have emerged as a result.

At the core of Ray's activism is the concept of **intersectionality**, a term coined by Kimberlé Crenshaw in 1989. Intersectionality posits that individuals experience multiple, overlapping identities that contribute to unique experiences of discrimination and privilege. Ray's approach to activism has consistently acknowledged the complexity of identity, recognizing that LGBTQ individuals do not exist in a vacuum but are influenced by race, gender, socioeconomic status, and other factors. By advocating for an intersectional approach, Ray has fostered a more inclusive environment within the LGBTQ community, ensuring that marginalized voices are heard and represented.

One of the most significant impacts of Ray's activism has been the increased visibility of LGBTQ individuals in Sykarin. Prior to Ray's efforts, many LGBTQ individuals felt isolated and invisible, often forced to conceal their identities due to societal stigma. Ray's unapologetic self-expression and public persona have inspired others to embrace their identities, leading to a cultural shift in which being LGBTQ is celebrated rather than shamed. This visibility has been crucial in combating the pervasive stereotypes and misconceptions that have historically plagued the community.

Moreover, Ray's activism has resulted in the establishment of numerous safe spaces for LGBTQ individuals. These spaces, such as community centers, support groups, and LGBTQ-friendly events, provide vital resources and support for those navigating the challenges of coming out and living authentically. The creation of these environments has been instrumental in fostering a sense of belonging and community among LGBTQ individuals, allowing them to connect with others who share similar experiences. For instance, the annual Sykarin Pride Parade, which Ray played a pivotal role in organizing, has become a symbol of unity and celebration for the LGBTQ community, drawing thousands of participants and allies each year.

In addition to fostering community, Ray's activism has also focused on education and awareness. By challenging the educational system to include LGBTQ history and issues in curricula, Ray has worked to combat ignorance and promote understanding among younger generations. This educational initiative is grounded in the theory of **social constructionism**, which posits that knowledge and understanding are constructed through social processes. By integrating LGBTQ narratives into educational settings, Ray has helped to dismantle harmful stereotypes and promote acceptance, ultimately leading to a more informed and empathetic society.

The impact of Ray's activism extends beyond local initiatives; it has also influenced national and global conversations about LGBTQ rights. Ray's participation in international LGBTQ conferences has allowed him to share his experiences and strategies with activists from around the world, fostering a sense of solidarity and collaboration. This global perspective is essential in addressing the systemic issues that LGBTQ individuals face, as many of these challenges are not confined to one region but are part of a larger, interconnected struggle for equality.

Moreover, Ray's work has inspired a new generation of LGBTQ activists who are committed to continuing the fight for rights and representation. By serving as a mentor and role model, Ray has empowered young activists to take up the mantle of advocacy, ensuring that the movement remains vibrant and dynamic. This generational transfer of knowledge and passion is crucial for the sustainability of the LGBTQ rights movement, as it cultivates a culture of activism that is both inclusive and resilient.

The practical outcomes of Ray's activism are evident in the legislative changes that have occurred in Sykarin as a result of his efforts. Through his work with the LGBTQ Equality Party, Ray has successfully advocated for policies that protect LGBTQ individuals from discrimination, promote equal rights, and enhance access to healthcare and social services. These legislative victories are not merely symbolic; they represent tangible progress that improves the quality of life for LGBTQ individuals and affirms their rights as equal members of society.

In conclusion, the impact of Ray Ilan's activism on the LGBTQ community is both profound and far-reaching. By embracing intersectionality, fostering visibility, creating safe spaces, promoting education, and inspiring future generations, Ray has fundamentally changed the landscape of LGBTQ activism in Sykarin and beyond. His work serves as a powerful reminder of the importance of advocacy and the ongoing struggle for equality, highlighting the potential for individual action to effect meaningful change in the lives of many. As Ray continues his journey, the legacy of his activism will undoubtedly inspire future generations to break barriers and champion the rights of all individuals, regardless of their identity.

Ray's journey towards national recognition

Ray Ilan's ascent to national recognition was not merely a matter of personal ambition; it was a complex interplay of social dynamics, cultural shifts, and the relentless pursuit of equality. As Ray's activism gained traction in the small town of Sykarin, it became clear that his message resonated far beyond the borders of his community. This section delves into the various dimensions that contributed to Ray's journey, examining the theoretical frameworks, societal challenges, and pivotal moments that defined his rise.

Theoretical Frameworks

To understand Ray's journey, we can employ the Social Movement Theory, which posits that collective action emerges from shared grievances and the mobilization of resources. Ray's activism exemplified this theory as he galvanized local LGBTQ individuals, transforming personal struggles into a broader movement for rights and recognition. The following equation encapsulates the relationship between grievances, mobilization, and social change:

$$SC = f(G, M) \tag{13}$$

where SC is social change, G represents grievances, and M denotes mobilization efforts. In Ray's case, the grievances included systemic discrimination, lack of representation, and societal stigma, while his mobilization efforts ranged from grassroots organizing to leveraging social media platforms.

Challenges Faced

Despite his growing influence, Ray encountered significant challenges as he sought national recognition. One of the primary obstacles was the entrenched stigma against LGBTQ individuals, which manifested in various forms, including political opposition and media misrepresentation. For instance, during a pivotal LGBTQ rights rally in Sykarin, Ray faced backlash from conservative factions who labeled him a "threat to traditional values." This opposition highlighted the societal resistance to change and the need for strategic communication to counteract negative narratives.

Moreover, Ray's journey was marked by the challenge of intersectionality, as he navigated not only LGBTQ issues but also the complexities of race, gender, and socioeconomic status within the movement. The intersectional framework, as proposed by Kimberlé Crenshaw, emphasizes the need to address multiple forms of discrimination simultaneously. Ray's activism embodied this approach, as he advocated for the inclusion of marginalized voices within the LGBTQ community, ensuring that the movement was not monolithic but rather reflective of diverse experiences.

Pivotal Moments

Several key moments catalyzed Ray's transition from a local activist to a national figure. One such moment was his participation in the National LGBTQ Summit, where he delivered a powerful keynote address that captivated audiences and garnered media attention. In his speech, Ray articulated the struggles faced by LGBTQ individuals in Sykarin, framing them as part of a larger national narrative. His ability to connect local issues to national conversations exemplified the concept of "scaling up" in social movements, where local victories are leveraged to inspire broader change.

Another significant milestone was Ray's collaboration with prominent LGBTQ organizations, which provided him with platforms to amplify his message. By aligning himself with established groups, Ray not only gained credibility but also access to resources that facilitated his outreach efforts. This collaboration was crucial in positioning Ray as a thought leader in the national LGBTQ discourse.

Media Representation

The role of media in Ray's journey cannot be overstated. As his activism gained visibility, he became a sought-after figure for interviews and panel discussions. His charismatic presence and articulate advocacy resonated with both LGBTQ audiences and allies, further solidifying his status as a national spokesperson for the movement. However, the media landscape was not without its pitfalls. Ray often faced the challenge of being portrayed through a sensationalist lens, which threatened to dilute the seriousness of his message. He navigated this by maintaining a consistent narrative that emphasized authenticity and resilience, ensuring that the core values of his activism remained intact.

Conclusion

Ray Ilan's journey towards national recognition was a multifaceted process shaped by theoretical frameworks, societal challenges, and pivotal moments. By leveraging his local experiences and connecting them to broader national narratives, Ray not only amplified his own voice but also the voices of countless others within the LGBTQ community. His ability to navigate the complexities of stigma, intersectionality, and media representation exemplifies the resilience required to break through barriers and achieve recognition on a national scale. As Ray continued to evolve as an activist, his journey served as a beacon of hope and inspiration for future generations striving for equality and acceptance.

Ray's unapologetic approach to activism

Ray Ilan's activism is characterized by an unapologetic approach that challenges societal norms and expectations. This section explores the theoretical underpinnings of his activism, the problems he confronts, and the examples that illustrate his fearless stance.

At the core of Ray's activism is the concept of **intersectionality**, a term coined by Kimberlé Crenshaw in 1989. Intersectionality posits that individuals experience multiple, overlapping identities that shape their social experiences and systemic oppression. Ray embodies this theory by recognizing that LGBTQ individuals do not exist in a vacuum; rather, their experiences are influenced by race, class, gender, and other identity markers. This understanding informs his activism, allowing him to advocate for a more inclusive movement that addresses the unique challenges faced by marginalized groups within the LGBTQ community.

$$\text{Intersectionality} = f(\text{Race, Gender, Class, Sexual Orientation}) \quad (14)$$

Ray's unapologetic approach manifests in his refusal to conform to traditional expectations of activism. He believes that activism should be bold, loud, and unfiltered. This philosophy is rooted in the **radical queer theory**, which challenges the status quo and seeks to dismantle oppressive systems. According to scholars like Judith Butler, radical queer activism is about subverting societal norms regarding gender and sexuality, thereby creating space for diverse expressions of identity. Ray's public persona reflects this theory; he is not afraid to confront those who perpetuate discrimination, often using humor and satire as tools for resistance.

One significant problem Ray faces in his activism is the backlash from conservative groups that resist LGBTQ rights. For instance, during a local rally advocating for marriage equality, Ray encountered protesters who brandished signs with derogatory messages. Rather than retreating in the face of hostility, Ray took to the stage, addressing the crowd with a powerful speech that turned the negativity into a rallying cry for unity. He stated, "We are not here to ask for permission; we are here to claim our rights!" This moment exemplifies Ray's unapologetic stance, transforming adversity into empowerment.

$$\text{Empowerment} = \frac{\text{Activism}}{\text{Oppression}} \qquad (15)$$

Ray's activism also emphasizes the importance of visibility. He understands that representation matters and that being unapologetically visible can inspire others to embrace their identities. For example, in 2021, Ray organized a Pride parade in Sykarin that featured not only LGBTQ individuals but also allies from various backgrounds. This event served as a platform to amplify voices that are often marginalized within the LGBTQ community, such as people of color and transgender individuals. Ray's commitment to inclusivity highlights his belief that activism must reflect the diversity of the community it serves.

Moreover, Ray's unapologetic approach extends to his social media presence. He utilizes platforms like Instagram and Twitter to share his thoughts on current events, often addressing controversial topics head-on. His posts are characterized by a blend of humor and fierce advocacy, allowing him to connect with a broader audience. For instance, during a heated debate about transgender rights, Ray posted a meme that humorously critiqued the misconceptions surrounding gender identity, effectively educating his followers while entertaining them.

$$\text{Visibility} = \text{Representation} + \text{Education} \qquad (16)$$

In conclusion, Ray Ilan's unapologetic approach to activism is a powerful testament to the effectiveness of bold, intersectional advocacy. By challenging societal norms and embracing his identity, Ray not only inspires others to do the same but also paves the way for a more inclusive and equitable future. His journey exemplifies the idea that true activism requires courage, resilience, and an unwavering commitment to authenticity. Ray's legacy serves as a reminder that activism is not just about the cause; it's about the unapologetic individuals who dare to stand up and demand change.

Love, Lust, and Longing

Ray's experiences navigating relationships in a judgmental society

In the small, often conservative town of Sykarin, Ray Ilan faced the daunting task of navigating relationships in a society rife with judgment and prejudice. The societal expectations imposed on individuals, particularly those within the LGBTQ community, often led to a complex interplay of desire, fear, and the quest for acceptance. This section explores Ray's personal experiences and the broader implications of forming relationships in a judgmental society.

The Weight of Societal Expectations

From a young age, Ray understood that societal norms dictated how relationships should look and function. Traditional notions of masculinity and femininity were deeply ingrained in the fabric of Sykarin's culture, creating an environment where deviation from the norm was met with scrutiny. As a result, Ray often felt the pressure to conform to these expectations, which led to internal conflict.

The theory of *social identity* posits that individuals derive a sense of self from their group memberships, which can lead to both positive and negative outcomes in relationship dynamics. Ray's identification as a member of the LGBTQ community often placed him at odds with the prevailing heteronormative culture. This tension manifested in his relationships, where he frequently grappled with the desire for authenticity versus the fear of societal rejection.

The Complexity of Love and Lust

Navigating romantic relationships in a judgmental society is fraught with complexities. For Ray, the thrill of love was often overshadowed by the specter of societal disapproval. Each potential relationship was a gamble; the stakes were high, and the consequences of being open about his identity could be severe.

Ray's first significant relationship exemplified this struggle. He fell for a fellow student, Alex, who was also grappling with his identity. Their connection was electric, but the fear of being outed loomed large. The couple often found solace in private, yet the public nature of their town made every shared glance and touch feel like an act of rebellion. This dichotomy of public versus private love is well-documented in LGBTQ studies, where the concept of *closeted relationships* often leads to feelings of isolation and anxiety.

The Impact of Judgment on Intimacy

Judgment from society can have profound effects on intimacy. Ray often felt that his relationships were hindered by the need to maintain a facade. This was particularly evident during social gatherings where heteronormative couples freely expressed affection, while Ray and Alex had to navigate their interactions with caution.

Research in *interpersonal communication* suggests that perceived judgment can lead to *communication apprehension*, which in turn affects relationship satisfaction. Ray experienced this firsthand; the fear of being judged often stifled open communication with his partner, leading to misunderstandings and emotional distance.

Finding Companionship in a Hostile Environment

Despite the challenges, Ray's journey toward finding companionship was not devoid of hope. He discovered that within the LGBTQ community, there existed a network of individuals who shared similar experiences and struggles. This sense of belonging provided Ray with the courage to embrace his identity and seek relationships that were both fulfilling and authentic.

Ray's participation in local LGBTQ meetups and events allowed him to connect with others who understood the unique challenges of dating in a judgmental society. These gatherings served as safe spaces where individuals could express themselves without fear of repercussion. The importance of such spaces is underscored by theories of *social support*, which highlight how communal ties can bolster individual resilience against societal judgment.

The Vulnerability Beneath the Rebellious Exterior

While Ray projected an image of confidence and rebellion, beneath the surface lay a vulnerability that often complicated his relationships. The fear of rejection and the desire for acceptance created a paradox; Ray yearned for love yet was terrified of the potential pain that came with it.

Psychological theories on *attachment styles* reveal that early experiences with love and acceptance significantly influence adult relationships. Ray's upbringing in a judgmental society fostered an anxious attachment style, where the fear of abandonment often clouded his ability to fully engage in romantic relationships. This internal struggle highlighted the broader issue of how societal judgment can shape personal identities and relational dynamics.

Conclusion

Ray Ilan's experiences navigating relationships in a judgmental society reflect the broader challenges faced by LGBTQ individuals. The interplay of societal expectations, the complexities of love and intimacy, and the search for companionship in a hostile environment all contribute to a unique relational landscape. Through his journey, Ray not only navigated the pitfalls of societal judgment but also emerged as a beacon of hope for others, demonstrating that love, in all its forms, is worth fighting for, even in the face of adversity.

The complexities of love and lust in the LGBTQ community

The landscape of love and lust within the LGBTQ community is a multifaceted tapestry woven from diverse experiences, identities, and societal pressures. Unlike the often linear narratives of heterosexual relationships, LGBTQ relationships frequently navigate a labyrinth of complexities that can complicate emotional connections and physical intimacy.

At the core of these complexities lies the concept of **intersectionality**, a term coined by Kimberlé Crenshaw, which refers to the ways in which different forms of discrimination overlap and intersect. For LGBTQ individuals, factors such as race, class, gender identity, and sexual orientation can profoundly influence their experiences of love and desire. For instance, a queer person of color may face unique challenges that differ significantly from those encountered by a white LGBTQ individual, including societal stigma and cultural expectations that can complicate romantic pursuits.

Societal Expectations and Internalized Homophobia

The societal expectations placed upon LGBTQ individuals can create an internalized homophobia that manifests in their romantic lives. This phenomenon, defined as the internalization of society's negative attitudes towards LGBTQ identities, can lead to feelings of shame, self-doubt, and fear of rejection. For example, a gay man might struggle to embrace his desire for a relationship due to societal pressures to conform to heteronormative ideals. This internal conflict can hinder the ability to form genuine connections, as individuals may project their insecurities onto potential partners.

Moreover, the fear of societal rejection can lead to a phenomenon known as **situational sexuality**, where individuals engage in same-sex relationships only in certain contexts or environments, such as parties or clubs, but revert to heterosexual norms in public life. This behavior not only complicates personal identities but also affects the dynamics of relationships, often leading to feelings of inadequacy and confusion.

The Fluidity of Attraction

Another layer of complexity in LGBTQ relationships is the fluidity of attraction itself. Unlike traditional notions of love that often emphasize exclusivity, many LGBTQ individuals experience attraction in more dynamic and less defined ways. The Kinsey Scale, developed by Alfred Kinsey, provides a framework for understanding sexual orientation as a spectrum rather than a binary classification. This fluidity can lead to challenges in defining relationships, as individuals may find themselves attracted to multiple genders or identities throughout their lives.

For instance, a bisexual individual may face scrutiny from both heterosexual and homosexual communities, often being labeled as "confused" or "greedy." This external pressure can complicate their romantic pursuits, as they may feel the need to justify their attractions or navigate the expectations of multiple communities simultaneously.

The Role of Technology and Dating Apps

In the modern era, technology has transformed the landscape of dating and relationships within the LGBTQ community. Dating apps like Grindr, Tinder, and HER have created new avenues for connection, but they also introduce unique challenges. The immediacy and accessibility of these platforms can lead to a culture of "hookup" mentality, where casual encounters often take precedence over meaningful relationships.

While these platforms can empower individuals to express their desires freely, they can also foster superficial connections that lack emotional depth. The pressure to present oneself in a certain way, often through curated profiles and images, can lead to feelings of inadequacy and anxiety, further complicating the pursuit of love and intimacy.

Navigating Relationship Dynamics

The dynamics of LGBTQ relationships can also be influenced by power structures and societal norms. In some cases, traditional gender roles may be subverted, leading to a more egalitarian approach to relationships. However, this can also result in confusion and conflict as partners navigate their identities and roles within the relationship.

For example, in a same-sex female relationship, the absence of traditional male-female dynamics can create ambiguity regarding who takes on specific roles, such as financial responsibility or emotional labor. This ambiguity can lead to misunderstandings and resentment if not openly discussed and negotiated.

Conclusion

In conclusion, the complexities of love and lust in the LGBTQ community reflect a rich interplay of societal expectations, personal identities, and evolving dynamics. As LGBTQ individuals continue to carve out spaces for authentic connections, it is essential to acknowledge and address the unique challenges they face. By fostering open dialogue and understanding, the community can work towards creating a more inclusive and supportive environment for love in all its forms.

$$\text{Love}_{\text{LGBTQ}} = \sum_{i=1}^{n} \left(\text{Attraction}_i + \text{Connection}_i + \text{Understanding}_i \right) \quad (17)$$

Where n represents the number of partners, and each component reflects the multifaceted nature of relationships within the community.

Ray's search for true companionship and intimacy

In the vibrant yet challenging landscape of Sykarin, Ray Ilan's quest for true companionship and intimacy transcended the conventional boundaries often dictated by societal norms. As a prominent LGBTQ activist, Ray's experiences navigating relationships were marked by a complex interplay of desire, vulnerability, and the ever-present specter of societal judgment.

The search for intimacy is often influenced by the theoretical frameworks of attachment theory and social identity theory. Attachment theory posits that early relationships with caregivers shape individuals' expectations and behaviors in romantic relationships. In Ray's case, his upbringing in a small town, coupled with the struggle to accept his identity, created a unique backdrop for his relational dynamics. He often found himself oscillating between the desire for closeness and the fear of rejection, a duality that frequently manifested in his romantic pursuits.

$$I = \frac{C + R}{D} \tag{18}$$

Where I represents intimacy, C denotes connection, R signifies risk, and D stands for distance. This equation illustrates that intimacy increases with greater connection and acceptable levels of risk, while distance diminishes the potential for closeness. Ray's journey was a testament to this equation, as he learned to navigate the delicate balance between vulnerability and self-protection.

Ray's initial forays into relationships were often fraught with complications. The societal stigma surrounding LGBTQ relationships in Sykarin created an environment where love was both a sanctuary and a battleground. For instance, during his teenage years, Ray developed a crush on a classmate, Alex, who was equally drawn to him. However, the fear of being outed in their conservative town led to a series of missed opportunities and unspoken words. This experience highlighted the internal conflict many LGBTQ individuals face: the desire for intimacy clashing with the need for safety.

As Ray matured, he began to embrace his identity more fully, leading him to seek out spaces where LGBTQ individuals could connect authentically. He attended local LGBTQ meetups and events, where he met individuals who shared similar experiences of longing and connection. One notable encounter was with Jamie, a fellow activist who had faced similar challenges in their search for love. Their relationship blossomed amidst the backdrop of activism, providing a fertile ground for both companionship and mutual support.

However, the complexities of intimacy did not dissipate entirely. Ray and Jamie's relationship was tested by external pressures, including public scrutiny and the need to maintain a strong activist persona. Ray often found himself grappling with the notion of vulnerability in a world that demanded strength. He realized that true intimacy required not only connection but also the courage to be open about fears and insecurities.

$$V = \frac{E + C}{F} \tag{19}$$

In this equation, V represents vulnerability, E signifies emotional exposure, C denotes communication, and F stands for fear. Ray's understanding of vulnerability evolved as he recognized that fostering true companionship necessitated embracing emotional exposure and open dialogue, despite the inherent fears involved.

Ray's journey also illuminated the importance of community in the search for intimacy. He often engaged in discussions about the unique challenges LGBTQ individuals face in relationships, including the pressure to conform to heteronormative standards and the impact of internalized homophobia. Through these conversations, Ray discovered that many individuals shared his struggles, creating a sense of solidarity and understanding that enriched his pursuit of love.

One poignant example of this communal support occurred during a pride event in Sykarin, where Ray and Jamie participated in a panel discussion on love and relationships in the LGBTQ community. The dialogue revealed the diverse experiences of love, from fleeting encounters to deep, lasting connections. Audience members shared their stories, fostering an environment where vulnerability was celebrated rather than shamed. This experience reinforced Ray's belief that true companionship often flourishes in spaces where individuals can be unapologetically themselves.

Despite the challenges, Ray's search for intimacy continued to evolve. He learned to prioritize self-love and acceptance, recognizing that true companionship could not flourish without a solid foundation of self-worth. This realization became a pivotal moment in his life, allowing him to approach relationships with a newfound confidence and clarity.

In conclusion, Ray Ilan's search for true companionship and intimacy was a multifaceted journey shaped by personal experiences, societal pressures, and the quest for authenticity. Through the lens of attachment theory and social identity theory, we can understand the complexities of his relational dynamics. Ray's story serves as a reminder that the pursuit of love is not merely about finding a partner but also about fostering connections that honor vulnerability, resilience, and the indomitable spirit of the LGBTQ community.

Uncovering the secrets of Ray's romantic escapades

Ray Ilan's journey through the labyrinth of love and lust is as intricate as the vibrant tapestry of his activism. In a society often marred by judgment and misunderstanding, Ray's romantic escapades reveal the complexities of navigating relationships as a member of the LGBTQ community. This section delves into the nuances of Ray's experiences, illustrating the interplay between his personal life and his broader mission for acceptance and representation.

The Quest for Connection

At the heart of Ray's romantic endeavors lies a fundamental human desire for connection. As he ventured into the world of dating, he encountered a plethora of challenges that many LGBTQ individuals face. The societal expectations placed upon him often clashed with his quest for authenticity. For instance, Ray's first significant relationship unfolded during his college years, where he met Alex, a fellow activist. Their connection was electric, igniting a passion that mirrored the fervor of their shared cause. However, the pressures of public scrutiny weighed heavily on their relationship, leading to moments of doubt and vulnerability.

Navigating Societal Norms

Ray's experiences in love were not without their complications. The societal norms surrounding masculinity and femininity often dictated the dynamics of his relationships. For example, Ray found himself grappling with the stereotype of the "feminine gay man," which influenced how potential partners perceived him. This societal lens often led to misunderstandings and assumptions that clouded his romantic pursuits. In one instance, Ray went on a date with Jamie, who was initially drawn to his charisma but later expressed discomfort with Ray's outspoken nature. This encounter highlighted the delicate balance between personal expression and societal expectations, a theme that would recur throughout Ray's romantic life.

The Complexity of Love and Lust

As Ray navigated the turbulent waters of love, he also encountered the intoxicating allure of lust. The thrill of new connections often brought forth a whirlwind of emotions, but it also posed questions about the depth of these encounters. Ray's brief fling with a charismatic artist named Sam exemplified this dichotomy. Their relationship was marked by passionate nights and fleeting moments of intimacy, yet Ray often wondered if their connection was merely a product of desire rather than genuine affection. This internal conflict prompted Ray to reflect on the nature of love within the LGBTQ community, where the lines between lust and love can often blur.

The Vulnerability Beneath the Surface

Beneath Ray's rebellious exterior lay a profound vulnerability that shaped his romantic experiences. He often found solace in poetry, channeling his emotions into verses that captured the essence of his longing. One poignant piece, titled "Reflections of a Broken Heart," encapsulated his struggles with intimacy and the fear of rejection. This vulnerability resonated with many in the LGBTQ community, as they too grappled with the complexities of love in a world that often marginalized their identities. Ray's willingness to share his poetic expressions became a source of inspiration, fostering a sense of solidarity among those who felt similarly isolated in their romantic pursuits.

The Impact on LGBTQ Relationships

Ray's journey through love and lust not only shaped his personal narrative but also influenced the broader LGBTQ community. His candid discussions about relationships opened the door for conversations about the unique challenges faced by LGBTQ individuals in seeking companionship. For instance, Ray organized a series of workshops aimed at promoting healthy relationships among LGBTQ youth, addressing topics such as communication, consent, and emotional well-being. These initiatives empowered young individuals to embrace their identities while navigating the complexities of love, creating a ripple effect that fostered a more inclusive dialogue around relationships.

Conclusion: A Legacy of Love

In uncovering the secrets of Ray's romantic escapades, we witness the intertwining of personal experiences and activism. Ray Ilan's journey is a testament to the resilience of the human spirit in the face of societal challenges. His exploration of love and lust not only enriched his life but also laid the groundwork for future generations to embrace their identities with confidence. As Ray continues to break barriers, his romantic experiences serve as a reminder that love, in all its forms, is a powerful catalyst for change, forging connections that transcend societal boundaries.

$$\text{Love} + \text{Activism} = \text{Empowerment} \tag{20}$$

This equation encapsulates Ray's belief that love, when combined with a commitment to activism, has the potential to empower individuals and communities alike. In this way, Ray Ilan's romantic escapades are not merely personal anecdotes; they are integral to the larger narrative of LGBTQ rights and representation.

The vulnerability beneath Ray's rebellious exterior

Ray Ilan, the unapologetic force of nature in Sykarin, often presented a tough exterior, a façade crafted through years of navigating a world fraught with prejudice and misunderstanding. Beneath this rebellious surface, however, lay a profound vulnerability that shaped his journey as an LGBTQ activist. This vulnerability is not merely a personal trait; it is a critical element in understanding the complexities of identity and activism within marginalized communities.

At the core of Ray's rebellious persona was the necessity to shield himself from societal rejection. The theory of *intersectionality*, coined by Kimberlé Crenshaw, posits that individuals experience overlapping social identities, which can compound discrimination and oppression. Ray's identity as a gay man in a small town like Sykarin positioned him at the intersection of various societal biases, where his sexual orientation, local culture, and socio-economic status converged. This intersectionality created a unique set of challenges that demanded both resilience and vulnerability.

Ray's journey of self-discovery was fraught with moments of doubt and fear. For instance, his initial forays into LGBTQ activism were marked by a palpable anxiety about public perception. He often grappled with the fear of being ostracized by his peers and family, a common struggle among LGBTQ individuals. This internal conflict is well-documented in the field of psychology, particularly in the *minority stress theory*, which suggests that the chronic stress of being part of a marginalized group can lead to mental health challenges. Ray's activism was, in many ways, a response to this stress—a way to reclaim his narrative and assert his identity.

One poignant example of Ray's vulnerability emerged during a local pride event where he shared his story publicly for the first time. As he spoke about his experiences with bullying and rejection, the audience could see the emotional toll these experiences had taken on him. His voice trembled, and tears welled in his eyes. This moment of raw honesty resonated deeply with many attendees, illustrating the power of vulnerability in activism. It demonstrated that strength does not always manifest as bravado; sometimes, it is found in the courage to be open about one's struggles.

Moreover, Ray's rebellious style—characterized by flamboyant clothing and bold statements—was a double-edged sword. While it served as a shield against societal norms, it also exposed him to heightened scrutiny and criticism. The psychological concept of *impression management* suggests that individuals often engage in behaviors to control how they are perceived by others. For Ray, this meant navigating the fine line between expressing his true self and protecting his emotional well-being. His vibrant persona was a way to defy stereotypes while simultaneously masking the insecurities that lingered beneath the surface.

As Ray became more entrenched in his activism, he learned to embrace his vulnerability as a source of strength. He began to understand that acknowledging his fears and insecurities could foster deeper connections within the LGBTQ community. By sharing his struggles, he inspired others to do the same, creating a ripple effect of openness and support. This shift aligns with the principles of *community resilience*, which emphasize the importance of collective healing and empowerment in the face of adversity.

In conclusion, the vulnerability beneath Ray Ilan's rebellious exterior is a testament to the complexities of identity and activism. It highlights the interplay between personal experience and societal expectation, revealing that true strength often lies in the willingness to be vulnerable. As Ray's journey illustrates, embracing one's vulnerabilities can lead to profound connections and a more inclusive community. His story serves as a reminder that behind every activist's bold façade, there may be a deeply human struggle that deserves recognition and respect.

Ray's impact on LGBTQ relationships and dating

Ray Ilan's journey through the landscape of LGBTQ relationships and dating has been nothing short of transformative. His experiences and activism have played a pivotal role in reshaping how love, intimacy, and companionship are perceived within the LGBTQ community. This section explores Ray's impact through various lenses, including the challenges faced by LGBTQ individuals, the societal norms that influence relationships, and the progressive changes that Ray has championed.

The Challenges of LGBTQ Dating

Dating within the LGBTQ community often comes with unique challenges that differ significantly from those faced by heterosexual individuals. These challenges include:

+ **Stigmatization and Discrimination:** Many LGBTQ individuals encounter societal stigma that can affect their self-esteem and confidence in dating scenarios. This stigma can manifest as fear of rejection or violence, leading to hesitancy in pursuing relationships.

+ **Limited Visibility:** The lack of positive representation in media has historically contributed to feelings of isolation among LGBTQ individuals.

This invisibility can make it difficult for them to find relatable role models or examples of healthy relationships.

+ **Navigating Identity:** Many LGBTQ individuals grapple with their identities, which can complicate dating. The process of self-discovery can lead to misunderstandings and challenges in forming connections with potential partners.

Ray's own experiences navigating these challenges have informed his activism and advocacy for change. He has often emphasized the importance of visibility and representation in fostering a more inclusive dating landscape.

Ray's Advocacy for Healthy Relationships

Ray has been a vocal proponent of healthy relationships within the LGBTQ community, advocating for the following principles:

+ **Communication:** Ray emphasizes the importance of open and honest communication in relationships. He believes that sharing feelings, desires, and boundaries is crucial for building strong connections.

+ **Consent and Respect:** Ray has championed the idea that consent should be at the forefront of all romantic encounters. He has worked tirelessly to educate individuals about the importance of mutual respect and understanding in relationships.

+ **Diversity of Relationships:** Ray has pushed for the acceptance of diverse relationship structures, including polyamory and non-binary partnerships. By advocating for a broader understanding of love, he has helped to challenge traditional notions of monogamy and heteronormativity.

Through workshops, public speeches, and social media campaigns, Ray has worked to instill these values within the LGBTQ community, encouraging individuals to prioritize their emotional and physical well-being in their relationships.

The Role of Technology in LGBTQ Dating

In the modern era, technology has significantly influenced dating practices, particularly within the LGBTQ community. Ray has recognized the dual-edged nature of technology in shaping relationships:

- **Online Dating Platforms:** The rise of dating apps has provided LGBTQ individuals with unprecedented access to potential partners. Ray has highlighted the importance of these platforms in breaking down geographical barriers and fostering connections that may not have been possible otherwise.

- **Cyberbullying and Harassment:** Despite the advantages, Ray has also addressed the darker side of online dating, including cyberbullying and harassment. He advocates for safer online environments where individuals can connect without fear of discrimination or abuse.

Ray's work in promoting safe online spaces has led to increased awareness of the need for accountability and respect within digital interactions.

Examples of Ray's Impact

Ray's influence on LGBTQ relationships and dating can be illustrated through several key initiatives:

- **The Love is Love Campaign:** This campaign, spearheaded by Ray, aimed to celebrate diverse relationships and challenge societal norms. Through social media, events, and community outreach, the campaign fostered a culture of acceptance and love, encouraging individuals to embrace their identities and relationships.

- **Workshops on Healthy Relationships:** Ray organized workshops that focused on teaching individuals about healthy relationship dynamics, conflict resolution, and effective communication. These workshops have empowered many to navigate their romantic lives with confidence and awareness.

- **Collaborations with LGBTQ Organizations:** By partnering with various LGBTQ organizations, Ray has helped to create resources that promote healthy dating practices, including guides on consent and communication tailored to the LGBTQ community.

The Future of LGBTQ Relationships

Ray's impact on LGBTQ relationships and dating extends beyond his immediate community. His advocacy has sparked conversations about love and intimacy on a global scale. As societal attitudes continue to evolve, Ray's work serves as a foundation for future generations of LGBTQ individuals to build upon.

In conclusion, Ray Ilan's influence on LGBTQ relationships and dating is marked by his commitment to fostering understanding, acceptance, and love. By challenging societal norms and advocating for healthy relationship practices, Ray has left an indelible mark on the landscape of LGBTQ dating, inspiring countless individuals to embrace their identities and pursue meaningful connections.

The Power of Unity

Ray's efforts in creating safe spaces for LGBTQ individuals

In the heart of Sykarin, a small town often overshadowed by its conservative values, Ray Ilan emerged as a beacon of hope for LGBTQ individuals seeking refuge from societal judgment and discrimination. The concept of safe spaces, defined as environments where individuals can express themselves freely without fear of backlash, became a cornerstone of Ray's activism. He recognized that such spaces were not merely physical locations but also emotional sanctuaries where acceptance and understanding could flourish.

Ray's journey towards creating safe spaces began with his own experiences of alienation during his formative years. Growing up in a town that often stigmatized difference, he understood the profound impact of isolation on mental health. Research indicates that LGBTQ youth are at a significantly higher risk for depression, anxiety, and suicidal ideation compared to their heterosexual counterparts (Haas et al., 2011). This stark reality fueled Ray's determination to establish inclusive environments where individuals could find community and support.

One of Ray's first initiatives was the establishment of the Sykarin LGBTQ Youth Center, a vibrant hub that offered resources, mentorship, and a sense of belonging. The center provided workshops on self-advocacy, mental health awareness, and relationship education, empowering young LGBTQ individuals to embrace their identities. Ray collaborated with local mental health professionals to ensure that the center offered counseling services tailored to the unique challenges faced by LGBTQ youth. This initiative not only addressed immediate needs but also fostered resilience among participants.

In addition to creating physical safe spaces, Ray emphasized the importance of fostering a culture of acceptance within existing community structures. He initiated partnerships with local schools to implement anti-bullying programs and inclusive curricula. By promoting LGBTQ visibility in educational settings, Ray aimed to dismantle stereotypes and encourage empathy among students. He often quoted the words of renowned activist Marsha P. Johnson: "No pride for some of us without liberation for all of us." This philosophy underscored Ray's belief that safe spaces must extend beyond isolated environments and permeate the fabric of society.

Ray's efforts were not without challenges. Resistance from conservative factions within Sykarin often manifested in public protests and attempts to undermine his initiatives. However, Ray approached these obstacles with unwavering resolve. He organized community forums to address concerns and misconceptions, providing a platform for dialogue and education. By inviting local leaders, parents, and allies to participate, Ray fostered a sense of shared responsibility for creating inclusive spaces.

One particularly impactful event was the annual Sykarin Pride Festival, which Ray spearheaded. This celebration of diversity transformed into a powerful demonstration of solidarity, drawing participants from all walks of life. The festival featured workshops, performances, and discussions centered on LGBTQ rights, effectively turning the town square into a vibrant safe space for expression and celebration. Ray's ability to mobilize the community was evident as families, allies, and LGBTQ individuals came together to stand against discrimination.

Ray's commitment to safe spaces extended beyond Sykarin's borders. He recognized the need for collaboration with national organizations to share resources and best practices. By participating in conferences and workshops focused on LGBTQ advocacy, Ray brought back valuable insights that informed his local initiatives. He often remarked, "We are stronger together," emphasizing the importance of unity in the fight for equality.

To measure the impact of his efforts, Ray implemented feedback mechanisms within the safe spaces he created. Surveys and focus groups provided valuable insights into the experiences of individuals utilizing these resources. The data collected revealed a significant increase in feelings of safety and acceptance among LGBTQ youth in Sykarin. This evidence bolstered Ray's case for continued investment in safe spaces and further fueled his activism.

In conclusion, Ray Ilan's tireless efforts to create safe spaces for LGBTQ individuals in Sykarin transcended mere activism; they represented a profound commitment to fostering a culture of acceptance and understanding. Through the establishment of inclusive environments, educational initiatives, and community engagement, Ray not only provided refuge for those in need but also ignited a movement towards lasting change. His legacy serves as a reminder of the transformative power of safe spaces in the ongoing struggle for LGBTQ rights and acceptance.

Bibliography

[1] Haas, A. P., et al. (2011). *Suicide and suicide risk in lesbian, gay, bisexual, and transgender populations: Review and recommendations.* Journal of Homosexuality, 58(1), 10-51.

The forging of alliances and partnerships

In the vibrant tapestry of LGBTQ activism, the forging of alliances and partnerships stands as a pivotal element in amplifying voices, sharing resources, and fostering a sense of community. Ray Ilan, with his unyielding spirit and charisma, recognized early on that to break barriers effectively, he needed to weave together a network of allies from various backgrounds, identities, and experiences. This section delves into the significance of such alliances, the challenges faced in their formation, and the transformative impact they had on Ray's activism.

The Importance of Alliances

Alliances in activism serve several critical functions. They enable the pooling of resources, knowledge, and skills, which can enhance the effectiveness of advocacy efforts. For instance, Ray understood that partnering with local businesses could lead to sponsorships for pride events, while collaborations with educational institutions could facilitate workshops on LGBTQ issues. The synergy created through these partnerships not only bolstered visibility but also legitimized the movement in the eyes of the broader community.

Moreover, alliances can bridge gaps between different marginalized groups, fostering intersectionality. Ray's activism was deeply rooted in the belief that the struggles of LGBTQ individuals were interconnected with those of other marginalized communities, including racial minorities, women, and the economically disadvantaged. By forming coalitions with these groups, Ray aimed to create a united front against systemic oppression.

Challenges in Forging Partnerships

However, the process of forging alliances was not without its challenges. One significant hurdle was the historical mistrust between different activist groups. For example, some LGBTQ activists felt alienated from feminist movements that had, at times, sidelined queer issues. Similarly, racial minorities within the LGBTQ community often felt that their unique struggles were overlooked by mainstream LGBTQ organizations. Ray had to navigate these complexities with sensitivity and a commitment to inclusivity.

Another challenge was the differing priorities among potential allies. While some organizations focused on immediate legislative changes, others prioritized grassroots community building. Ray's ability to articulate a shared vision that encompassed various goals was crucial in aligning these diverse interests. He often employed the strategy of hosting roundtable discussions, where representatives from different groups could voice their concerns and aspirations, fostering a collaborative spirit.

Examples of Successful Partnerships

One of Ray's notable partnerships was with the Sykarin Youth Coalition, a group dedicated to empowering young people through education and advocacy. Together, they launched the "Pride in Our Schools" initiative, which aimed to integrate LGBTQ history and rights into the school curriculum. This partnership not only educated students but also created a safe space for LGBTQ youth to express themselves, significantly reducing instances of bullying and discrimination.

Additionally, Ray collaborated with local businesses to establish the "Sykarin Pride Month." This initiative included a series of events, such as parades, workshops, and art exhibitions, that celebrated LGBTQ culture and history. The involvement of local businesses not only provided financial support but also encouraged community members to engage with LGBTQ issues in a celebratory and inclusive manner.

The Impact of Alliances on Ray's Activism

The alliances Ray forged had a profound impact on his activism and the broader LGBTQ movement in Sykarin. By creating a diverse coalition of supporters, Ray was able to amplify the voices of those who had historically been marginalized within the LGBTQ community. This approach not only strengthened the movement but also fostered a sense of solidarity among various groups.

Moreover, the partnerships facilitated the sharing of best practices and resources, leading to more effective advocacy strategies. For instance, the collaboration with the Sykarin Youth Coalition resulted in the development of training programs for teachers, equipping them with the tools to create inclusive classrooms. This ripple effect of knowledge sharing ultimately contributed to a more informed and compassionate society.

Conclusion

In conclusion, the forging of alliances and partnerships was a cornerstone of Ray Ilan's activism. Through his efforts to unite diverse groups, Ray not only enhanced the visibility and impact of LGBTQ issues in Sykarin but also laid the groundwork for a more inclusive and equitable society. The challenges faced in building these alliances were met with determination and creativity, ultimately leading to transformative change. As Ray often said, "Together, we are unstoppable," a mantra that encapsulated the essence of his collaborative approach to activism.

Ray's journey towards bridging the gap between LGBTQ and non-LGBTQ communities

Ray Ilan's journey towards bridging the gap between LGBTQ and non-LGBTQ communities began with a deep understanding of the underlying societal structures that perpetuate division. Drawing on theories of social identity and intersectionality, Ray recognized that the barriers between communities were not merely individual prejudices but systemic issues rooted in historical contexts.

Theoretical Framework

Social identity theory, as proposed by Henri Tajfel, posits that individuals derive a sense of self from their group memberships, leading to in-group favoritism and out-group discrimination. This framework helped Ray understand the dynamics at play in Sykarin, where LGBTQ individuals often found themselves marginalized. By emphasizing common humanity rather than differences, Ray aimed to shift perceptions and foster empathy across communities.

$$\text{Social Identity} = \text{Personal Identity} + \text{Group Identity} \qquad (21)$$

Additionally, the concept of intersectionality, introduced by Kimberlé Crenshaw, informed Ray's activism. He understood that the experiences of LGBTQ individuals are not monolithic; rather, they intersect with race, class, gender, and other identities. This nuanced understanding allowed Ray to advocate for a more inclusive approach that acknowledged the diverse experiences within the LGBTQ community.

Community Engagement Initiatives

To bridge the gap, Ray initiated community engagement programs that brought together LGBTQ and non-LGBTQ individuals. One notable initiative was the "Unity in Diversity" festival, which celebrated cultural differences while promoting dialogue. The festival featured art, music, and workshops that encouraged collaboration between community members.

For example, a workshop titled "Understanding Each Other" facilitated discussions on stereotypes and misconceptions. Participants shared personal stories, fostering empathy and understanding. This approach aligned with the contact hypothesis, which suggests that increased interaction between groups can reduce prejudice.

$$\text{Prejudice Reduction} \propto \text{Increased Contact} \qquad (22)$$

Ray also established partnerships with local businesses and organizations. By collaborating on initiatives such as inclusive hiring practices and diversity training, he created opportunities for non-LGBTQ allies to engage actively in the fight for equality. This not only empowered LGBTQ individuals but also educated the broader community about the importance of inclusivity.

Challenges Encountered

Despite these efforts, Ray faced significant challenges. Resistance from conservative factions within Sykarin posed obstacles to his initiatives. Many non-LGBTQ individuals held entrenched beliefs that made them resistant to change. Ray addressed this by employing a strategy of gradual exposure, introducing LGBTQ narratives through relatable mediums such as film screenings and art exhibits.

One poignant example was the screening of a documentary highlighting the lives of LGBTQ individuals in Sykarin. By showcasing personal stories, Ray aimed to humanize the LGBTQ experience and dismantle stereotypes. The documentary sparked discussions that led to increased awareness and understanding among non-LGBTQ audiences.

Impact and Legacy

Ray's efforts to bridge the gap were not without impact. Over time, he witnessed a shift in attitudes within Sykarin. Non-LGBTQ individuals began to participate actively in LGBTQ events, and alliances formed around shared goals of equality and justice. The annual "Pride and Allies March," which began as a small gathering, grew into a city-wide event that celebrated diversity and unity.

Moreover, Ray's work laid the groundwork for future initiatives aimed at fostering inclusivity. The establishment of the "Ray Ilan Foundation" provided resources for ongoing education and advocacy, ensuring that the dialogue between LGBTQ and non-LGBTQ communities continued.

In conclusion, Ray Ilan's journey towards bridging the gap between LGBTQ and non-LGBTQ communities exemplifies the power of empathy, dialogue, and collaboration. By applying theoretical frameworks and engaging in community initiatives, Ray not only broke down barriers but also fostered a culture of understanding and acceptance in Sykarin. His legacy serves as a reminder that bridging divides requires commitment, creativity, and an unwavering belief in the potential for change.

The importance of intersectionality in Ray's activism

In the vibrant tapestry of LGBTQ activism, Ray Ilan stands as a beacon of intersectionality, a concept that underscores the interconnected nature of social categorizations such as race, class, and gender, and how these overlapping identities contribute to unique experiences of discrimination and privilege. Coined by legal scholar Kimberlé Crenshaw in 1989, intersectionality offers a framework for understanding how various forms of inequality and oppression intersect, particularly within marginalized communities.

Ray's activism is deeply rooted in this principle, recognizing that the fight for LGBTQ rights cannot be divorced from the broader struggles against racism, sexism, and economic inequality. For Ray, intersectionality is not merely an academic concept; it is a lived reality that informs every aspect of his activism.

Theoretical Framework Intersectionality posits that individuals experience overlapping systems of oppression, which can compound their struggles. For example, a Black transgender woman may face discrimination not only because of her gender identity but also due to her race. This dual marginalization highlights the necessity for an inclusive approach in activism, one that addresses the specific needs of diverse subgroups within the LGBTQ community.

Mathematically, we can represent intersectionality as follows:

$$I = f(R, G, C, E) \qquad (23)$$

where:

+ I = Intersectionality

+ R = Race

+ G = Gender

+ C = Class

+ E = Other identities (e.g., ability, age, nationality)

This equation illustrates that intersectionality is a function of multiple identities that shape an individual's experience of oppression and privilege.

Challenges in Activism   Ray encountered significant challenges in advocating for intersectionality within the LGBTQ movement.   Many mainstream LGBTQ organizations historically prioritized issues affecting white, cisgender, middle-class individuals, often sidelining the voices of people of color, transgender individuals, and those from lower socioeconomic backgrounds.   This exclusion not only perpetuated existing inequalities but also weakened the movement's overall effectiveness.

For instance, during a pivotal rally in Sykarin, Ray addressed the issue of police violence against transgender individuals, particularly focusing on the alarming rates of violence faced by transgender women of color. He stated, "When we fight for our rights, we must ensure that no one is left behind. The struggle for justice is not a monolith; it is a chorus of voices that must harmonize."

Examples of Intersectional Activism   Ray's approach to intersectionality is evident in his initiatives aimed at creating inclusive spaces that cater to the diverse needs of the LGBTQ community.   One of his notable projects was the establishment of the Sykarin LGBTQ Resource Center, which offered tailored programs for various demographic groups, including workshops on the unique challenges faced by LGBTQ youth of color and support groups for LGBTQ individuals with disabilities.

Moreover, Ray collaborated with local organizations that focused on racial justice, women's rights, and economic equity, effectively broadening the scope of

LGBTQ activism. By forging these alliances, Ray demonstrated that the fight for LGBTQ rights is inherently linked to other social justice movements.

The Impact of Intersectionality on Ray's Activism Ray's commitment to intersectionality has significantly shaped the landscape of LGBTQ activism in Sykarin. By amplifying the voices of marginalized individuals within the community, he has fostered a more inclusive movement that recognizes the complexity of identity. This approach has not only empowered those who have historically been silenced but has also attracted a broader coalition of supporters, strengthening the fight for equality.

In conclusion, the importance of intersectionality in Ray Ilan's activism cannot be overstated. It serves as a guiding principle that informs his strategies, challenges, and collaborations. By embracing the multifaceted nature of identity, Ray has not only advanced LGBTQ rights in Sykarin but has also set a precedent for future activists to follow—a testament to the power of unity in diversity.

Celebrating the strength and resilience of the LGBTQ community

The LGBTQ community has long been a tapestry woven from the threads of diverse identities, experiences, and histories. This section aims to spotlight the remarkable strength and resilience that has characterized LGBTQ individuals and groups, particularly in the face of systemic discrimination and societal challenges.

Theoretical Framework

To understand the resilience of the LGBTQ community, we can draw upon several theoretical frameworks, including resilience theory, intersectionality, and social identity theory. Resilience theory posits that individuals and groups can adapt and thrive despite adversity, often through the support of their communities. Intersectionality, introduced by Kimberlé Crenshaw, emphasizes that individuals experience oppression and privilege differently based on overlapping social identities, such as race, gender, and sexual orientation. Social identity theory, developed by Henri Tajfel and John Turner, suggests that a person's sense of who they are is based on their group membership, which can offer both a source of pride and a basis for discrimination.

Historical Context

Historically, the LGBTQ community has faced significant challenges, including criminalization, discrimination, and social ostracism. The Stonewall Riots of 1969 marked a pivotal moment in LGBTQ history, serving as a catalyst for the modern LGBTQ rights movement. The resilience exhibited during and after these riots laid the groundwork for future activism, demonstrating that the community could unite in the face of oppression.

Community Support and Solidarity

One of the most potent sources of strength within the LGBTQ community is its capacity for solidarity and support. Organizations such as The Trevor Project, Human Rights Campaign, and local LGBTQ centers provide essential resources, advocacy, and safe spaces for individuals. These organizations not only offer support but also mobilize community action, fostering a sense of belonging and collective empowerment.

For instance, during the COVID-19 pandemic, many LGBTQ organizations adapted to the challenges by providing virtual support groups and online resources, showcasing resilience in a time of crisis. The ability to pivot and continue offering support exemplifies the community's strength.

Cultural Expression and Activism

Art and cultural expression have historically served as powerful tools for LGBTQ individuals to assert their identities and share their stories. From the works of poets like Allen Ginsberg to contemporary artists like Lady Gaga, cultural expression has played a crucial role in challenging stereotypes and fostering pride.

Activism, too, has been a means of celebrating resilience. Events like Pride parades are not only celebrations of identity but also acts of defiance against societal norms. They symbolize the collective strength of the LGBTQ community, showcasing vibrant expressions of identity, love, and unity.

Intersectionality and Resilience

The LGBTQ community is not monolithic; it encompasses a diverse range of identities, including people of color, those with disabilities, and individuals from various socioeconomic backgrounds. The intersection of these identities can complicate experiences of oppression but also highlights the multifaceted nature of resilience.

For example, LGBTQ individuals of color often face compounded discrimination, leading to a unique set of challenges. However, many have emerged as leaders within the movement, advocating for a more inclusive approach that recognizes the importance of intersectionality. This collective advocacy not only strengthens the LGBTQ movement but also fosters resilience among its members.

Personal Narratives of Resilience

Personal narratives play a vital role in illustrating the resilience of the LGBTQ community. Stories of individuals overcoming adversity, such as coming out in unsupportive environments or battling mental health challenges, serve as powerful testaments to the strength of the community.

For instance, the story of Marsha P. Johnson, a Black transgender activist and key figure in the Stonewall Riots, highlights resilience in the face of systemic oppression. Johnson's unwavering commitment to activism and community support exemplifies the indomitable spirit that characterizes many within the LGBTQ community.

Conclusion

In conclusion, the strength and resilience of the LGBTQ community are celebrated through its rich history, community support, cultural expression, and personal narratives. By understanding the theoretical frameworks that underpin these experiences, we can better appreciate the complexities of resilience within the community. As we continue to advocate for equality and justice, it is essential to recognize and honor the strength that has propelled the LGBTQ movement forward, ensuring that future generations can thrive in an inclusive and supportive environment.

$$R = \sum_{i=1}^{n} \left(\frac{S_i}{D_i} \right) \tag{24}$$

where R represents resilience, S_i signifies the support systems available to individuals, and D_i represents the discrimination faced. This equation encapsulates the balance of support and adversity that defines resilience in the LGBTQ community.

Ray's role in fostering a sense of community

Ray Ilan's journey through the tumultuous landscape of LGBTQ activism in Sykarin was not merely about breaking barriers; it was fundamentally about building a community. In a world where individuals often felt isolated due to their identities, Ray recognized the profound importance of connection and solidarity.

His efforts to foster a sense of community can be understood through several key frameworks: social identity theory, community psychology, and intersectionality.

Social Identity Theory

Social identity theory, proposed by Henri Tajfel and John Turner, posits that individuals derive a sense of self from their group memberships. Ray understood that for many LGBTQ individuals in Sykarin, their sexual orientation or gender identity was a significant part of their identity. By creating spaces where these identities were celebrated, Ray helped individuals to embrace their authentic selves.

For example, Ray organized regular meet-ups at local cafes and community centers, where LGBTQ individuals could gather without fear of judgment. These events fostered a sense of belonging, allowing individuals to share their experiences and support one another. The informal nature of these gatherings encouraged participants to express their identities freely, reinforcing their social connections.

Community Psychology

The field of community psychology emphasizes the importance of community-based interventions in promoting mental health and well-being. Ray's initiatives were deeply rooted in this principle. He launched the "Sykarin Pride Network," a grassroots organization aimed at providing resources and support to LGBTQ individuals. This network not only offered counseling services but also organized workshops on topics such as self-advocacy and resilience.

By addressing the psychological needs of the community, Ray facilitated a support system that empowered individuals to confront societal challenges. The success of the Sykarin Pride Network can be measured through participant feedback, with 85% of attendees reporting increased confidence in their identities and a greater sense of community belonging.

Intersectionality

Ray's approach to community building was also informed by the concept of intersectionality, introduced by Kimberlé Crenshaw. He recognized that LGBTQ individuals do not exist in a vacuum; their experiences are shaped by intersecting identities, including race, gender, and socioeconomic status. Ray's activism sought to include voices from marginalized intersections within the LGBTQ community.

For instance, Ray collaborated with local organizations representing people of color and those with disabilities to ensure that their needs were addressed. This collaboration culminated in the "Unity Festival," an annual event celebrating the diversity within the LGBTQ community. The festival featured performances from artists of various backgrounds, workshops on intersectional issues, and discussions on how to collectively combat discrimination.

Challenges and Resilience

Despite Ray's unwavering commitment to fostering community, he faced significant challenges. Resistance from conservative factions within Sykarin often manifested in protests against LGBTQ events and initiatives. However, Ray's resilience shone through during these times. He organized counter-protests that not only defended the LGBTQ community but also educated the broader public about LGBTQ issues.

One notable example was the "March for Acceptance," where Ray led a peaceful demonstration that attracted over 1,000 participants, showcasing the strength of community solidarity. This event not only countered negative narratives but also galvanized support from allies, further strengthening the community fabric.

The Ripple Effect

Ray's role in fostering community extended beyond immediate support. By creating a robust network of LGBTQ individuals and allies, he sparked a ripple effect that encouraged others to take action. Many participants from his events went on to become advocates themselves, forming their own groups and initiatives. This organic growth of activism exemplifies the power of community in driving social change.

As Ray often stated, "When we stand together, we are unstoppable." This mantra became a rallying cry for the community, encapsulating the essence of collective strength. The sense of community that Ray fostered in Sykarin became a model for other regions, demonstrating how localized efforts can lead to broader societal shifts.

In conclusion, Ray Ilan's role in fostering a sense of community was pivotal to his activism. By utilizing social identity theory, community psychology principles, and an intersectional approach, he created a safe haven for LGBTQ individuals in Sykarin. His legacy is one of resilience, unity, and empowerment, leaving an indelible mark on the community he fought to uplift. The sense of belonging that Ray cultivated continues to inspire future generations of activists, proving that community is not just a support system but a catalyst for change.

Chapter 2: Shattering Glass Ceilings

Chapter 2: Shattering Glass Ceilings

Chapter 2: Shattering Glass Ceilings

In the heart of Sykarin, where the sun sets over the horizon like a golden promise of change, Ray Ilan began to carve a path that would not only redefine the landscape of LGBTQ rights but also challenge the very foundations of societal norms. This chapter, "Shattering Glass Ceilings," encapsulates Ray's introduction to the tumultuous world of politics and LGBTQ rights, where he would soon become a beacon of hope and resilience.

Ray's Introduction to Politics and LGBTQ Rights

Ray's journey into the political arena was not a mere coincidence; it was a culmination of years spent grappling with his identity and the societal expectations that sought to confine him. The political landscape of Sykarin was riddled with outdated beliefs and stereotypes that marginalized LGBTQ individuals. Ray recognized that to effect real change, he had to step into the ring and fight for his community.

$$\text{Activism} = \text{Awareness} \times \text{Engagement} \qquad (25)$$

This equation represents Ray's belief that true activism arises from a combination of raising awareness about LGBTQ issues and engaging with the community to foster change. Ray began attending town hall meetings, where he would voice the concerns of the LGBTQ community, often facing backlash but never backing down.

Challenging the Status Quo in Sykarin's Political Landscape

As Ray navigated the political landscape, he encountered a myriad of challenges. The status quo was entrenched, and the existing political figures were often resistant to change. However, Ray's determination was unwavering. He organized rallies, created awareness campaigns, and began to build a coalition of like-minded individuals who believed in equality and justice.

One notable example of Ray's challenge to the status quo was the "Pride in Politics" campaign, which aimed to highlight the contributions of LGBTQ individuals in the community. The campaign was met with resistance from conservative factions, but it ultimately garnered significant support from the younger generation, who were eager for change.

Ray's Iconic Speeches that Rallied the LGBTQ Community

Ray's ability to communicate effectively became one of his most powerful tools. His speeches were not just words; they were calls to action. During the annual Sykarin Pride Parade, Ray delivered a speech that ignited the crowd, stating:

> "We are not just fighting for our rights; we are fighting for the right to love, to exist, and to thrive in a world that often seeks to silence us. Together, we will shatter these glass ceilings and pave the way for future generations."

This moment marked a turning point in Ray's activism, as it united the LGBTQ community and allies in a shared vision of hope and resilience.

The Formation of the LGBTQ Equality Party

Recognizing the need for a structured approach to advocacy, Ray spearheaded the formation of the LGBTQ Equality Party. This political entity aimed to represent the voices of LGBTQ individuals in Sykarin's government. The party's platform included key issues such as anti-discrimination laws, healthcare access, and education reform.

The formation of the party was not without its challenges. Internal conflicts arose regarding the party's direction and strategies, but Ray's leadership skills shone through as he mediated discussions and fostered unity among members.

Ray's Journey Towards Becoming the Face of LGBTQ Political Activism

As the LGBTQ Equality Party gained traction, Ray emerged as its charismatic leader. His journey was marked by both triumphs and tribulations. He faced smear campaigns, personal attacks, and even threats to his safety. Yet, each challenge only fueled his resolve to advocate for his community.

Ray's ability to connect with people from all walks of life became his greatest asset. He understood that to break through the glass ceilings of political resistance, he needed to build bridges, not walls. This approach led to collaborations with other marginalized groups, emphasizing intersectionality in activism.

Ray's Impact on Sykarin's Political Atmosphere

Ray's influence began to permeate the political atmosphere of Sykarin. Policies that once seemed impossible to implement were now being discussed at the highest levels of government. The LGBTQ community felt empowered, and allies rallied behind Ray's vision for a more inclusive society.

The impact of Ray's activism was evident in the changing attitudes of the local populace. The once quiet whispers of dissent transformed into loud calls for equality and justice. Ray had not only shattered glass ceilings but had also inspired a movement that would echo through the halls of Sykarin's government for years to come.

In conclusion, this chapter illustrates how Ray Ilan's journey into the political realm was characterized by courage, resilience, and an unwavering commitment to breaking barriers. His introduction to politics was not just about gaining power; it was about empowering those who had been silenced for far too long. As we move forward, we will explore the obstacles Ray faced in the political arena and the strategies he employed to combat discrimination, ensuring that his legacy as a trailblazer in LGBTQ rights continues to inspire future generations.

A Trailblazing Movement

Ray's introduction to politics and LGBTQ rights

Ray Ilan's journey into the world of politics was not merely a career choice; it was a response to the urgent need for representation and advocacy for LGBTQ rights in Sykarin. As Ray navigated the complexities of his identity and the challenges of growing up in a small town, he began to recognize the profound impact that political decisions had on the lives of LGBTQ individuals. This realization served as a catalyst for Ray's entry into activism, as he sought to challenge the systemic injustices faced by his community.

The political landscape in Sykarin was characterized by a lack of representation for LGBTQ voices, which often resulted in policies that marginalized and discriminated against individuals based on their sexual orientation or gender identity. This was evident in various forms, including the absence of anti-discrimination laws, limited access to healthcare for LGBTQ individuals, and the criminalization of same-sex relationships. Ray understood that to effect meaningful change, he needed to engage with the political system directly.

Ray's introduction to politics began with grassroots organizing. He started attending local meetings and forums, where he could voice the concerns of the LGBTQ community. It was here that he encountered the harsh realities of political engagement; many politicians were resistant to discussing LGBTQ issues, viewing them as divisive or unnecessary. This resistance only fueled Ray's determination to push forward. He began to study political theory, focusing on the works of scholars such as Judith Butler and Michel Foucault, who emphasized the importance of identity politics and the role of power in shaping social norms.

$$P = \frac{F}{A} \tag{26}$$

Where P represents the political pressure exerted by marginalized groups, F is the force of activism, and A is the area of influence. In this context, Ray recognized that the force of activism needed to be amplified to affect change in the political arena.

Ray's first significant political action came when he organized a protest against a local ordinance that sought to ban pride parades in Sykarin. This event marked a turning point, not only for Ray but for the entire LGBTQ community. The protest attracted a diverse crowd, including allies from various sectors of society, demonstrating that the fight for LGBTQ rights was not solely an LGBTQ issue but a human rights issue that resonated with many. The media coverage of the protest brought national attention to the struggles faced by LGBTQ individuals in Sykarin, and Ray quickly became a recognizable figure in the movement.

The success of the protest inspired Ray to delve deeper into political activism. He began to collaborate with established LGBTQ organizations, learning the ropes of political advocacy and lobbying. This experience was instrumental in shaping his understanding of the legislative process. Ray quickly realized that advocacy was not just about raising awareness; it required strategic planning, coalition-building, and a deep understanding of the political landscape.

One of the key theories that influenced Ray's approach was the concept of intersectionality, as articulated by Kimberlé Crenshaw. Ray understood that the struggles faced by LGBTQ individuals were often compounded by other forms of discrimination, including race, class, and gender. This understanding led him to advocate for a more inclusive approach to LGBTQ rights, one that considered the diverse experiences of individuals within the community.

As Ray became more involved in politics, he faced numerous challenges, including pushback from conservative factions within Sykarin. These groups often employed fear tactics, suggesting that LGBTQ rights would undermine traditional family values. Ray countered these arguments with data and personal stories, emphasizing that LGBTQ individuals deserved the same rights and protections as everyone else. He utilized social media as a platform to share these narratives, effectively humanizing the issues at stake.

$$R = \frac{C}{S} \qquad (27)$$

Where R is the reach of LGBTQ advocacy, C is the number of communities engaged, and S is the societal stigma present. Ray's ability to engage with multiple communities while addressing stigma was crucial in expanding the reach of LGBTQ advocacy in Sykarin.

Ray's introduction to politics culminated in his decision to run for office. Fueled by a desire to create tangible change, he launched a campaign that focused on LGBTQ rights, healthcare access, and anti-discrimination laws. His platform resonated with a broad audience, as he articulated a vision for a more inclusive Sykarin. Ray's candidacy was not just about personal ambition; it was about representing those who had been silenced for too long.

In conclusion, Ray Ilan's introduction to politics and LGBTQ rights was marked by a series of strategic actions and theoretical understandings that shaped his activism. From grassroots organizing to running for office, Ray's journey exemplifies the power of political engagement in advocating for marginalized communities. His commitment to challenging the status quo and amplifying diverse voices set the stage for a transformative movement in Sykarin, one that would continue to evolve as Ray's activism gained momentum.

Challenging the status quo in Sykarin's political landscape

In the small town of Sykarin, the political landscape was traditionally dominated by conservative values and a reluctance to embrace change. The status quo was characterized by a lack of representation for LGBTQ individuals, who often faced discrimination and marginalization in both social and political spheres. Ray Ilan's entry into this landscape marked a seismic shift, challenging long-held beliefs and practices that had stifled the voices of many.

One of the primary theories that underpin Ray's challenge to the status quo is the concept of **social constructivism**, which posits that societal norms and values are not inherent but rather constructed through social processes. Ray recognized that the prevailing attitudes towards LGBTQ individuals in Sykarin were not immutable truths but rather constructs that could be deconstructed and reshaped through activism and political engagement. This understanding fueled Ray's determination to redefine what was considered acceptable and normal within the political discourse of Sykarin.

Ray's first major challenge to the status quo came during a local council meeting, where he presented a motion advocating for the inclusion of LGBTQ rights in the town's official policies. This was met with significant resistance from conservative council members, who argued that such measures would undermine traditional family values. Ray countered this argument by presenting data that highlighted the psychological and social benefits of inclusivity, citing studies such as:

$$\text{Well-being} = f(\text{Inclusion, Acceptance, Support}) \quad\quad (28)$$

This equation illustrates that well-being is a function of inclusion, acceptance, and support, all of which are critical for the mental health of LGBTQ individuals. By framing his arguments in terms of community well-being rather than merely rights, Ray was able to appeal to a broader audience, including those who may have initially opposed LGBTQ inclusion.

Despite his efforts, Ray faced significant backlash. Many in Sykarin viewed his activism as a direct threat to their way of life. For instance, during a town hall meeting, a local pastor delivered a vehement speech against Ray's initiatives, claiming they would lead to the moral decay of the community. This incident highlighted the deep-seated fears that many residents had regarding change. Ray, however, remained undeterred. He began to organize community forums where residents could express their concerns and engage in open dialogue about LGBTQ issues. This approach demonstrated Ray's commitment to not only advocating for LGBTQ rights but also fostering understanding and empathy among all community members.

Moreover, Ray's activism was not limited to local politics; it also encompassed a broader critique of systemic injustices. He frequently referenced the **Intersectionality Theory**, developed by Kimberlé Crenshaw, which emphasizes that individuals experience overlapping forms of discrimination based on various social identities, including race, gender, and sexual orientation. Ray's application of this theory was evident in his speeches, where he highlighted the unique challenges faced by LGBTQ individuals of color, women, and those from low-income backgrounds. By doing so, he expanded the conversation beyond mere representation to include the complexities of identity and the need for comprehensive solutions.

One notable example of Ray's challenge to the political status quo occurred during the election season when he decided to run for a local council seat. His campaign was unconventional; it focused not only on LGBTQ issues but also on broader social justice themes, such as affordable housing, education reform, and healthcare access. Ray's slogan, "A Voice for All," resonated with many voters who felt disenfranchised by the traditional political elite. His ability to connect LGBTQ rights with universal human rights issues helped to galvanize support from diverse groups within Sykarin.

As Ray campaigned, he faced numerous obstacles, including a lack of funding and resources compared to his opponents, who were backed by established political machines. However, he leveraged social media platforms to engage younger voters and build a grassroots movement. This strategy not only challenged the status quo but also disrupted traditional campaigning methods, demonstrating that political engagement could be accessible to all, regardless of financial status.

Ray's efforts culminated in a pivotal moment when he organized a rally that drew hundreds of supporters from across Sykarin and neighboring towns. This event not only showcased the growing support for LGBTQ rights but also served as a powerful statement against the entrenched political norms that had long silenced marginalized voices. The rally featured speakers from various backgrounds, each sharing personal stories of discrimination and resilience, creating a tapestry of experiences that illustrated the urgent need for change.

In conclusion, Ray Ilan's challenge to the status quo in Sykarin's political landscape was marked by a strategic blend of theory, grassroots activism, and community engagement. By framing LGBTQ rights within the broader context of social justice and well-being, Ray not only advocated for his community but also inspired others to join the fight against systemic discrimination. His legacy serves as a testament to the power of challenging societal norms and the importance of representation in fostering a more inclusive political environment.

Ray's iconic speeches that rallied the LGBTQ community

Ray Ilan's journey through the political landscape of Sykarin was marked by a series of iconic speeches that not only galvanized the local LGBTQ community but also challenged societal norms and expectations. Each speech was a carefully crafted blend of personal narrative, emotional resonance, and powerful calls to action, embodying Ray's unique style and passion for advocacy.

The Art of Persuasion

At the heart of Ray's speeches was the art of persuasion, a skill that allowed him to connect with diverse audiences. According to Aristotle's rhetorical framework, effective persuasion relies on three key elements: ethos (credibility), pathos (emotional appeal), and logos (logical argument). Ray masterfully employed these elements to create compelling narratives that resonated with both LGBTQ individuals and allies.

$$P = E + A + R \tag{29}$$

Where P represents persuasion, E represents ethos, A represents pathos, and R represents logos. Ray's ability to weave his personal experiences into a broader narrative of struggle and triumph helped establish his credibility (ethos), while his passionate delivery invoked deep emotional responses (pathos), and his logical arguments laid out the necessity for change (logos).

Key Themes in Ray's Speeches

Ray's speeches often revolved around several key themes that reflected the challenges faced by the LGBTQ community in Sykarin:

+ **Identity and Acceptance:** Ray spoke candidly about his own journey of self-discovery, emphasizing the importance of embracing one's true self. This theme resonated deeply with many individuals who had faced similar struggles.

+ **Unity and Solidarity:** In a society often divided by prejudice, Ray's messages of unity served as a rallying cry for the LGBTQ community. He frequently reminded his audience that together, they could overcome any obstacle.

+ **Advocacy and Action:** Ray consistently called for action, urging his audience to not only advocate for their rights but also to engage in the political process. He believed that change was possible through collective effort and determination.

Memorable Moments

One of Ray's most memorable speeches occurred during the annual Sykarin Pride Parade. Standing atop a makeshift stage, he addressed a crowd of thousands, declaring:

> "We are not just fighting for our rights; we are fighting for the very essence of who we are. We are here, we are proud, and we will not be silenced!"

This moment encapsulated Ray's ability to inspire and mobilize. The crowd erupted in cheers, a testament to the profound impact of his words.

Impact and Legacy

Ray's speeches not only rallied the LGBTQ community but also attracted attention from local media and political figures. His ability to articulate the struggles faced by LGBTQ individuals in a manner that was both relatable and inspiring helped shift public perception and foster a greater understanding of LGBTQ issues.

The ripple effect of Ray's speeches can be seen in the increased visibility of LGBTQ rights in Sykarin's political discourse. Following one of his speeches, a local newspaper published an editorial endorsing LGBTQ rights, marking a significant shift in the community's dialogue.

Conclusion

In conclusion, Ray Ilan's iconic speeches were pivotal in rallying the LGBTQ community in Sykarin. Through a combination of personal storytelling, emotional resonance, and compelling calls to action, Ray not only inspired individuals to embrace their identities but also galvanized a movement for change. His legacy as a powerful orator continues to influence LGBTQ activism, proving that words have the power to ignite passion and drive progress.

The formation of the LGBTQ Equality Party

In the vibrant political landscape of Sykarin, the need for a dedicated platform advocating for LGBTQ rights became increasingly apparent. As Ray Ilan's activism gained momentum, it became clear that the existing political parties were not adequately representing the interests and rights of the LGBTQ community. This realization catalyzed Ray's vision for a new political entity—the LGBTQ Equality Party.

Identifying the Need for Representation

The LGBTQ community in Sykarin faced systemic discrimination, social stigmatization, and a lack of political voice. The existing political parties often overlooked LGBTQ issues, prioritizing traditional concerns over the nuanced challenges faced by sexual and gender minorities. Ray recognized that without a dedicated party, the community's needs would continue to be marginalized.

Building a Coalition

To form the LGBTQ Equality Party, Ray embarked on a mission to unite diverse voices within the LGBTQ community. This coalition-building process involved extensive outreach efforts, engaging with individuals from various backgrounds—transgender activists, queer youth, and allies. Ray organized town hall meetings, where community members could express their concerns and aspirations. This grassroots approach ensured that the party's foundation was built on the lived experiences of its constituents.

Drafting a Manifesto

Central to the formation of the LGBTQ Equality Party was the development of a comprehensive manifesto. This document outlined the party's core principles and policy goals, including:

- **Equality and Non-Discrimination:** Advocating for laws that protect LGBTQ individuals from discrimination in housing, employment, and public services.

- **Healthcare Access:** Ensuring equitable access to healthcare services, including mental health support and gender-affirming care.

- **Education:** Promoting inclusive curricula that educate students about LGBTQ history and issues, fostering a culture of acceptance in schools.

- **Safety and Support:** Establishing safe spaces and resources for LGBTQ individuals facing violence or harassment.

Ray's commitment to inclusivity was reflected in the manifesto, which emphasized intersectionality, recognizing that issues of race, class, and gender identity intersect with sexual orientation.

Launching the Party

The official launch of the LGBTQ Equality Party was a landmark event in Sykarin's political history. Ray organized a rally in the town square, drawing a diverse crowd of supporters. The atmosphere was electric, with speeches that resonated with the community's hopes and struggles. Ray's passionate oratory highlighted the urgency of the moment, stating:

> "We are not just fighting for our rights; we are fighting for our lives. The LGBTQ Equality Party will be the voice of the voiceless, the hope for the hopeless, and the change that Sykarin desperately needs."

The rally culminated in the formal announcement of the party's formation, accompanied by a call to action for community members to register and participate in the political process.

Challenges and Opposition

The formation of the LGBTQ Equality Party was not without its challenges. Opposition from conservative factions within Sykarin was swift and fierce. Critics questioned the legitimacy of the party, often resorting to derogatory language and unfounded accusations. Ray and his team faced significant hurdles in gaining recognition and respect within the broader political landscape.

Despite these challenges, the party's grassroots support continued to grow. Ray's strategy involved engaging with the community through door-to-door campaigns, educational workshops, and social media outreach. By fostering dialogue and building relationships, the LGBTQ Equality Party began to shift perceptions and challenge the status quo.

Establishing Political Infrastructure

As the party gained traction, Ray understood the importance of establishing a robust political infrastructure. This included forming local chapters, recruiting candidates for local elections, and developing a fundraising strategy to support campaign initiatives. The party's structure was designed to empower grassroots activists, ensuring that leadership positions were accessible to individuals from diverse backgrounds.

Achievements and Milestones

Within a short period, the LGBTQ Equality Party achieved significant milestones. They successfully lobbied for the inclusion of LGBTQ rights in the local government agenda, leading to the implementation of policies that protected against discrimination. Additionally, the party's candidates began to win seats in local councils, further amplifying the community's voice in political decision-making.

Ray's leadership was instrumental in these achievements, as he tirelessly advocated for the rights of LGBTQ individuals both within and outside the party. His ability to articulate the party's vision and mobilize support was critical to its success.

Conclusion

The formation of the LGBTQ Equality Party marked a pivotal moment in Sykarin's political landscape. Under Ray Ilan's leadership, the party emerged as a powerful advocate for LGBTQ rights, challenging existing norms and pushing for systemic change. The party not only provided a platform for marginalized voices but also inspired a new generation of activists to engage in the political process. As Ray often reminded his supporters, "Together, we are unstoppable. Together, we will break the barriers that have held us back for too long."

Ray's journey towards becoming the face of LGBTQ political activism

Ray Ilan's journey towards becoming the face of LGBTQ political activism was not merely a personal evolution; it was a powerful convergence of societal dynamics, personal resilience, and the relentless pursuit of justice. This section explores the theoretical frameworks underpinning Ray's activism, the significant challenges he faced, and the milestones that marked his ascent to prominence in the political landscape of Sykarin.

Theoretical Frameworks

To understand Ray's emergence as a political figure, we must first consider the theoretical frameworks that informed his activism. Drawing from *Critical Theory*, particularly the works of Theodor Adorno and Max Horkheimer, Ray recognized the importance of challenging the status quo. Critical Theory posits that societal structures often perpetuate oppression, and thus, activism must aim to unveil these structures. Ray's activism was rooted in the belief that visibility and representation were essential to dismantling systemic discrimination against LGBTQ individuals.

Additionally, Ray embraced *Intersectionality*, a term coined by Kimberlé Crenshaw. This framework highlights how various forms of identity—such as race, gender, and sexual orientation—intersect to create unique modes of discrimination. Ray's activism was deeply informed by this perspective, as he sought to address not only LGBTQ rights but also the interconnected struggles faced by marginalized communities within Sykarin.

Challenges Faced

Ray's ascent to political activism was fraught with challenges. Initially, he encountered the pervasive stigma surrounding LGBTQ individuals in Sykarin. The local political landscape was dominated by conservative ideologies that viewed LGBTQ rights as a threat to traditional values. This environment posed significant barriers to Ray's efforts to advocate for equality.

One of the primary challenges was the lack of representation in political offices. LGBTQ individuals were often sidelined in political discussions, leading to policies that failed to address their needs. Ray's determination to change this narrative was met with resistance from established political figures who were reluctant to embrace progressive change.

Moreover, Ray faced personal challenges, including threats and harassment aimed at silencing his voice. However, he viewed these adversities as fuel for his activism, reinforcing his commitment to advocating for LGBTQ rights.

Milestones in Ray's Ascent

Despite the myriad challenges, Ray's journey was marked by significant milestones that solidified his status as a leading figure in LGBTQ political activism.

- **Founding the LGBTQ Equality Party:** One of Ray's most significant achievements was the establishment of the LGBTQ Equality Party. This political party aimed to create a platform specifically addressing the rights and needs of LGBTQ individuals. The party's formation was a pivotal moment in Sykarin's political landscape, as it provided a voice for those who had been historically marginalized.

- **Iconic Speeches:** Ray's ability to articulate the struggles and aspirations of the LGBTQ community resonated deeply with the public. His speeches became a rallying cry for change, emphasizing the importance of unity and resilience. For instance, during a major rally in Sykarin, Ray stated,

> "We are not just fighting for our rights; we are fighting for the right to exist, to love, and to be who we are without fear."

This statement encapsulated the essence of his activism and inspired many to join the movement.

+ **Legislative Advocacy:** Ray's political activism extended to legislative efforts aimed at advancing LGBTQ rights. He played a crucial role in advocating for anti-discrimination laws and policies that protected LGBTQ individuals in employment, housing, and healthcare. His relentless pursuit of legislative change demonstrated that political activism could lead to tangible improvements in people's lives.

+ **Building Alliances:** Recognizing the importance of coalition-building, Ray forged alliances with other marginalized groups, including racial minorities and women. This approach not only amplified the LGBTQ movement's voice but also highlighted the interconnectedness of various social justice struggles. By collaborating with these groups, Ray was able to broaden the scope of his activism and create a more inclusive movement.

Conclusion

Ray Ilan's journey towards becoming the face of LGBTQ political activism in Sykarin was a testament to his unwavering commitment to justice and equality. By grounding his activism in critical theory and intersectionality, he was able to challenge societal norms and advocate for meaningful change. Despite facing significant challenges, Ray's milestones—such as founding the LGBTQ Equality Party, delivering iconic speeches, and advocating for legislative change—solidified his status as a prominent political figure. His journey serves as an inspiration for future activists, illustrating that the path to political representation is fraught with obstacles but ultimately achievable through resilience, unity, and a steadfast commitment to justice.

Ray's impact on Sykarin's political atmosphere

Ray Ilan's emergence as a pivotal figure in Sykarin's political landscape marked a significant turning point not only for the LGBTQ community but for the entire socio-political fabric of the town. His influence can be analyzed through several theoretical frameworks, including social movement theory, intersectionality, and the concept of political representation.

Social Movement Theory

Social movement theory posits that collective action can lead to social change, driven by the shared experiences and goals of marginalized groups. Ray's activism exemplified this theory as he galvanized the LGBTQ community in Sykarin, transforming individual struggles into a powerful collective voice. His ability to mobilize allies and supporters was instrumental in challenging the status quo. For instance, during his first major rally, Ray's impassioned speech drew a crowd of over a thousand attendees, a clear demonstration of the community's willingness to unite for change. The equation that encapsulates this mobilization can be represented as:

$$\text{Social Change} = f(\text{Collective Action, Awareness, Support})$$

Here, the function f illustrates that social change in Sykarin is a direct outcome of the synergy between collective action, increased awareness of LGBTQ issues, and community support.

Intersectionality in Politics

Ray's activism also brought to light the importance of intersectionality in political discourse. By recognizing that LGBTQ issues intersect with race, gender, and socio-economic status, Ray advocated for policies that addressed the unique challenges faced by diverse groups within the LGBTQ community. This approach not only broadened the scope of LGBTQ activism in Sykarin but also fostered alliances with other marginalized groups, creating a more inclusive political atmosphere. For example, Ray partnered with local organizations advocating for racial equality, leading to a series of joint initiatives that highlighted the interconnectedness of their struggles. The impact of this intersectional approach can be summarized by the equation:

$$\text{Inclusive Policies} = g(\text{Intersectionality, Collaboration, Advocacy})$$

Where g reflects how inclusive policies are a product of recognizing intersectionality, fostering collaboration, and sustained advocacy.

Political Representation and Visibility

Ray's rise to prominence also significantly impacted political representation in Sykarin. As the first openly LGBTQ individual to hold a political office, Ray challenged the prevailing norms and stereotypes that often marginalized LGBTQ voices in governance. His presence in the political arena inspired a new generation of activists and politicians, demonstrating that representation matters. The visibility of LGBTQ individuals in political spaces can be expressed as:

$$\text{Visibility} = h(\text{Representation, Media Coverage, Public Perception})$$

In this case, h indicates that increased visibility is contingent upon representation in political offices, positive media coverage, and a shift in public perception towards acceptance.

Challenges and Backlash

Despite his significant impact, Ray faced considerable challenges and backlash from conservative factions within Sykarin. These groups often employed rhetoric that sought to undermine his achievements, framing his activism as a threat to traditional values. However, Ray's resilience in the face of adversity only strengthened his resolve and further galvanized support from the LGBTQ community and its allies. The dynamics of this backlash can be analyzed through the lens of conflict theory, which suggests that social change often emerges from the tensions between opposing groups.

Legacy and Future Implications

Ray Ilan's influence on Sykarin's political atmosphere is multifaceted and profound. By advocating for LGBTQ rights, fostering intersectional alliances, and challenging societal norms, he has laid the groundwork for a more inclusive political environment. His legacy is evident in the increased representation of LGBTQ individuals in local politics and the ongoing dialogues surrounding LGBTQ rights and social justice in Sykarin. As future generations of activists continue to build upon his work, Ray's impact will undoubtedly resonate, shaping the trajectory of LGBTQ activism and political representation for years to come.

In conclusion, Ray Ilan's contributions to Sykarin's political atmosphere exemplify the power of activism in effecting change. His journey reflects the complexities of navigating a landscape rife with challenges while simultaneously pushing for progress. The equations presented illustrate the interconnectedness of social movements, intersectionality, and political representation, underscoring the significance of Ray's work in fostering a more equitable society.

Navigating the Political Battlefield

The obstacles faced by Ray in the political arena

Ray Ilan's journey into the political arena was not without its challenges. As an openly LGBTQ individual in a small town like Sykarin, he faced a myriad of obstacles that tested his resolve and commitment to advocacy. The political landscape was fraught with traditional values and deep-rooted prejudices, which manifested in various forms of discrimination and resistance. This section will explore the key challenges Ray encountered, supported by relevant theories and examples.

Societal Prejudice and Discrimination

One of the primary obstacles Ray faced was societal prejudice against LGBTQ individuals. According to *Social Identity Theory* (Tajfel & Turner, 1979), individuals derive a sense of identity from their group memberships. In Sykarin, where heteronormative values dominated, Ray's identity as a gay man placed him at odds with the prevailing social norms. This conflict often resulted in hostility from constituents who viewed his sexual orientation as a threat to traditional family values.

$$\text{Prejudice} = f(\text{Social Norms, Ingroup Bias, Stereotypes}) \qquad (30)$$

This equation illustrates how societal prejudice is a function of prevailing social norms, ingroup biases, and stereotypes. Ray encountered aggressive opposition during town hall meetings, where he was often met with derogatory remarks and attempts to delegitimize his platform.

Political Opposition

Ray's entry into politics also meant facing established political figures who were resistant to change. The *Status Quo Bias* (Samuelson & Zeckhauser, 1988) explains how individuals prefer things to remain the same, leading to resistance against new ideas or candidates. Many local politicians viewed Ray's candidacy as a direct challenge to their authority and the status quo.

$$\text{Status Quo Bias} = \frac{\text{Preference for Current State}}{\text{Risk of Change}} \tag{31}$$

This bias was evident in the smear campaigns launched against Ray, which aimed to undermine his credibility and portray him as unfit for office. For instance, opponents circulated false narratives suggesting that Ray's policies would lead to the moral decay of Sykarin, invoking fear to sway public opinion against him.

Internal Community Divisions

In addition to external opposition, Ray also faced challenges within the LGBTQ community itself. The *Intersectionality Theory* (Crenshaw, 1989) posits that individuals experience overlapping social identities, which can lead to unique forms of discrimination. Within the LGBTQ community, differing opinions on activism strategies and priorities sometimes created rifts.

$$\text{Intersectionality} = \sum_{i=1}^{n} \text{Identity}_i \cdot \text{Discrimination}_i \tag{32}$$

This equation highlights how various identities contribute to one's overall experience of discrimination. Some members of the LGBTQ community in Sykarin felt that Ray's approach was too radical and alienated potential allies. This internal division complicated Ray's efforts to unify the community under a common cause.

Media Scrutiny and Representation

Ray's visibility as a public figure also brought intense media scrutiny, which often skewed public perception. The *Framing Theory* (Entman, 1993) suggests that the way issues are presented in the media can significantly influence public opinion. Media coverage of Ray often focused on sensationalist aspects of his personal life rather than his political agenda.

$$\text{Public Perception} = f(\text{Media Coverage, Public Discourse}) \tag{33}$$

Ray's efforts to shift the narrative towards substantive policy discussions were often overshadowed by tabloid-style reporting that emphasized his sexuality over his qualifications. This media framing not only impacted his campaign but also affected the broader perception of LGBTQ candidates in Sykarin.

Resource Limitations

Lastly, Ray encountered significant resource limitations that hampered his political ambitions. The *Resource Dependence Theory* (Pfeffer & Salancik, 1978) posits that organizations depend on resources from their environment, which can dictate their power and influence. Ray, as a newcomer to politics, lacked the financial backing and institutional support that established candidates enjoyed.

$$\text{Power} = \frac{\text{Access to Resources}}{\text{Dependence on Others}} \tag{34}$$

Ray's campaign was often underfunded, making it difficult to compete with opponents who had access to substantial financial resources. This limitation forced Ray to rely on grassroots support and innovative fundraising strategies, which, while effective, placed additional pressure on his campaign efforts.

Conclusion

In conclusion, Ray Ilan's political journey was marked by significant obstacles, including societal prejudice, political opposition, internal community divisions, media scrutiny, and resource limitations. Each of these challenges tested his resolve and commitment to advocating for LGBTQ rights in Sykarin. However, through resilience and determination, Ray navigated these barriers, laying the groundwork for future generations of LGBTQ activists. His experiences serve as a testament to the complexities of political activism within marginalized communities and highlight the importance of solidarity, representation, and perseverance in the face of adversity.

Ray's strategies for combatting discrimination in politics

In the realm of politics, discrimination can manifest in various forms, including systemic bias, societal prejudice, and institutional barriers that hinder the representation and rights of LGBTQ individuals. Ray Ilan, as a pioneering activist in Sykarin, developed a series of strategic approaches to combat these forms of discrimination, leveraging both grassroots mobilization and high-level political engagement.

1. Building Coalitions

One of Ray's primary strategies was the formation of coalitions with other marginalized groups. By uniting various social movements, Ray emphasized the importance of intersectionality, as described by Crenshaw (1989), which posits that individuals experience overlapping systems of oppression. Ray's coalition-building efforts included partnerships with racial justice organizations, women's rights groups, and disability advocacy networks. This approach not only amplified the voices of LGBTQ individuals but also highlighted the interconnected nature of discrimination.

$$\text{Intersectionality} = \sum_{i=1}^{n} \text{Oppression}_i \qquad (35)$$

Where n represents the number of intersecting identities, and Oppression_i denotes the unique experiences of discrimination faced by each identity.

2. Grassroots Mobilization

Ray recognized the power of grassroots mobilization as a means to challenge discriminatory practices. He organized community forums and town hall meetings to engage residents in discussions about LGBTQ rights. These events served as platforms for education and awareness, allowing community members to share their experiences and advocate for change collectively. Ray's grassroots efforts were grounded in the theory of participatory democracy, which emphasizes the importance of citizen involvement in political processes.

3. Legislative Advocacy

To combat discrimination at the policy level, Ray employed targeted legislative advocacy. He identified key pieces of legislation that would directly impact the LGBTQ community, such as anti-discrimination laws and marriage equality bills. By mobilizing constituents to contact their representatives, Ray effectively demonstrated the demand for change. This strategy aligns with the theory of agenda-setting in political communication, which suggests that public opinion can influence policymakers' priorities.

$$\text{Public Pressure} = \text{Mobilization} \times \text{Visibility} \qquad (36)$$

Where Mobilization refers to the active engagement of community members, and Visibility denotes the public awareness of LGBTQ issues.

4. Utilizing Media Platforms

Understanding the role of media in shaping public perception, Ray strategically utilized various media platforms to amplify LGBTQ issues. He engaged with local and national news outlets, participated in interviews, and utilized social media to reach broader audiences. By sharing personal stories and highlighting the impact of discrimination, Ray humanized the LGBTQ experience and fostered empathy among the general public. This approach is supported by the cultivation theory, which posits that media exposure can shape societal attitudes over time.

5. Training and Empowerment

Ray also focused on training and empowering other LGBTQ individuals to become advocates for their rights. He organized workshops that equipped participants with the skills necessary to navigate the political landscape, including public speaking, lobbying, and community organizing. This strategy aligns with Freire's (1970) concept of critical pedagogy, which emphasizes the importance of education as a tool for social change.

$$\text{Empowerment} = \text{Education} + \text{Action} \qquad (37)$$

Where Education refers to the knowledge gained through training, and Action denotes the application of that knowledge in advocacy efforts.

6. Challenging Institutional Barriers

Ray was acutely aware of the institutional barriers that perpetuated discrimination within political systems. He actively challenged these barriers by advocating for policy reforms that promoted inclusivity and representation. For instance, Ray lobbied for the implementation of diversity training programs within government agencies to address biases and improve the treatment of LGBTQ individuals. This approach reflects the critical race theory, which asserts that systemic racism and discrimination are embedded in legal systems and institutions.

7. Engaging in Public Discourse

Lastly, Ray engaged in public discourse to confront discriminatory rhetoric directly. He participated in debates and public forums, where he challenged misconceptions and stereotypes about the LGBTQ community. By presenting factual information and personal narratives, Ray aimed to shift the narrative surrounding LGBTQ issues. This strategy aligns with the social movement theory, which highlights the significance of discourse in shaping public attitudes and mobilizing support for social change.

$$\text{Discourse} = \text{Narrative} + \text{Fact} \tag{38}$$

Where Narrative represents the personal stories shared, and Fact denotes the empirical evidence presented.

In conclusion, Ray Ilan's multifaceted strategies for combatting discrimination in politics were instrumental in advancing LGBTQ rights in Sykarin. Through coalition-building, grassroots mobilization, legislative advocacy, media engagement, empowerment, institutional reform, and public discourse, Ray not only challenged the status quo but also inspired a new generation of activists to continue the fight for equality. His legacy serves as a testament to the power of strategic action in the face of discrimination.

Ray's legislative triumphs in advancing LGBTQ rights

Ray Ilan's journey through the political landscape of Sykarin was marked by a series of legislative triumphs that significantly advanced LGBTQ rights and representation. As he stepped into the political arena, Ray faced an uphill battle against entrenched societal norms and a political system that had historically marginalized LGBTQ voices. However, through strategic planning, coalition-building, and an unwavering commitment to equality, Ray was able to effectuate substantial changes that would resonate through the community and beyond.

One of Ray's most notable legislative achievements was the introduction and passage of the **LGBTQ Equality Act**, which aimed to prohibit discrimination based on sexual orientation and gender identity in employment, housing, and public accommodations. This act was not merely a piece of legislation; it was a bold statement affirming the rights of LGBTQ individuals in Sykarin. The act's passage marked a significant shift in the legal framework protecting marginalized communities.

$$P(E) = P(E|H)P(H) + P(E|\neg H)P(\neg H) \tag{39}$$

In this equation, $P(E)$ represents the probability of experiencing equality in employment, H denotes the hypothesis that LGBTQ individuals are treated equally, and $\neg H$ represents the hypothesis of inequality. Ray's efforts were focused on increasing $P(E|H)$ while decreasing $P(E|\neg H)$, thereby shifting the balance toward equality.

Ray's legislative strategy involved extensive outreach and education efforts. He organized town hall meetings, engaging directly with constituents to discuss the importance of LGBTQ rights. By sharing personal stories and statistics illustrating the discrimination faced by LGBTQ individuals, Ray was able to humanize the issue and garner support from both allies and skeptics alike. His approach was rooted in the theory of **social constructivism**, which posits that understanding and meaning are constructed through social interactions. By fostering dialogue, Ray dismantled misconceptions and built a coalition of support that transcended traditional political boundaries.

Additionally, Ray championed the establishment of the **Sykarin LGBTQ Advisory Council**, a body designed to provide ongoing input on policies affecting the LGBTQ community. This council not only served as a platform for advocacy but also ensured that LGBTQ voices were included in the policymaking process. The creation of this advisory body exemplified the principles of **participatory democracy**, emphasizing the importance of inclusive governance and community engagement.

Ray's legislative victories were not without challenges. He faced significant opposition from conservative factions within the government, who argued that expanding LGBTQ rights would undermine traditional values. This resistance was compounded by a lack of understanding and awareness regarding LGBTQ issues. In response, Ray employed strategic framing techniques to reframe the narrative surrounding LGBTQ rights. He positioned the fight for equality as a fundamental human rights issue, drawing parallels to other civil rights movements throughout history.

For instance, during a pivotal debate on the LGBTQ Equality Act, Ray delivered a powerful speech that resonated with both the emotional and rational aspects of the audience. He stated:

"We are not asking for special treatment; we are demanding the same rights that every citizen of Sykarin deserves. Equality is not a privilege; it is a right. When we uplift the voices of the marginalized, we strengthen the fabric of our society."

This speech was pivotal in swaying undecided lawmakers and mobilizing public support. Ray's ability to articulate the need for legislative change exemplified the effectiveness of narrative in political advocacy.

Ultimately, Ray's legislative triumphs culminated in the successful passage of several key bills, including the establishment of comprehensive anti-discrimination protections and the introduction of inclusive policies within educational institutions. These legislative achievements not only improved the lives of countless LGBTQ individuals in Sykarin but also set a precedent for other regions to follow.

In conclusion, Ray Ilan's legislative triumphs in advancing LGBTQ rights were characterized by strategic planning, community engagement, and a commitment to inclusivity. Through his efforts, Ray not only transformed the legal landscape of Sykarin but also inspired a new generation of activists to continue the fight for equality. His legacy serves as a testament to the power of advocacy and the importance of legislative action in creating a more just and equitable society.

The backlash and opposition faced by Ray in his political career

Ray Ilan's ascent in the political arena was not without significant backlash and opposition. As he began to challenge the status quo in Sykarin, he became a lightning rod for criticism, drawing the ire of traditionalists and those resistant to change. This section explores the multifaceted nature of the opposition Ray encountered, the societal implications of such resistance, and the strategies he employed to navigate these turbulent waters.

Understanding the Opposition

The backlash Ray faced can be understood through the lens of social identity theory, which posits that individuals derive a sense of identity from their membership in social groups. In Sykarin, the dominant social groups—rooted in conservative values—saw Ray's activism as a direct threat to their established norms and beliefs. This led to a variety of responses, ranging from vocal opposition to more insidious forms of discrimination.

$$\text{Opposition} = f(\text{Social Identity, Cultural Norms, Political Climate}) \quad (40)$$

Where: - Opposition is the backlash Ray faced. - Social Identity refers to the collective identity of traditionalist groups. - Cultural Norms encapsulates the prevailing societal expectations. - Political Climate denotes the existing political landscape in Sykarin.

Public Criticism and Media Scrutiny

One of the most immediate forms of backlash came through public criticism and media scrutiny. Local newspapers and television stations often sensationalized Ray's initiatives, framing them as radical or outlandish. For instance, when Ray proposed a city-wide LGBTQ pride event, media outlets ran stories that questioned the appropriateness of such an event in Sykarin, labeling it as a "disruption" to the community's traditional values.

This negative media portrayal not only affected public perception but also emboldened opponents to voice their dissent. Ray found himself the target of organized protests, with conservative groups rallying against his initiatives, claiming they undermined family values and societal stability.

Legislative Roadblocks

As Ray sought to implement progressive policies, he encountered significant legislative roadblocks. Many of his proposals aimed at enhancing LGBTQ rights were met with fierce opposition in the local council. Traditionalist council members employed various tactics to stall or derail legislation, including:

- **Filibustering:** Lengthy debates that delayed voting on key measures.

- **Amendments:** Introducing amendments that diluted the impact of Ray's proposals.

- **Public Hearings:** Organizing hearings that attracted vocal opponents, creating a hostile environment for discussion.

For example, during the debate over a proposed anti-discrimination ordinance, Ray faced relentless questioning and opposition from council members who argued that such measures would lead to "reverse discrimination" against non-LGBTQ individuals. This rhetoric not only stalled the legislation but also fostered a climate of fear and misinformation among constituents.

Personal Attacks and Threats

The backlash Ray faced also turned personal. As he became a more prominent figure in Sykarin, he received threats, both online and offline. Social media became a battleground where opponents launched smear campaigns, attempting to tarnish his reputation. These attacks often included:

- **Cyberbullying:** Targeted harassment through social media platforms.

- **Doxxing:** The public release of Ray's personal information, leading to safety concerns.

+ **Physical Threats:** Instances of intimidation at public events and rallies.

Ray's resilience was tested as he navigated these challenges. He often emphasized the importance of mental health and community support, urging his followers to remain steadfast in the face of adversity.

Community Divisions

The opposition Ray faced also highlighted deep divisions within the Sykarin community. While many rallied behind him, others felt alienated by his progressive stance. This polarization manifested in various ways, such as:

+ **Community Forums:** Divisive discussions that often ended in heated arguments.

+ **Social Segregation:** A split in local organizations, with some distancing themselves from Ray's initiatives.

+ **Economic Boycotts:** Attempts by opponents to undermine businesses that supported Ray's activism.

Ray recognized the need to bridge these divides. He initiated community dialogues aimed at fostering understanding and empathy, striving to create a more inclusive environment where differing viewpoints could coexist.

Conclusion: Rising Above the Challenges

Despite the backlash and opposition, Ray Ilan emerged as a symbol of resilience and determination. His ability to confront and navigate these challenges not only solidified his position as a leader but also galvanized support for LGBTQ rights in Sykarin. Through strategic communication, community engagement, and unwavering commitment to his principles, Ray demonstrated that the path to progress is often fraught with obstacles, but it is a journey worth undertaking.

In the face of adversity, Ray's mantra became clear: "We rise by lifting others." This philosophy guided him through the tumultuous waters of political opposition, ultimately shaping his legacy as a transformative figure in the fight for LGBTQ rights.

Ray's resilience in the face of adversity

Ray Ilan's journey through the political landscape of Sykarin was not merely a tale of triumph; it was also a testament to resilience in the face of adversity. The LGBTQ community has historically faced significant challenges, including discrimination, societal rejection, and systemic barriers. For Ray, these obstacles were not deterrents but rather catalysts that fueled his determination to succeed and advocate for change.

One of the most pressing issues Ray confronted was the entrenched stigma surrounding LGBTQ identities. According to the *Social Identity Theory* (Tajfel & Turner, 1979), individuals derive part of their self-concept from their perceived membership in social groups. For Ray, the struggle to assert his identity while facing societal prejudice was a constant battle. This theory underscores the psychological impact of discrimination, which can lead to internalized homophobia and a diminished sense of self-worth. Yet, Ray transformed this challenge into a source of strength. Instead of succumbing to the negativity, he embraced his identity and used it as a platform to uplift others.

Ray's resilience was further tested during his initial foray into politics. The local political landscape was rife with opposition, and many viewed his candidacy through a lens of skepticism. In a poignant example, during a town hall meeting, Ray faced a barrage of hostile questions regarding his qualifications and intentions. Rather than retreating or becoming defensive, he employed a technique known as *reframing*, which involves changing the way a situation is perceived. Ray responded to the criticism by highlighting the importance of diverse representation in politics, stating, "If we want to change the narrative, we must first change the storytellers." This approach not only disarmed his critics but also resonated with many in the audience, transforming skepticism into support.

Moreover, Ray's resilience was evident in his strategic response to legislative setbacks. For instance, when a proposed bill aimed at protecting LGBTQ rights was defeated in the city council, many activists were disheartened. However, Ray organized a series of community forums to discuss the implications of the defeat and strategize for future efforts. This proactive approach exemplified the concept of *adaptive resilience*, which is characterized by the ability to bounce back from setbacks while remaining focused on long-term goals. Ray's ability to mobilize the community and pivot towards a renewed strategy not only demonstrated his resilience but also inspired others to remain engaged and hopeful.

Ray's personal experiences also played a critical role in his resilience. Growing up in Sykarin, he faced bullying and isolation during his formative years. These experiences, while painful, instilled in him a profound understanding of the importance of community support. He often quoted the adage, "What doesn't kill you makes you stronger," emphasizing that his struggles shaped his character and fueled his passion for activism. This perspective aligns with the *Post-Traumatic Growth Theory*, which posits that individuals can experience personal development following adversity. Ray's journey exemplified this theory as he transformed his pain into purpose, advocating for mental health resources and support networks for LGBTQ youth.

In the political arena, Ray encountered not only opposition from conservative factions but also betrayal from within his circle. A former ally publicly denounced him, claiming that his activism was merely a publicity stunt. Instead of allowing this betrayal to derail his mission, Ray publicly acknowledged the pain of betrayal while reiterating his commitment to his cause. He stated, "In the face of adversity, I choose to rise. I choose to be the voice for those who feel voiceless." This statement resonated deeply within the community, reinforcing his position as a leader who was unafraid to confront challenges head-on.

Ultimately, Ray's resilience in the face of adversity was not just about enduring hardships; it was about transforming them into opportunities for growth and advocacy. His journey illustrates the profound impact of resilience on individual and collective empowerment within the LGBTQ community. Through his unwavering commitment to justice, Ray became a beacon of hope, inspiring countless others to stand firm in their identities and fight for their rights.

In conclusion, Ray Ilan's resilience amidst adversity is a powerful narrative that highlights the importance of perseverance in the face of societal challenges. His ability to navigate the turbulent waters of politics, coupled with his personal experiences and commitment to community, serves as a blueprint for aspiring activists. As Ray himself once said, "Resilience is not just about bouncing back; it's about bouncing forward." This philosophy not only defined his journey but also left an indelible mark on the LGBTQ movement in Sykarin and beyond.

Ray's impact on LGBTQ political representation

Ray Ilan's journey through the political landscape of Sykarin marked a transformative era for LGBTQ representation. His rise to prominence not only shattered glass ceilings but also catalyzed a broader conversation about inclusivity and equality within political spheres. This section explores the profound impact Ray had on LGBTQ political representation, highlighting the theoretical frameworks, challenges, and tangible outcomes of his activism.

Theoretical Framework: Intersectionality in Politics

At the core of Ray's activism was the concept of *intersectionality*, a theory developed by Kimberlé Crenshaw that emphasizes the interconnected nature of social categorizations such as race, class, and gender. Ray's approach to LGBTQ representation was deeply informed by this framework, as he recognized that the experiences of LGBTQ individuals were not monolithic. By advocating for policies that addressed the unique challenges faced by individuals at the intersections of various identities, Ray ensured that the voices of the most marginalized within the LGBTQ community were heard.

Challenges in Political Representation

Despite Ray's determination, he faced significant challenges in advancing LGBTQ political representation. The entrenched norms within Sykarin's political landscape often favored traditional views, leading to resistance against progressive policies. Discrimination and homophobia were pervasive, manifesting not only in public sentiment but also within political institutions.

Ray encountered numerous obstacles, including:

+ **Legislative Barriers:** Many proposed LGBTQ rights initiatives faced immediate opposition, often resulting in stalled legislation.

+ **Public Backlash:** Ray's visibility as an LGBTQ leader attracted both support and hostility, complicating his efforts to unite the community and garner broad political support.

+ **Internal Divisions:** The LGBTQ community itself was not immune to divisions based on race, class, and gender, which sometimes hindered collective action.

Tangible Outcomes of Ray's Activism

Despite these challenges, Ray's impact on LGBTQ political representation was significant and multifaceted:

1. **Increased Visibility:** Ray's candidness about his identity and experiences brought LGBTQ issues to the forefront of political discourse in Sykarin. His presence at rallies, debates, and public forums helped normalize LGBTQ representation in spaces where it had previously been absent.

2. **Policy Advancements:** Under Ray's leadership, several key policies were enacted that advanced LGBTQ rights. These included anti-discrimination laws, healthcare access initiatives, and educational reforms aimed at promoting LGBTQ inclusivity in schools.

3. **Building Alliances:** Ray recognized the importance of coalition-building. By forming alliances with other marginalized groups, he fostered a broader movement for social justice that transcended LGBTQ issues alone. This strategy not only amplified the voices of LGBTQ individuals but also highlighted the interconnectedness of various social justice movements.

4. **Youth Engagement:** Ray's initiatives inspired a new generation of activists. By prioritizing LGBTQ education in schools, he empowered young people to engage in political activism, creating a pipeline of future leaders committed to advocating for LGBTQ rights.

5. **National Recognition:** Ray's efforts did not go unnoticed beyond Sykarin. His work garnered national attention, positioning him as a key figure in the LGBTQ rights movement. This recognition helped to elevate the issues faced by LGBTQ individuals on a larger scale, influencing policy discussions at the national level.

Case Studies: Local to National Impact

To illustrate Ray's impact on LGBTQ political representation, we can examine specific case studies:

+ **The Equality Bill:** Ray spearheaded the campaign for the Equality Bill, which aimed to protect LGBTQ individuals from discrimination in employment and housing. His passionate speeches and strategic outreach efforts mobilized public support, ultimately leading to the bill's passage.

+ **The Sykarin Pride March:** Ray organized the first Pride march in Sykarin, which not only celebrated LGBTQ identity but also served as a platform for political expression. This event drew thousands of participants and received extensive media coverage, further solidifying LGBTQ visibility in the political landscape.

+ **Youth Advocacy Programs:** Through the establishment of youth advocacy programs, Ray created spaces for LGBTQ youth to voice their concerns and engage in political processes. These programs not only educated young people about their rights but also encouraged them to participate in local governance.

Conclusion: A Lasting Legacy

Ray Ilan's impact on LGBTQ political representation in Sykarin serves as a testament to the power of activism rooted in authenticity and intersectionality. By challenging the status quo and advocating for inclusive policies, Ray not only transformed the political landscape of his hometown but also inspired a movement that resonated far beyond its borders. His legacy continues to influence the ongoing struggle for LGBTQ rights, reminding us that representation matters and that every voice has the power to effect change.

As we reflect on Ray's journey, we are reminded of the importance of perseverance in the face of adversity and the need for continued advocacy for marginalized communities. The work of Ray Ilan is far from over; it is a call to action for future generations to carry the torch of activism and ensure that the fight for equality and representation endures.

The International Stage: Ray Goes Global

Ray's influence beyond Sykarin's borders

Ray Ilan's activism transcended the confines of his small town, Sykarin, and resonated across national and international landscapes. His journey from a local LGBTQ activist to a global figure exemplifies the power of grassroots movements and the ripple effect they can create when fueled by passion and resilience. This section delves into the ways Ray's influence expanded beyond Sykarin, shaping LGBTQ discourse on a broader scale.

The Global Ripple Effect

Ray's activism began with localized efforts, but as he gained recognition, his message reached audiences far beyond Sykarin. The concept of *networked activism,* as described by Bennett and Segerberg (2013), posits that social movements can gain momentum through interconnected networks, both online and offline. Ray utilized social media platforms to share his experiences, strategies, and successes, effectively creating a global community of supporters and activists. This digital engagement allowed for the rapid dissemination of information regarding LGBTQ rights, fostering solidarity among marginalized groups worldwide.

Participation in International LGBTQ Conferences

Ray's journey took a significant turn when he was invited to speak at international LGBTQ conferences. These platforms provided him with opportunities to connect with activists from diverse backgrounds, each facing unique challenges. His speeches, characterized by their raw authenticity and powerful narratives, inspired many to adopt similar strategies in their local contexts. For example, during the *Global Pride Summit* in 2022, Ray emphasized the importance of intersectionality, urging attendees to consider how overlapping identities—such as race, gender, and class—affect the LGBTQ experience. His call to action resonated with activists from various countries, prompting discussions on how to tailor advocacy efforts to address specific community needs.

Advocating for LGBTQ Rights on a Global Scale

Ray's influence also manifested in his advocacy for LGBTQ rights on a global scale. He collaborated with international organizations such as *ILGA World* and *OutRight Action International*, focusing on pressing issues such as anti-LGBTQ legislation, violence against LGBTQ individuals, and the need for comprehensive health services. His efforts highlighted the disparities faced by LGBTQ communities in different regions, such as the criminalization of homosexuality in several African and Middle Eastern countries. By raising awareness about these issues, Ray not only educated his audience but also mobilized resources to support grassroots organizations working in these regions.

International Recognition and Accolades

As a result of his tireless work, Ray received numerous accolades that further solidified his status as a global LGBTQ leader. He was awarded the *International LGBTQ Activist of the Year* in 2023, recognizing his contributions to advancing LGBTQ rights and representation. This recognition not only validated his efforts but also amplified his voice on the international stage. The award ceremony, attended by dignitaries and activists from around the world, served as a platform for Ray to articulate his vision for a more inclusive future, emphasizing that the fight for LGBTQ rights is a universal struggle.

Ray's Vision for a More Inclusive World

Ray's influence extended to shaping the narrative around LGBTQ rights globally. He advocated for a vision of inclusivity that encompassed not just legal rights but also cultural acceptance and representation. He often referenced the work of theorists like Judith Butler, who argues that gender and sexuality are performative constructs influenced by societal norms. Ray's activism challenged these norms, urging communities worldwide to embrace diverse expressions of identity. His campaigns encouraged individuals to celebrate their uniqueness, fostering an environment where LGBTQ individuals could thrive without fear of persecution.

Challenges Faced by Ray in Spreading His Message Globally

Despite his successes, Ray encountered challenges in spreading his message globally. Cultural differences, varying levels of acceptance, and political resistance posed significant obstacles. For instance, during his visit to a conference in Eastern Europe, he faced backlash from conservative groups who viewed his presence as a threat to traditional values. Ray addressed these challenges head-on, employing dialogue and education as tools for change. He emphasized the importance of listening to local activists, understanding their struggles, and offering support without imposing external narratives.

Ray's Enduring Commitment to Creating a More Inclusive World

Ray's commitment to fostering inclusivity extended beyond mere advocacy; it became a personal mission. He established the *Ray Ilan Foundation*, which aimed to provide resources and support for LGBTQ activists worldwide. The foundation funded initiatives focused on mental health, education, and legal assistance, ensuring that those on the front lines of the fight for LGBTQ rights had the tools they needed to succeed. Through these efforts, Ray solidified his legacy as a leader who not only broke barriers in his own community but also inspired a global movement towards equality and acceptance.

In conclusion, Ray Ilan's influence beyond Sykarin's borders is a testament to the power of grassroots activism and the importance of global solidarity. His journey illustrates how localized efforts can inspire change on a larger scale, encouraging individuals and communities worldwide to join the fight for LGBTQ rights. As Ray continues to break barriers, his legacy serves as a reminder that the struggle for equality is a collective endeavor, transcending geographical boundaries and cultural differences.

Ray's participation in international LGBTQ conferences

Ray Ilan's journey as a prominent LGBTQ activist took a transformative turn when he began participating in international LGBTQ conferences. These conferences served as a vital platform for Ray to amplify his voice, share his experiences, and connect with activists from around the globe. Ray's participation was not just about representation; it was about creating a ripple effect that would resonate throughout the LGBTQ community.

The Importance of International Conferences

International LGBTQ conferences are crucial for fostering dialogue, sharing best practices, and building solidarity among activists. They provide a unique opportunity for individuals from diverse cultural backgrounds to come together and discuss the challenges and triumphs faced by LGBTQ communities worldwide. As Ray often articulated, "When we unite, we become a force that cannot be ignored."

These conferences often cover a range of topics, including:

+ Legislative advancements in LGBTQ rights

+ Health and wellness issues affecting LGBTQ individuals

+ Strategies for combating discrimination and violence

+ The intersectionality of LGBTQ identities with race, gender, and socioeconomic status

Ray's involvement in these discussions not only highlighted the issues faced by the LGBTQ community in Sykarin but also positioned him as a key figure in the global movement for equality.

Ray's Key Contributions

One of Ray's most notable contributions at these conferences was his ability to articulate the specific challenges faced by LGBTQ individuals in smaller, often overlooked communities. He emphasized that while large cities might have more visible LGBTQ support systems, rural areas like Sykarin often lacked the resources and visibility needed for advocacy.

For instance, during the International LGBTQ Rights Conference in Berlin, Ray presented a compelling case study on the impact of rural isolation on mental health within the LGBTQ community. He utilized statistical data to illustrate the correlation between geographical isolation and increased rates of mental health issues among LGBTQ individuals. The data can be represented as follows:

$$MHI = f(I, R, E) \tag{41}$$

Where:

- MHI = Mental Health Issues

- I = Isolation level

- R = Resources available

- E = Environmental acceptance

Ray argued that as isolation (I) increases, mental health issues (MHI) also rise, particularly when resources (R) are scarce and environmental acceptance (E) is low. This framework helped attendees understand the nuanced challenges faced by those in less urbanized areas.

Networking and Building Alliances

Ray's participation in these conferences also allowed him to network with other activists, policymakers, and organizations dedicated to LGBTQ rights. Through these connections, he was able to forge alliances that would later prove instrumental in advancing LGBTQ rights both locally and internationally.

For example, at the Global Pride Summit in Toronto, Ray met with representatives from various LGBTQ organizations, leading to the formation of a coalition aimed at addressing the unique needs of rural LGBTQ communities. This coalition focused on:

- Developing outreach programs to provide mental health support

- Creating educational resources tailored for rural schools

- Advocating for policy changes at the local and national levels

Ray's ability to articulate the needs of rural LGBTQ individuals resonated with many, leading to increased funding and resources directed towards these initiatives.

Global Recognition and Impact

Ray's contributions to international LGBTQ conferences did not go unnoticed. His passionate speeches and compelling presentations earned him accolades and recognition from global LGBTQ organizations. This recognition was not just a personal achievement; it served to elevate the visibility of Sykarin's LGBTQ community on the world stage.

For instance, Ray was awarded the Global LGBTQ Activist Award at the International Pride Conference in Paris, which highlighted his innovative approaches to activism and his commitment to breaking barriers. This accolade not only celebrated Ray's work but also brought attention to the ongoing struggles faced by LGBTQ individuals in less visible regions.

In conclusion, Ray Ilan's participation in international LGBTQ conferences was a pivotal aspect of his activism. It allowed him to share his experiences, build alliances, and advocate for the unique challenges faced by rural LGBTQ communities. Through his efforts, Ray was able to amplify the voices of those often left unheard, fostering a sense of unity and purpose within the global LGBTQ movement. His work continues to inspire future generations of activists, proving that even from a small town like Sykarin, one can make a significant impact on the world stage.

Advocating for LGBTQ rights on a global scale

Ray Ilan's journey transcended the borders of Sykarin, as he emerged as a formidable voice advocating for LGBTQ rights on an international platform. Recognizing that the fight for equality is a universal struggle, Ray's activism began to gain traction beyond his small town, resonating with countless individuals facing similar challenges worldwide.

Theoretical Framework

At the heart of Ray's advocacy lies the understanding of intersectionality, a theory proposed by Kimberlé Crenshaw. Intersectionality emphasizes that individuals experience oppression in varying configurations and degrees of intensity based on their overlapping identities, such as race, gender, sexuality, and class. This framework guided Ray in recognizing that LGBTQ rights are not isolated from other social justice issues. He understood that advocating for LGBTQ rights necessitated addressing systemic inequalities that affect marginalized communities globally.

Identifying Global Problems

Ray's advocacy was informed by the myriad of issues faced by LGBTQ individuals around the world. In many countries, homosexuality remains criminalized, leading to severe penalties, including imprisonment and violence. For instance, in regions such as parts of Africa and the Middle East, LGBTQ individuals often face persecution simply for being who they are. Ray highlighted these injustices at international conferences, using his platform to amplify the voices of those who could not speak for themselves.

Furthermore, Ray addressed the issue of global disparities in healthcare access for LGBTQ individuals. The HIV/AIDS epidemic disproportionately affects LGBTQ communities, particularly in countries where stigma and discrimination hinder access to essential health services. Ray advocated for comprehensive healthcare policies that include LGBTQ individuals, emphasizing the need for culturally competent care and education.

Global Advocacy Initiatives

Ray's advocacy took various forms, including participation in international LGBTQ conferences, where he shared his experiences and strategies with activists from different countries. One notable event was the Global LGBTQ Rights Summit in Amsterdam, where Ray delivered a powerful keynote address that captivated the audience. He spoke about the importance of solidarity among LGBTQ activists worldwide, stating:

> "Our fight is not just for ourselves but for every person who dares to love freely, regardless of where they are born. Together, we can break the chains of oppression."

Ray also launched initiatives aimed at fostering international alliances. He collaborated with organizations such as ILGA (International Lesbian, Gay, Bisexual, Trans and Intersex Association) to create a global network of activists committed to advancing LGBTQ rights. This collaboration resulted in the formation of the "Global LGBTQ Coalition," which aimed to provide resources, training, and support to grassroots activists in countries with restrictive laws.

Case Studies of Impact

One significant example of Ray's impact was his involvement in the campaign against the anti-LGBTQ laws in Uganda. By leveraging social media, Ray mobilized international support, encouraging thousands to sign petitions and participate in global demonstrations. His efforts drew attention to the draconian measures being enacted against LGBTQ individuals in Uganda, leading to increased pressure on the Ugandan government from international bodies and human rights organizations.

Additionally, Ray's advocacy contributed to the successful passage of a resolution at the United Nations Human Rights Council, calling for the decriminalization of homosexuality worldwide. This landmark resolution was a testament to the collective efforts of activists like Ray, who worked tirelessly to ensure that LGBTQ rights were recognized as fundamental human rights.

Challenges and Resistance

Despite his successes, Ray faced significant challenges in his global advocacy efforts. Resistance from conservative groups and governments was rampant, often manifesting in threats and backlash against both Ray and his allies. In some instances, Ray received hostile responses from political leaders who sought to undermine his credibility. Nevertheless, he remained undeterred, employing strategic communication and coalition-building to counteract these challenges.

Ray also recognized the importance of addressing the internal divisions within the LGBTQ community. He often emphasized the need for unity among various factions, advocating for a more inclusive approach that considers the diverse experiences and identities within the community. This approach was essential in building a cohesive movement capable of confronting global challenges.

Conclusion

Ray Ilan's advocacy for LGBTQ rights on a global scale exemplifies the power of intersectional activism. By addressing systemic inequalities and fostering international solidarity, Ray not only raised awareness of LGBTQ issues but also inspired a new generation of activists committed to the cause. His legacy serves as a reminder that the fight for equality knows no borders and that the collective strength of the LGBTQ community can indeed change the world.

International recognition and accolades for Ray's activism

Ray Ilan's activism transcended the borders of Sykarin, garnering international recognition and accolades that underscored the significance of his contributions to the LGBTQ movement. His journey from a small-town advocate to a global icon exemplified the potential for grassroots activism to effect change on a larger scale.

Global Impact and Visibility

Ray's participation in international LGBTQ conferences, such as the *International LGBTQ Rights Summit* and the *Global Pride Conference*, positioned him as a thought leader in the movement. During these events, Ray delivered powerful speeches that resonated with audiences worldwide. He emphasized the importance of intersectionality, stating:

$$I = \sum_{i=1}^{n} \text{Intersectionality}(i) \tag{42}$$

where I represents the total impact of intersectional advocacy, and n is the number of intersecting identities represented in the LGBTQ community. This equation highlights the multifaceted nature of oppression and the necessity of inclusive activism.

Ray's approach to activism was not without challenges. He faced criticism from various factions within the LGBTQ community, particularly regarding his methods and the pace of change. However, his resilience and unwavering commitment to his principles led to a growing recognition of his efforts.

Accolades and Honors

In recognition of his tireless work, Ray received several prestigious awards, including:

+ **The Global LGBTQ Activist Award** (2022): This accolade was bestowed upon Ray for his outstanding contributions to advancing LGBTQ rights on an international scale. The award highlighted his ability to mobilize communities and inspire change across borders.

+ **The Sykarin Human Rights Medal** (2023): This honor was awarded to Ray for his exceptional leadership in the fight for LGBTQ rights within Sykarin, emphasizing his local impact that resonated globally.

+ **The International Unity Prize** (2023): Recognizing his efforts in fostering alliances between LGBTQ and non-LGBTQ communities, this prize celebrated Ray's commitment to inclusivity and dialogue.

These accolades not only validated Ray's work but also served as a beacon of hope for LGBTQ activists around the world, illustrating that change is possible through dedication and resilience.

Media Recognition

Ray's activism caught the attention of global media outlets, leading to features in prominent publications such as *The Advocate*, *Out Magazine*, and *Time*. Articles highlighted his unique approach to activism, which combined traditional advocacy with innovative strategies, including social media campaigns and grassroots organizing.

One notable campaign, *#RayRevolution*, became a viral sensation, encouraging individuals to share their stories of LGBTQ discrimination and resilience. This campaign not only amplified marginalized voices but also fostered a sense of solidarity among LGBTQ individuals globally. The campaign's success can be quantified through engagement metrics, demonstrating a significant increase in visibility for LGBTQ issues:

$$E = \frac{V + C + S}{T} \qquad (43)$$

where E represents engagement, V is the number of views, C is the number of comments, S is the number of shares, and T is the total time the campaign was active. This formula illustrates the effectiveness of Ray's social media strategy in mobilizing support and raising awareness.

Legacy of Global Advocacy

Ray's international recognition solidified his legacy as a transformative figure in the LGBTQ movement. His work inspired a new generation of activists to pursue advocacy with passion and purpose. As Ray often stated:

"To break barriers, we must first build bridges."

This philosophy guided his efforts in fostering international alliances and collaborations. Ray's vision for a world where LGBTQ rights are universally recognized continues to inspire activists worldwide.

The accolades and recognition Ray received were not merely personal triumphs; they represented the collective efforts of countless individuals who fought for LGBTQ rights. His story serves as a reminder that activism knows no borders and that the pursuit of equality is a global endeavor.

In conclusion, Ray Ilan's international recognition and accolades reflect the profound impact of his activism. Through his unwavering commitment to LGBTQ rights, he not only changed the landscape of Sykarin but also inspired a global movement for equality and justice. His legacy is a testament to the power of activism and the importance of standing up for what is right, no matter the odds.

Ray's vision for a more inclusive world

Ray Ilan's vision for a more inclusive world is rooted in the belief that diversity is not merely a characteristic to be tolerated but a fundamental strength that enriches society as a whole. This vision encompasses various aspects of life, including social, political, and cultural dimensions, and aims to dismantle the systemic barriers that marginalize LGBTQ individuals and other minority groups.

At the core of Ray's philosophy is the understanding that inclusivity is a multifaceted concept, often described through the lens of intersectionality. As defined by Crenshaw (1989), intersectionality refers to the way different forms of discrimination—such as those based on race, gender, sexual orientation, and class—interact and overlap. Ray emphasizes the importance of recognizing these intersections to create a comprehensive approach to activism that addresses the unique challenges faced by individuals at the crossroads of multiple identities.

$$I = f(R, G, S, C) \tag{44}$$

Where:

+ I = Inclusivity

+ R = Race

+ G = Gender

+ S = Sexual orientation

+ C = Class

Ray advocates for policies that promote equal rights and opportunities across these intersecting identities. He often cites the lack of representation in political spaces as a significant barrier to achieving inclusivity. For instance, during his campaign for Sykarin's highest political office, Ray highlighted the underrepresentation of LGBTQ individuals in local government, arguing that diverse voices are essential for crafting policies that reflect the needs of all constituents.

In addressing systemic issues, Ray points to the ongoing discrimination faced by LGBTQ individuals in various sectors, including healthcare, employment, and education. He argues that these inequalities are not just personal grievances but societal failures that require collective action. As an example, Ray references the disparities in mental health outcomes among LGBTQ youth, which are exacerbated by stigma and lack of support. According to the Trevor Project (2021), LGBTQ youth are more than twice as likely to experience a mental health crisis compared to their heterosexual peers. Ray believes that fostering inclusivity in schools—through comprehensive LGBTQ education and supportive environments—can significantly improve these outcomes.

$$MHO = \frac{LQ + SE + SC}{3} \tag{45}$$

Where:

+ MHO = Mental health outcomes

+ LQ = Level of queer representation

+ SE = Supportive environments

+ SC = School climate

Ray's vision extends beyond local boundaries; he aspires to create a global movement for LGBTQ rights. He emphasizes the importance of international solidarity, recognizing that the struggle for equality is not confined to any one nation. In his speeches at international LGBTQ conferences, Ray often draws parallels between the challenges faced by LGBTQ communities worldwide, advocating for a united front against discrimination. He believes that by sharing strategies and resources, activists can amplify their impact and foster a more inclusive global society.

An example of this global vision in action is Ray's collaboration with international organizations to promote LGBTQ rights in countries where such identities are criminalized. He emphasizes that the fight for inclusivity is a shared human struggle, one that transcends borders and cultures. Ray's participation in initiatives aimed at providing asylum for LGBTQ individuals fleeing persecution is a testament to his commitment to this cause.

Furthermore, Ray envisions a world where inclusivity is woven into the fabric of societal norms. He challenges traditional notions of gender and sexuality, advocating for a broader understanding of identity that includes non-binary and gender non-conforming individuals. By promoting visibility and representation in media and culture, Ray aims to shift perceptions and foster acceptance. He often cites the importance of positive portrayals of LGBTQ individuals in popular culture, arguing that representation can dismantle stereotypes and foster empathy.

In conclusion, Ray Ilan's vision for a more inclusive world is a call to action. It is a vision that demands recognition of intersecting identities, a commitment to dismantling systemic barriers, and a dedication to fostering global solidarity.

Through his activism, Ray inspires others to join the movement for inclusivity, reminding us that a world where everyone is valued and respected is not just a dream, but a goal that can be achieved through collective effort and unwavering determination.

Ray's impact on the global LGBTQ community

Ray Ilan's activism transcended the borders of Sykarin, resonating deeply within the global LGBTQ community. His unique blend of charisma, tenacity, and unyielding commitment to equality positioned him as a formidable advocate on the international stage. The impact of Ray's work can be examined through various lenses, including his influence on global policies, the fostering of international coalitions, and the promotion of LGBTQ rights in diverse cultural contexts.

Influencing Global Policies

Ray's participation in international LGBTQ conferences allowed him to advocate for significant policy changes. His speeches often highlighted the universal struggle for LGBTQ rights, emphasizing that while cultural contexts may differ, the fundamental right to love and live freely is a shared human right. For instance, during the Global LGBTQ Rights Summit in 2022, Ray presented a compelling argument for the adoption of the **Universal Declaration of LGBTQ Rights**, which aimed to standardize protections for LGBTQ individuals across nations.

The theoretical framework underpinning Ray's advocacy can be linked to *Intersectionality*, a term coined by Kimberlé Crenshaw, which explores how various social identities intersect and impact individuals' experiences of oppression. Ray utilized this theory to argue that LGBTQ rights cannot be viewed in isolation; they are inextricably linked to issues of race, gender, and socioeconomic status. His ability to weave these narratives into his speeches garnered attention and support from a multitude of global leaders, ultimately influencing policy discussions in several countries.

Fostering International Coalitions

Ray's work extended beyond mere rhetoric; he actively sought to build coalitions among LGBTQ organizations worldwide. By establishing the **Global LGBTQ Alliance**, Ray created a platform where activists could share resources, strategies, and support. This coalition not only amplified the voices of marginalized LGBTQ individuals but also facilitated the exchange of best practices in advocacy.

One of the notable outcomes of this coalition was the **Safe Spaces Initiative**, which aimed to create safe environments for LGBTQ individuals in regions where they faced severe discrimination. For example, in regions of Eastern Europe where anti-LGBTQ sentiment is prevalent, the initiative provided funding and resources for local organizations to establish shelters and support networks.

Ray's approach was grounded in the theory of *Social Movement Theory*, which posits that collective action can lead to social change. By uniting diverse groups under a common cause, Ray demonstrated the power of solidarity in the fight for LGBTQ rights. This collective action not only strengthened local movements but also garnered international attention, leading to increased pressure on governments to enact progressive policies.

Promoting LGBTQ Rights in Diverse Cultural Contexts

Ray's impact was also evident in his ability to navigate and respect cultural differences while advocating for LGBTQ rights. He understood that the fight for equality must be sensitive to local customs and beliefs. For instance, during his visit to a LGBTQ festival in Brazil, Ray emphasized the importance of cultural representation in activism. He collaborated with local artists to create a campaign that celebrated Brazilian LGBTQ culture while addressing issues of violence and discrimination.

This approach aligns with the concept of *Cultural Relativism*, which posits that beliefs and practices should be understood based on an individual's own culture. Ray's respect for cultural differences allowed him to build trust and rapport with local activists, fostering a sense of ownership over the issues that affected their communities. His ability to adapt his message to resonate with different cultural contexts exemplified his effectiveness as a global advocate.

Examples of Ray's Global Influence

Ray's influence on the global LGBTQ community can be illustrated through several key examples:

1. **International Recognition**: In 2023, Ray received the **Global LGBTQ Advocate Award** for his outstanding contributions to the movement. This accolade not only recognized his work but also elevated the visibility of LGBTQ issues on a global scale.

2. **Collaborative Campaigns**: Ray spearheaded the **Rainbow Rights Campaign**, which united activists from over 30 countries to advocate for LGBTQ rights at the United Nations. This campaign resulted in a historic resolution

supporting LGBTQ rights, marking a significant milestone in international human rights law.

3. **Educational Initiatives**: Ray established the **Global LGBTQ Youth Empowerment Program**, which provided scholarships and mentorship for LGBTQ youth worldwide. By investing in the next generation of activists, Ray ensured that the fight for equality would continue to thrive.

In conclusion, Ray Ilan's impact on the global LGBTQ community is profound and multifaceted. Through his advocacy, coalition-building, and cultural sensitivity, he has not only influenced policies and practices but has also inspired countless individuals to join the fight for equality. Ray's legacy serves as a reminder that the struggle for LGBTQ rights is a global endeavor, requiring solidarity, understanding, and a shared commitment to justice for all.

Breaking the Glass Ceiling: Ray's Historic Achievement

Ray's groundbreaking campaign for Sykarin's highest political office

In the vibrant political landscape of Sykarin, Ray Ilan emerged as a beacon of hope and change, launching a groundbreaking campaign for the highest political office in the region. This campaign was not merely a quest for power; it was a bold declaration of identity, resilience, and the relentless pursuit of equality. Ray's journey to this pivotal moment was marked by a series of strategic decisions, grassroots mobilization, and the unwavering support of the LGBTQ community and its allies.

The Political Landscape of Sykarin

To understand the significance of Ray's campaign, one must first grasp the political environment of Sykarin. Historically, the political arena had been dominated by traditional values, often marginalizing voices that deviated from the norm. The LGBTQ community faced systemic discrimination, and representation was nearly non-existent. This backdrop set the stage for Ray's audacious bid for office, challenging the status quo and advocating for a more inclusive governance model.

Crafting a Vision

Ray's campaign was built on a compelling vision that resonated with the diverse population of Sykarin. He articulated a platform that emphasized equality, social justice, and economic empowerment. Central to his vision was the idea that every individual, regardless of their sexual orientation or gender identity, deserved a seat at the table. Ray's slogan, "Sykarin for All," encapsulated this ethos, signaling a departure from exclusionary politics.

Grassroots Mobilization

A hallmark of Ray's campaign was its grassroots nature. Recognizing that true change comes from the ground up, Ray mobilized volunteers from various backgrounds, creating a coalition that transcended traditional political boundaries. This coalition was instrumental in organizing community events, rallies, and town halls, fostering a sense of belonging and ownership among constituents. The campaign utilized social media platforms to amplify its message, creating viral moments that galvanized support and raised awareness about LGBTQ issues.

Challenges and Opposition

Despite the enthusiasm surrounding Ray's campaign, it was not without challenges. The opposition was fierce, with detractors attempting to undermine his credibility through misinformation and fear-mongering. One notable instance involved a smear campaign that sought to portray Ray as unfit for leadership due to his sexual orientation. However, Ray confronted these challenges head-on, employing a strategy rooted in transparency and authenticity. He publicly addressed the false narratives, reinforcing his commitment to serve all constituents, regardless of their beliefs.

Building Alliances

Ray understood that to achieve his goals, he needed to build alliances beyond the LGBTQ community. He reached out to various advocacy groups, including those focused on women's rights, racial equality, and environmental justice. By highlighting the intersections of these movements, Ray demonstrated that the fight for LGBTQ rights was part of a broader struggle for human rights. This approach not only expanded his support base but also fostered a sense of unity among diverse groups.

The Power of Representation

Ray's candidacy was historic, as he became the first openly LGBTQ individual to run for Sykarin's highest political office. This milestone was not merely symbolic; it represented a shift in the narrative surrounding LGBTQ individuals in politics. By stepping into the spotlight, Ray challenged stereotypes and inspired countless others to embrace their identities and pursue their political aspirations. His campaign became a source of empowerment for marginalized communities, proving that representation matters.

The Role of Media

The media played a crucial role in shaping public perception of Ray's campaign. Coverage ranged from supportive articles that highlighted his groundbreaking platform to critical pieces questioning his viability as a candidate. Ray adeptly navigated this landscape, leveraging media attention to amplify his message. He participated in interviews, debates, and public forums, using each opportunity to articulate his vision and connect with voters on a personal level.

A Historic Election Day

As election day approached, the energy surrounding Ray's campaign reached a fever pitch. Voter turnout was unprecedented, with many individuals motivated by the desire to support a candidate who truly represented their values. On the day of the election, the streets of Sykarin were alive with excitement, as supporters donned campaign merchandise and rallied at polling stations.

The results were a testament to the power of grassroots organizing and the hunger for change. Ray Ilan emerged victorious, becoming Sykarin's first openly LGBTQ mayor. This historic achievement not only shattered glass ceilings but also signified a pivotal moment in the fight for LGBTQ rights in the region.

Conclusion

Ray's groundbreaking campaign for Sykarin's highest political office was a transformative journey that redefined the political landscape. It exemplified the power of resilience, community, and the unwavering belief that change is possible. As Ray took office, he carried with him the hopes and dreams of countless individuals, committed to fostering an inclusive and equitable Sykarin for all.

$$\text{Victory} = \text{Grassroots Support} + \text{Authenticity} + \text{Coalition Building} \qquad (46)$$

The obstacles and opposition faced by Ray in the race

In the pursuit of his groundbreaking campaign for Sykarin's highest political office, Ray Ilan encountered a plethora of obstacles and opposition that tested his resolve and commitment to LGBTQ representation. These challenges can be categorized into social, political, and personal dimensions, each contributing to the complex landscape of his electoral journey.

Social Stigmas and Prejudices

One of the most formidable barriers Ray faced was the deeply ingrained social stigmas and prejudices against LGBTQ individuals in Sykarin. Despite the progress made in the realm of LGBTQ rights, many residents held onto traditional views that perceived homosexuality as an aberration. This societal backdrop created a hostile environment for Ray's candidacy.

$$\text{Social Acceptance} = \frac{\text{Positive Perception of LGBTQ}}{\text{Negative Stereotypes}} \tag{47}$$

As this equation suggests, the level of social acceptance Ray could achieve was inversely proportional to the prevalence of negative stereotypes. Many voters were influenced by misconceptions regarding LGBTQ individuals, often viewing them as unfit for leadership roles. This perception was exacerbated by sensationalist media portrayals that focused on Ray's identity rather than his qualifications.

Political Opposition

In the political arena, Ray encountered significant opposition from established political figures who were resistant to change. Many of these opponents utilized fear-mongering tactics to sway public opinion against Ray's campaign. They framed his candidacy as a threat to traditional values, claiming that electing an openly gay mayor would undermine the fabric of Sykarin's community.

$$\text{Political Resistance} = \text{Fear Tactics} + \text{Traditionalism} \tag{48}$$

This equation highlights how political resistance stemmed from both fear tactics employed by opponents and a strong adherence to traditionalism among the electorate. Ray's opponents capitalized on these sentiments, launching smear campaigns that aimed to discredit his character and question his leadership abilities.

Internal Struggles and Self-Doubt

Alongside external opposition, Ray grappled with internal struggles and self-doubt. The pressure of being a trailblazer weighed heavily on him, as he often questioned whether he was adequately prepared for the challenges of political life. This self-doubt was compounded by the fear of failure, not just for himself, but for the entire LGBTQ community that looked to him for representation.

$$\text{Self-Doubt} = \text{Pressure} \times \text{Expectations} \qquad (49)$$

In this equation, the intensity of self-doubt Ray experienced was directly proportional to the pressure he felt and the expectations placed upon him by both supporters and detractors. This internal conflict manifested in moments of vulnerability, where Ray had to remind himself of his purpose and the importance of his candidacy for future generations.

Mobilizing Support Amidst Opposition

Despite these formidable challenges, Ray worked tirelessly to mobilize support from the LGBTQ community and allies. He organized grassroots campaigns, leveraging social media platforms to amplify his message and counteract the negative narratives propagated by his opponents.

For instance, Ray hosted town hall meetings where he addressed concerns, dispelled myths, and highlighted the importance of inclusivity in leadership. His ability to connect with voters on a personal level helped to humanize his campaign and build a coalition of supporters who believed in his vision for Sykarin.

$$\text{Community Support} = \text{Engagement} + \text{Visibility} \qquad (50)$$

This equation illustrates that community support was a function of Ray's engagement with constituents and the visibility of his campaign. By fostering open dialogues and encouraging participation, Ray was able to create a movement that transcended his identity, focusing instead on shared values and the common good.

Conclusion

In summary, the obstacles and opposition faced by Ray Ilan in his race for Sykarin's highest political office were multifaceted, encompassing social stigmas, political resistance, and personal challenges. However, through resilience, strategic campaigning, and community mobilization, Ray was able to navigate these hurdles, ultimately paving the way for a more inclusive political landscape in Sykarin. His journey serves as a testament to the power of perseverance in the face of adversity, inspiring future generations of LGBTQ activists to continue breaking barriers.

Ray's landslide victory and the impact on LGBTQ representation

Ray Ilan's historic campaign for Sykarin's highest political office culminated in a landslide victory that not only transformed the political landscape of his hometown but also served as a monumental step forward for LGBTQ representation across the nation. This victory is best understood through the lens of social movement theory, which posits that collective action can lead to significant political change. As Ray harnessed the power of grassroots activism, he mobilized a diverse coalition of supporters who resonated with his message of inclusivity and equality.

In the months leading up to the election, Ray's campaign faced numerous challenges, including entrenched homophobia and skepticism from both political opponents and segments of the electorate. However, Ray's strategic use of media and innovative outreach methods allowed him to effectively communicate his vision for Sykarin. By utilizing social media platforms, community events, and public forums, he not only raised awareness about LGBTQ issues but also humanized the struggles faced by the community.

One of the key elements that contributed to Ray's landslide victory was his ability to articulate a clear and compelling narrative that underscored the importance of representation. He framed his candidacy not merely as an LGBTQ campaign but as a movement for all marginalized groups seeking a voice in the political arena. This intersectional approach resonated with a broader audience, allowing Ray to build coalitions with various advocacy groups, including those focused on racial justice, women's rights, and economic equity.

The impact of Ray's victory extended beyond the confines of Sykarin. It symbolized a shift in societal attitudes towards LGBTQ individuals, demonstrating that a candidate's sexual orientation should not preclude them from holding public office. This shift is supported by the concept of "descriptive representation," which asserts that having representatives who share the same identities and experiences as their constituents can lead to more inclusive policy-making.

Mathematically, we can represent the increase in LGBTQ representation through the following equation:

$$R = \frac{N_{LGBTQ}}{N_{Total}} \times 100$$

where R is the representation rate, N_{LGBTQ} is the number of LGBTQ elected officials, and N_{Total} is the total number of elected officials. Following Ray's election, the representation rate R saw a significant increase from 5% to 15%, illustrating the profound impact of his victory on the visibility of LGBTQ individuals in politics.

Ray's administration prioritized policies that directly benefited the LGBTQ community, including anti-discrimination laws, comprehensive healthcare access, and educational initiatives aimed at fostering inclusivity. These policies not only addressed the immediate needs of the community but also served as a blueprint for other jurisdictions looking to enhance their own LGBTQ representation and rights.

Moreover, Ray's victory inspired a new generation of LGBTQ activists and politicians, who recognized that change was possible. The ripple effect of his success can be seen in the subsequent elections, where an increasing number of LGBTQ candidates emerged, emboldened by Ray's groundbreaking achievement. The phenomenon of "the rainbow wave" became evident, as more LGBTQ individuals sought office, leading to a more representative political landscape.

In conclusion, Ray Ilan's landslide victory was not just a personal triumph; it was a watershed moment for LGBTQ representation in Sykarin and beyond. By challenging the status quo and advocating for inclusive policies, Ray not only changed the narrative surrounding LGBTQ individuals in politics but also laid the groundwork for future advancements in equality and representation. His legacy serves as a reminder that when marginalized voices are empowered, the entire community can thrive, paving the way for a more just and equitable society.

Ray's transformative policies as Sykarin's first LGBTQ mayor

As Ray Ilan took office as Sykarin's first LGBTQ mayor, his administration was poised to implement a series of transformative policies that not only aimed to elevate the status of the LGBTQ community but also sought to integrate inclusivity into the very fabric of Sykarin's governance. Ray understood that the journey toward equality was not merely a political endeavor but a cultural revolution that required a multifaceted approach.

Policy Framework

Ray's policy framework was built on three foundational pillars: equality, representation, and education. Each of these pillars was designed to address systemic issues faced by the LGBTQ community while fostering an environment of acceptance and understanding.

$$\text{Inclusivity} = \frac{\text{Equality} + \text{Representation} + \text{Education}}{3} \tag{51}$$

This equation illustrates Ray's belief that true inclusivity could only be achieved by balancing these critical components.

Equality Initiatives

One of Ray's landmark policies was the introduction of the **Equality Ordinance**, which prohibited discrimination based on sexual orientation and gender identity in employment, housing, and public accommodations. This ordinance was not merely a legal document; it was a declaration of Sykarin's commitment to civil rights. Ray championed this initiative by leveraging data that illustrated the rampant discrimination faced by LGBTQ individuals.

For example, a study conducted by the Sykarin Institute of Social Research revealed that over 40% of LGBTQ residents had experienced discrimination in the workplace. Ray utilized this data to advocate for the ordinance, emphasizing that a thriving community could only exist when all its members were treated with dignity and respect.

Representation in Government

Understanding the importance of representation, Ray initiated the **LGBTQ Advisory Council**, a body composed of diverse voices from the LGBTQ community. This council served not only as a platform for dialogue but also as a mechanism for ensuring that the needs and concerns of LGBTQ residents were directly communicated to the mayor's office.

The council's first major project was to conduct a comprehensive survey assessing the needs of LGBTQ residents. The results were telling: issues such as mental health support, housing security, and access to healthcare were at the forefront. Ray responded by implementing targeted programs that addressed these needs, such as mental health workshops and partnerships with local health providers to ensure LGBTQ-friendly services.

Education Initiatives

Education was another cornerstone of Ray's policies. He spearheaded the **Inclusive Education Initiative**, which aimed to integrate LGBTQ history and issues into the school curriculum. This initiative was critical for fostering understanding and acceptance among young people, thereby reducing bullying and discrimination in schools.

The initiative included:

- **Curriculum Development**: Collaborating with educators to develop age-appropriate materials that reflect LGBTQ contributions to history and society.

- **Training Programs**: Implementing training programs for teachers on LGBTQ issues, ensuring they were equipped to create safe and supportive classroom environments.

- **Community Workshops**: Organizing workshops for parents and community members to discuss LGBTQ topics, aiming to bridge the gap between families and schools.

An example of the initiative's success came when a local high school reported a 30% decrease in bullying incidents related to sexual orientation and gender identity after the curriculum was introduced.

Public Safety and Health Policies

Ray also prioritized public safety and health policies that addressed the unique challenges faced by the LGBTQ community. His administration worked closely with local law enforcement to develop training programs focused on LGBTQ sensitivity and awareness. This initiative aimed to rebuild trust between the LGBTQ community and the police, which had historically been strained.

Moreover, Ray launched the **Health Equity Program**, which ensured that LGBTQ individuals had access to comprehensive healthcare services. This program included partnerships with local clinics to provide free health screenings, mental health services, and support groups tailored specifically for LGBTQ residents.

Legacy of Change

Ray's transformative policies as Sykarin's first LGBTQ mayor not only reshaped the political landscape but also instilled a sense of pride and belonging within the LGBTQ community. His administration's commitment to equality, representation, and education laid the groundwork for future leaders to continue the fight for LGBTQ rights in Sykarin.

In conclusion, Ray Ilan's tenure as mayor was marked by a series of bold and innovative policies that challenged the status quo and championed the rights of marginalized communities. His legacy is a testament to the power of leadership grounded in empathy, courage, and a relentless pursuit of justice.

$$\text{Legacy} = \int_0^T \text{Impact}(t)\,dt \qquad (52)$$

Where T is the time of Ray's tenure and $\text{Impact}(t)$ represents the positive changes enacted during his administration, illustrating that the true measure of leadership is found in the lasting impact on the community.

The legacy of Ray's achievement and its ripple effect on LGBTQ politics

Ray Ilan's election as Sykarin's first LGBTQ mayor marked a watershed moment not only for the town but also for LGBTQ politics on a broader scale. His victory was not merely a personal triumph; it represented a seismic shift in the political landscape, challenging deeply entrenched norms and inspiring a new generation of activists and politicians. The implications of Ray's achievement can be analyzed through several theoretical lenses, including social movement theory, intersectionality, and the concept of representation.

Social Movement Theory

Social movement theory posits that collective action can lead to significant social change. Ray's campaign was emblematic of this theory, as it galvanized the LGBTQ community and its allies to mobilize around a common cause. The grassroots strategies employed during his campaign, such as community organizing, coalition-building, and the use of social media, exemplified successful tactics outlined in social movement literature. According to Tilly and Tarrow (2015), successful social movements often exhibit a "political opportunity structure" that allows for the emergence of new leaders. Ray's rise to prominence can be seen as a response to such an opportunity, as the socio-political climate in Sykarin had begun to shift towards greater acceptance of LGBTQ rights.

Intersectionality

Ray's legacy also underscores the importance of intersectionality in contemporary LGBTQ politics. Intersectionality, a term coined by Kimberlé Crenshaw (1989), highlights how various forms of identity—such as race, gender, and sexual orientation—intersect to create unique experiences of oppression and privilege. Ray's advocacy was not limited to LGBTQ issues alone; he also addressed the needs of marginalized groups within the community, including people of color and those from lower socio-economic backgrounds. This holistic approach not only broadened the scope of LGBTQ activism in Sykarin but also set a precedent for future political leaders to adopt intersectional frameworks in their advocacy efforts.

The Ripple Effect on LGBTQ Politics

The ripple effect of Ray's achievement can be observed in several key areas:

+ **Increased Representation:** Ray's election opened the door for more LGBTQ candidates to run for office, creating a pipeline of diverse voices in politics. This increase in representation is vital for ensuring that the unique needs of the LGBTQ community are addressed in policy-making processes.

+ **Policy Changes:** As mayor, Ray implemented transformative policies that directly impacted the LGBTQ community, such as anti-discrimination laws and initiatives aimed at improving mental health services for LGBTQ youth. These policies not only benefited the local community but also served as models for other jurisdictions looking to enhance their own LGBTQ protections.

+ **National Attention:** Ray's success garnered national media attention, thrusting Sykarin into the spotlight as a beacon of progressive change. This visibility inspired similar movements in other towns and cities, creating a network of LGBTQ political activists who shared strategies and resources.

+ **Cultural Shifts:** Beyond policy, Ray's election signaled a cultural shift in attitudes towards LGBTQ individuals. His visibility as a public figure challenged stereotypes and misconceptions, fostering a more inclusive environment for future generations.

Examples of Impact

An illustrative example of Ray's ripple effect can be seen in the subsequent election of LGBTQ candidates in neighboring regions. For instance, the election of Maria Torres, an openly bisexual councilwoman in the adjacent town of Eldridge, was directly inspired by Ray's campaign. Maria's platform focused on intersectional issues, advocating for both LGBTQ rights and immigrant rights, thereby continuing Ray's legacy of inclusivity.

Moreover, Ray's policies have had lasting implications. The anti-discrimination laws he championed have led to a measurable decrease in hate crimes against LGBTQ individuals in Sykarin, as documented by the Sykarin Department of Justice (2022). This data illustrates the tangible impact of Ray's leadership on community safety and well-being.

Conclusion

In conclusion, Ray Ilan's achievement as Sykarin's first LGBTQ mayor transcended personal success; it initiated a transformative ripple effect in LGBTQ politics. By leveraging social movement strategies, embracing intersectionality, and fostering increased representation, Ray set a powerful precedent for future activists and leaders. His legacy continues to inspire, reminding us that the fight for equality is ongoing and that every barrier broken paves the way for others to follow. As Ray himself often said, "We are not just breaking barriers; we are building bridges."

Ray's impact on the LGBTQ community in Sykarin

Ray Ilan's ascent to the highest political office in Sykarin marked a transformative moment for the LGBTQ community, catalyzing a series of changes that fundamentally altered the socio-political landscape of the town. His historic victory as Sykarin's first LGBTQ mayor not only shattered glass ceilings but also served as a beacon of hope and inspiration for countless individuals who had previously felt marginalized and voiceless.

The impact of Ray's leadership can be understood through several key dimensions: representation, policy reform, community empowerment, and cultural change.

Representation

Ray's election fundamentally shifted the representation of LGBTQ individuals in Sykarin's political sphere. Prior to his tenure, the political landscape was predominantly heteronormative, often overlooking the needs and rights of LGBTQ constituents. Ray's presence in office challenged this status quo, providing a visible role model for LGBTQ youth who previously lacked representation. According to social identity theory, individuals who identify with a marginalized group benefit from seeing members of their community in positions of power, as it enhances their sense of belonging and self-worth (Tajfel & Turner, 1979).

Ray's visibility also encouraged other LGBTQ individuals to engage in politics, leading to a diversification of voices within local governance. His administration actively promoted the inclusion of LGBTQ individuals in decision-making processes, ensuring that policies reflected the needs of a broader constituency.

Policy Reform

Ray's tenure was marked by significant policy reforms aimed at advancing LGBTQ rights and protections. He championed legislation that addressed discrimination in housing, employment, and public accommodations. For instance, the introduction of the Fair Housing Act of Sykarin, which explicitly prohibited discrimination based on sexual orientation and gender identity, was a landmark achievement during his administration.

The impact of these reforms can be quantified through the following equation, which illustrates the relationship between policy implementation (P) and community well-being (W):

$$W = f(P) \quad \text{where } W \text{ is community well-being and } P \text{ is policy implementation}$$

As policies were enacted, surveys indicated a marked increase in the sense of safety and belonging among LGBTQ residents, with a reported 40% decrease in incidents of discrimination following the implementation of these reforms.

Community Empowerment

Ray's impact extended beyond policy; he fostered a culture of empowerment within the LGBTQ community. His administration established various programs aimed at supporting LGBTQ youth, including mentorship initiatives and safe spaces for dialogue. The establishment of the Sykarin LGBTQ Community Center under his leadership provided a physical space where individuals could gather, seek resources, and build community connections.

Ray's approach to community empowerment was rooted in the principles of participatory action research, which emphasizes the importance of community involvement in identifying and addressing issues. By facilitating workshops and forums, Ray encouraged LGBTQ individuals to voice their concerns and actively participate in shaping the policies that affected their lives.

Cultural Change

Culturally, Ray's leadership had a profound effect on the perception of LGBTQ individuals in Sykarin. His unapologetic authenticity and commitment to visibility challenged longstanding stereotypes and misconceptions. The media coverage surrounding his election and subsequent initiatives highlighted LGBTQ stories, celebrating diversity and fostering a more inclusive narrative.

The phenomenon of "Raymania" emerged, characterized by an increase in LGBTQ representation in local media, arts, and culture. This cultural shift not only validated the experiences of LGBTQ individuals but also educated the broader community, fostering empathy and understanding.

Ray's influence can be encapsulated in the following model of cultural change:

$$C = g(R) \quad \text{where } C \text{ is cultural acceptance and } R \text{ is representation}$$

As representation increased, cultural acceptance followed suit, with surveys indicating a 50% rise in support for LGBTQ rights within the general population of Sykarin.

In conclusion, Ray Ilan's impact on the LGBTQ community in Sykarin was multifaceted and profound. Through his leadership, he not only advanced policy reforms but also fostered a sense of empowerment and belonging among LGBTQ individuals. His legacy serves as a testament to the power of representation and the importance of inclusive governance in creating a more equitable society. As Ray once stated, "Breaking barriers is not just about changing laws; it's about changing hearts and minds." The ripple effect of his work continues to inspire future generations of activists and leaders within the LGBTQ community and beyond.

Ray's Unfiltered Truth

Ray's candid reflections on his journey as an LGBTQ activist

Ray Ilan's journey as an LGBTQ activist has been marked by a series of transformative experiences that shaped not only his identity but also the landscape of activism in Sykarin. Reflecting on this journey, Ray often emphasizes the importance of authenticity and vulnerability in activism. He believes that true change begins when individuals embrace their identities and share their stories, allowing others to see the human side of the struggle for equality.

One of the foundational theories that underpins Ray's activism is the **Intersectionality Theory**, introduced by Kimberlé Crenshaw. This theory posits that various social identities—such as race, gender, sexual orientation, and class—intersect to create unique modes of discrimination and privilege. Ray's reflections often highlight how intersectionality has played a critical role in his work, particularly in addressing the diverse needs of the LGBTQ community in Sykarin. He recalls a pivotal moment during a local pride event, where he witnessed the marginalization of LGBTQ individuals of color. This experience ignited a passion within him to advocate for a more inclusive approach to activism.

Ray's candid reflections also touch upon the challenges he faced as an activist. He recounts the initial resistance he encountered from both the LGBTQ community and the broader society. In the early days of his activism, Ray often felt like an outsider, struggling to find his place among established organizations that did not always prioritize the issues he deemed critical. For instance, he recalls organizing a community forum aimed at addressing mental health issues within the LGBTQ youth population, only to be met with skepticism from older activists who viewed such topics as secondary to marriage equality. This experience taught Ray the importance of perseverance and the need to advocate for all aspects of LGBTQ life, not just the most visible issues.

In his reflections, Ray also highlights the significance of mentorship and solidarity within the activist community. He credits many seasoned activists with guiding him through the complexities of advocacy, helping him navigate the political landscape of Sykarin. One such mentor, a local elder named Marcus, taught Ray the value of storytelling in activism. Marcus often said, "Our stories are our weapons; they can break down walls and build bridges." Inspired by this wisdom, Ray began to share his own story—his struggles with identity, the pain of rejection, and the joy of acceptance. This shift not only empowered him but also resonated with many in the community, fostering a sense of unity and shared purpose.

Ray's journey has not been without its emotional toll. He candidly discusses the mental health challenges that accompany activism, including burnout and anxiety. He believes that acknowledging these struggles is crucial for sustaining long-term engagement in activism. Ray advocates for self-care practices and the importance of creating supportive environments where activists can share their burdens. He often organizes wellness workshops that focus on mindfulness and resilience, emphasizing that taking care of oneself is not a sign of weakness but a necessary component of effective activism.

Through his reflections, Ray also addresses the evolution of LGBTQ activism over the years. He notes that while significant progress has been made, there are still many barriers to break. For example, he points to the ongoing fight for transgender rights, particularly in healthcare access and legal recognition. Ray's commitment to these issues is evident in his work with local organizations that focus on providing resources and support for transgender individuals. He believes that activism must continually adapt to address emerging challenges, ensuring that no one is left behind.

In conclusion, Ray Ilan's candid reflections on his journey as an LGBTQ activist reveal a profound understanding of the complexities of identity, community, and advocacy. His experiences highlight the importance of authenticity, intersectionality, mentorship, and self-care in the pursuit of equality. As Ray continues to break barriers and inspire others, his journey serves as a testament to the power of resilience and the enduring spirit of the LGBTQ movement.

$$\text{Activism} = \text{Authenticity} + \text{Intersectionality} + \text{Solidarity} + \text{Resilience} \quad (53)$$

The highs and lows of Ray's personal and professional life

Ray Ilan's journey as an LGBTQ activist is marked by a series of significant highs and lows that shaped not only his career but also his personal life. The complexity of navigating both realms is a testament to the challenges faced by many activists in the LGBTQ community.

The Highs: Triumphs and Achievements

Ray's ascent in the activist community began with his passionate speeches that ignited a fire in the hearts of those who felt marginalized. One of the most notable highs in his professional life was the formation of the LGBTQ Equality Party, which he spearheaded. This party not only provided a platform for LGBTQ rights but also served as a beacon of hope for those who had long been silenced. The success of the party is often attributed to Ray's charismatic leadership and ability to connect with people on a personal level.

$$\text{Activism Success} = \frac{\text{Community Engagement} \times \text{Effective Messaging}}{\text{Opposition}} \quad (54)$$

This equation illustrates that the success of Ray's activism was a product of his ability to engage the community while effectively communicating the party's vision, all while navigating significant opposition from conservative factions within Sykarin.

Another high point in Ray's life was his election as Sykarin's first LGBTQ mayor. This historic achievement was not merely a personal victory; it represented a monumental shift in the political landscape of Sykarin. Ray's policies focused on inclusivity, education, and healthcare for LGBTQ individuals, and his administration was celebrated for its progressive stance. The pride and joy he felt during his inaugural speech were palpable, as he stood before a crowd that included supporters who had fought alongside him for years.

The Lows: Struggles and Setbacks

Despite these highs, Ray's journey was fraught with challenges. One of the most significant lows occurred during his campaign for mayor. The backlash from conservative groups was intense, with protests and smear campaigns aimed at undermining his credibility. Ray faced personal attacks that questioned his character and motives, leading to moments of self-doubt.

$$\text{Mental Strain} = \text{Public Scrutiny} + \text{Personal Sacrifice} - \text{Support Network} \quad (55)$$

This equation highlights the mental strain Ray experienced, which was exacerbated by public scrutiny and personal sacrifices made in the name of activism. The lack of a robust support network during these trying times left him feeling isolated, a sentiment echoed by many activists who find themselves in similar situations.

Moreover, Ray's personal relationships suffered as he dedicated more time to his activism. The complexities of love and lust in a judgmental society often left him feeling vulnerable. His romantic escapades, while exciting, were often marred by the fear of public judgment.

Navigating Personal and Professional Life

Balancing personal and professional life became a delicate dance for Ray. He often found solace in the LGBTQ community, where friendships blossomed into family-like bonds. However, the pressure to maintain a public persona while grappling with personal issues created a dichotomy that was hard to reconcile.

Ray's experiences underscore a broader theory in activism: the **Emotional Labor Theory**, which posits that activists often expend emotional energy to maintain their roles in public life. This theory is particularly relevant in understanding the psychological toll that activism can take, as individuals like Ray navigate their identities while striving for social change.

$$\text{Emotional Labor} = \text{Authenticity} + \text{Public Image} - \text{Self-Care} \quad (56)$$

Ray's commitment to authenticity often clashed with the demands of maintaining a polished public image, leading to neglect of self-care. This neglect manifested in burnout and moments of despair, where Ray questioned the impact of his work and whether it was worth the personal cost.

Lessons Learned

Through these highs and lows, Ray learned invaluable lessons about resilience, community, and the importance of mental health. He realized that vulnerability is not a weakness but a strength that can foster deeper connections and understanding.

Ray's candid reflections on his journey serve as a reminder that the path of an activist is not a straight line; it is filled with peaks and valleys that shape one's identity and purpose. His story resonates with many who strive to break barriers, highlighting that the journey is as important as the destination.

In conclusion, the highs and lows of Ray Ilan's personal and professional life illustrate the complexities of being an LGBTQ activist. His triumphs inspire hope, while his struggles remind us of the resilience required to navigate this challenging yet rewarding path.

Ray's ongoing mission to inspire future LGBTQ activists

Ray Ilan's journey as an LGBTQ activist has not only transformed his local community in Sykarin but has also set a precedent for future generations of activists. His ongoing mission is rooted in the belief that empowerment through education, mentorship, and visibility is essential for fostering a vibrant and resilient LGBTQ movement. This section explores Ray's strategies and initiatives aimed at inspiring the next wave of activists, while also addressing the challenges they face in an ever-evolving socio-political landscape.

The Importance of Mentorship

Ray recognizes that mentorship plays a pivotal role in shaping the identities and activism of young LGBTQ individuals. By establishing mentorship programs, he creates safe spaces where aspiring activists can seek guidance, share experiences, and gain insights from those who have navigated the complexities of LGBTQ advocacy. This approach aligns with the theory of *social learning*, which posits that individuals learn behaviors through observation and imitation of role models.

For example, Ray's mentorship initiatives have paired seasoned activists with youth from marginalized backgrounds, ensuring that they receive the support needed to develop their own voices and strategies. This not only empowers the mentees but also enriches the activist community with fresh perspectives and innovative ideas.

Education as a Catalyst for Change

Ray's commitment to integrating LGBTQ education into school curricula is another cornerstone of his mission. He believes that education is a powerful tool for dismantling prejudice and fostering understanding. By advocating for comprehensive LGBTQ studies, Ray aims to equip future generations with the knowledge and empathy necessary to combat discrimination.

The implementation of LGBTQ-inclusive education has been shown to improve the school climate for all students, reducing bullying and increasing feelings of safety among LGBTQ youth. Research indicates that when students learn about diverse sexual orientations and gender identities, they are more likely to develop a positive attitude towards their peers. Ray's initiatives have led to the creation of educational materials that highlight LGBTQ history, culture, and contributions, thus normalizing LGBTQ identities within the fabric of society.

Utilizing Technology and Social Media

In a digital age where social media serves as a platform for activism, Ray leverages technology to inspire and mobilize future activists. He conducts online workshops, webinars, and social media campaigns that engage young people in discussions about LGBTQ rights and activism. This approach not only broadens the reach of his message but also fosters a sense of community among activists across geographical boundaries.

The use of social media allows for rapid dissemination of information and the ability to organize events quickly, making it an invaluable tool in contemporary activism. Ray's campaigns often utilize hashtags to create movements, such as #SykarinPride and #BreakTheSilence, which encourage participation and solidarity among LGBTQ individuals and allies.

Addressing Intersectionality

Ray's activism is deeply informed by the principles of intersectionality, recognizing that the LGBTQ community is not monolithic. He emphasizes the importance of addressing the unique challenges faced by individuals at the intersections of race, gender, class, and sexuality. By advocating for inclusive practices within the movement, Ray ensures that the voices of marginalized groups are heard and prioritized.

For instance, Ray has collaborated with organizations that focus on the specific needs of LGBTQ people of color, transgender individuals, and those with disabilities. This intersectional approach not only strengthens the movement but also creates a more equitable platform for all activists to thrive.

Celebrating Diversity in Activism

Ray believes that diversity in activism is a source of strength. He actively promotes the idea that every individual has a unique story and perspective to contribute to the movement. By celebrating diverse narratives, Ray inspires future activists to embrace their identities and experiences, encouraging them to share their stories as a means of advocacy.

This celebration of diversity is exemplified in events such as the annual *Sykarin Pride Festival*, where activists from various backgrounds come together to showcase their talents, share their stories, and foster a sense of belonging. Such events not only empower individuals but also create visibility for underrepresented groups within the LGBTQ community.

Ray's Legacy of Inspiration

Ultimately, Ray Ilan's ongoing mission to inspire future LGBTQ activists is characterized by a commitment to empowerment, education, and inclusivity. Through mentorship, educational initiatives, and the celebration of diversity, Ray is cultivating a new generation of activists who are equipped to face the challenges ahead. His legacy is one of resilience and hope, reminding us that the fight for equality is a collective journey that requires the participation of all.

As Ray often states, "The future of our movement lies in the hands of those we uplift today." This ethos drives his work and serves as a guiding principle for aspiring activists who seek to follow in his footsteps. By fostering a culture of support and inclusivity, Ray ensures that the flame of activism will continue to burn brightly for generations to come.

The challenges and triumphs of being a public figure

Being a public figure in the realm of LGBTQ activism is akin to navigating a high-octane race, where every turn can either lead to triumph or disaster. Ray Ilan, as a prominent activist, faced a unique set of challenges and triumphs that shaped his journey and influenced his impact on the community.

Challenges Faced

One of the primary challenges Ray encountered was the scrutiny that comes with visibility. The public eye can be unforgiving, especially for those who defy societal norms. Ray often found himself at the center of media attention, where every action and statement was analyzed and critiqued. This constant scrutiny can lead to a phenomenon known as *imposter syndrome*, where individuals doubt their accomplishments and fear being exposed as a "fraud." According to research by Clance and Imes (1978), this phenomenon is particularly prevalent among high-achieving individuals, including activists like Ray.

$$\text{Imposter Syndrome} = \frac{\text{Self-Doubt}}{\text{Public Scrutiny}} \qquad (57)$$

Ray's experiences were compounded by the backlash from conservative factions within Sykarin, who opposed his activism. This opposition often manifested in online harassment, protests, and even threats to his safety. Such hostile reactions can lead to significant psychological stress, with studies indicating that public figures in marginalized communities are at a higher risk for mental health issues, including anxiety and depression (Meyer, 2003).

Furthermore, Ray had to navigate the delicate balance between being authentic and maintaining a public persona. The pressure to conform to certain expectations can dilute one's message, leading to a phenomenon known as *performative activism*, where actions are taken more for show than for genuine impact. Ray often grappled with this tension, striving to remain true to himself while also being an effective advocate.

Triumphs Achieved

Despite these challenges, Ray's journey was not devoid of triumphs. His ability to leverage his public platform allowed him to amplify the voices of others within the LGBTQ community. By sharing his personal story, Ray humanized the struggles faced by many, fostering empathy and understanding among those outside the community. This aligns with the *social identity theory*, which posits that individuals derive part of their identity from the groups to which they belong (Tajfel & Turner, 1986). Ray's visibility helped to reshape public perceptions of LGBTQ individuals, promoting a more inclusive narrative.

$$\text{Public Perception} = \text{Visibility} \times \text{Authenticity} \qquad (58)$$

Moreover, Ray's activism led to tangible policy changes in Sykarin. His iconic speeches and passionate advocacy not only rallied support within the LGBTQ community but also garnered attention from allies and policymakers. This culminated in the formation of the LGBTQ Equality Party, which became a significant political force in the region. Ray's success in this arena exemplifies the potential for public figures to effect change through strategic engagement and coalition-building.

Ray also found triumph in the creation of safe spaces for LGBTQ individuals. His efforts to foster community and support networks provided a refuge for those grappling with their identities in a judgmental society. This initiative not only empowered individuals but also contributed to a growing sense of solidarity within the LGBTQ community. Research indicates that social support is crucial for the well-being of marginalized individuals, reinforcing the importance of Ray's work (Cohen & Wills, 1985).

Conclusion

In summary, the journey of being a public figure in LGBTQ activism is fraught with challenges, yet it is equally rich with opportunities for triumph. Ray Ilan's experiences illustrate the complexities of navigating public scrutiny, the pressures of authenticity, and the potential for meaningful impact. By embracing both the challenges and triumphs, Ray not only advanced the cause of LGBTQ rights in Sykarin but also inspired countless others to join the fight for equality. His legacy serves as a testament to the power of resilience and the importance of unwavering commitment to one's truth.

Ray's unapologetic authenticity and commitment to breaking barriers

Ray Ilan's journey as an LGBTQ activist is marked by an unwavering commitment to authenticity, a quality that has not only defined his personal narrative but has also galvanized a movement in Sykarin and beyond. This section explores how Ray's unapologetic authenticity has served as a catalyst for change, challenging societal norms and inspiring countless individuals to embrace their true selves.

The Essence of Authenticity

Authenticity, in the context of LGBTQ activism, can be understood through the lens of self-acceptance and visibility. According to [?], authenticity involves being true to oneself, which is particularly significant for marginalized communities that have historically faced pressure to conform to heteronormative standards. Ray's refusal to hide his identity or conform to societal expectations exemplifies this principle. He often states, "To be authentic is to be free; freedom is the first step to breaking barriers."

Breaking Down Barriers

Ray's commitment to authenticity manifests in various forms of activism, including public speaking, social media campaigns, and grassroots organizing. By openly sharing his experiences, including the struggles and triumphs of his journey, Ray has created a relatable narrative that resonates with many. His iconic speeches, filled with raw emotion and personal anecdotes, serve as both a rallying cry and a source of comfort for those grappling with their identities.

For example, during the *Sykarin Pride March*, Ray delivered a powerful speech that addressed the challenges faced by LGBTQ individuals in the community. He articulated the importance of embracing one's identity, stating, "When we stand tall in our truth, we dismantle the chains of ignorance and fear." This moment not only highlighted his authenticity but also inspired attendees to embrace their identities and advocate for change.

Theoretical Framework

Ray's approach can be analyzed through the *Social Identity Theory* proposed by Tajfel and Turner (1979), which posits that individuals derive part of their identity from the groups to which they belong. By openly identifying as a member of the LGBTQ community, Ray has fostered a sense of belonging among others who share similar experiences. This shared identity creates a supportive network that empowers individuals to express their true selves without fear of judgment.

Moreover, Ray's activism aligns with the principles of *Intersectionality*, as discussed by Crenshaw (1989). He recognizes that the LGBTQ experience is not monolithic; rather, it intersects with various identities, including race, gender, and socioeconomic status. By advocating for inclusivity within the LGBTQ movement, Ray ensures that all voices are heard and represented, further reinforcing the importance of authenticity in activism.

Challenges of Authenticity

Despite the power of authenticity, Ray has faced significant challenges. The backlash from conservative factions in Sykarin, who view his openness as a threat to traditional values, underscores the societal resistance to change. This opposition often manifests in public protests and derogatory campaigns aimed at discrediting his activism. However, Ray remains undeterred, viewing these challenges as opportunities to further emphasize the importance of authenticity.

In his interviews, Ray often reflects on the emotional toll of such adversity. He admits that the journey has not been easy, stating, "Every insult, every attack, only fuels my fire. Authenticity is my armor; it protects me while I break barriers." This resilience highlights how authenticity can serve as both a personal strength and a powerful tool for activism.

Real-World Examples

One notable example of Ray's commitment to authenticity is his involvement in the *LGBTQ Youth Empowerment Program*. This initiative, designed to provide support and resources for LGBTQ youth, emphasizes the importance of self-acceptance and visibility. Ray frequently shares his own story with participants, illustrating that embracing one's identity can lead to empowerment and success.

Additionally, Ray's use of social media platforms has allowed him to connect with a broader audience. His candid posts about personal struggles and victories have garnered significant attention, creating a virtual community of support. Through hashtags like #BeYourself and #BreakTheBarriers, Ray encourages individuals to share their stories, fostering a culture of authenticity and acceptance.

Conclusion

Ray Ilan's unapologetic authenticity is a cornerstone of his activism, driving his commitment to breaking barriers within the LGBTQ community. By embracing his true self and encouraging others to do the same, Ray has created a ripple effect that challenges societal norms and inspires a new generation of activists. His journey serves as a powerful reminder that authenticity is not just a personal journey; it is a collective movement towards liberation and equality. As Ray himself puts it, "When we are true to ourselves, we ignite the spark of change. Together, we can break every barrier."

Ray's lasting impact on the LGBTQ community

Ray Ilan's journey from a small-town activist to a national icon has left an indelible mark on the LGBTQ community, not only in Sykarin but across the globe. His impact can be analyzed through several lenses, including the evolution of LGBTQ rights, the cultivation of community, and the promotion of representation and visibility.

Evolution of LGBTQ Rights

Ray's activism has played a pivotal role in the evolution of LGBTQ rights in Sykarin. Through his tireless efforts, he has successfully challenged discriminatory laws and practices, advocating for legal recognition of same-sex relationships and the protection of LGBTQ individuals from discrimination. His campaigns have led to significant legal reforms, including the introduction of anti-discrimination legislation, which has provided a framework for protecting LGBTQ individuals in various sectors, including employment, housing, and healthcare.

The theoretical framework underpinning Ray's activism can be linked to the concept of *social justice*, which emphasizes the importance of equitable treatment and the dismantling of systemic barriers. As articulated by theorists like Iris Marion Young, social justice involves recognizing and addressing the injustices faced by marginalized groups. Ray's work exemplifies this theory as he mobilizes the community to advocate for their rights, fostering a sense of empowerment among LGBTQ individuals.

Cultivation of Community

Ray's impact extends beyond legal reforms; he has been instrumental in fostering a sense of community among LGBTQ individuals in Sykarin. By creating safe spaces and organizing events such as pride parades and LGBTQ forums, Ray has provided platforms for individuals to express their identities freely. This sense of belonging is crucial, as it combats the isolation often experienced by LGBTQ individuals in conservative environments.

The concept of *community building* is central to understanding Ray's legacy. According to sociologist Robert Putnam, community engagement is vital for social capital, which refers to the networks of relationships among people who live and work in a particular society. Ray's initiatives have not only strengthened bonds within the LGBTQ community but have also bridged gaps with allies and supporters from the broader society, fostering a culture of inclusivity and solidarity.

Promotion of Representation and Visibility

Representation is another critical aspect of Ray's impact on the LGBTQ community. His unapologetic approach to activism has challenged stereotypes and misconceptions surrounding LGBTQ individuals, paving the way for more authentic portrayals in media and politics. By amplifying diverse voices within the

LGBTQ spectrum, Ray has contributed to a richer narrative that goes beyond the binary understanding of gender and sexuality.

Theoretical perspectives on representation, such as those articulated by Stuart Hall, highlight the importance of visibility in shaping societal perceptions. Hall argues that representation is a powerful tool for challenging dominant narratives and fostering understanding. Ray's influence in popular culture, through collaborations with artists and media figures, has significantly enhanced the visibility of LGBTQ issues, enabling broader societal acceptance and understanding.

Legacy of Inspiration

Ray's lasting impact is also evident in his role as a mentor and inspiration for future generations of LGBTQ activists. His candid reflections on the challenges and triumphs of his journey serve as a guiding light for those who aspire to follow in his footsteps. By sharing his experiences, Ray emphasizes the importance of resilience and authenticity in activism.

The concept of *transformative leadership* is relevant here, as articulated by theorists like James MacGregor Burns. Transformative leaders inspire change by motivating others to transcend their self-interests for the sake of a larger cause. Ray's leadership style embodies this principle, as he encourages young activists to embrace their identities and advocate for their rights passionately.

Conclusion

In conclusion, Ray Ilan's lasting impact on the LGBTQ community is multifaceted, encompassing legal advancements, community building, representation, and mentorship. His work has not only transformed the landscape of LGBTQ rights in Sykarin but has also inspired a global movement toward inclusivity and equality. As future generations continue to build upon his legacy, Ray's indomitable spirit and commitment to breaking barriers will undoubtedly resonate, ensuring that the fight for LGBTQ rights remains a vibrant and essential part of the social justice narrative.

Chapter 3: Ray's Revolution Continues

Chapter 3: Ray's Revolution Continues

Chapter 3: Ray's Revolution Continues

In the vibrant landscape of Sykarin, Ray Ilan's journey is far from over. The revolution he ignited is not merely a moment in time; it is a continuous wave that challenges the very fabric of societal norms and expectations. As Ray steps into this new chapter, he embodies the spirit of resilience, pushing boundaries and redefining what it means to be an LGBTQ activist in a world still rife with prejudice and misunderstanding.

The Call for Change

Ray's revolution is propelled by a simple yet profound premise: the necessity of redefining "normal." The term itself has been historically laden with connotations that marginalize and exclude. In the context of LGBTQ rights, "normal" often implies conformity to heteronormative standards that have long dictated societal behavior. Ray's mission is to dismantle this concept, advocating for a broader, more inclusive understanding of identity and expression.

The challenge lies in addressing the entrenched beliefs that define societal norms. For instance, traditional gender roles have perpetuated stereotypes that confine individuals to binary classifications, often leading to discrimination against those who dare to deviate. Ray's approach is grounded in the theory of intersectionality, which posits that various forms of social stratification, such as race, gender, and sexual orientation, intersect to create unique dynamics of oppression and privilege. By embracing intersectionality, Ray acknowledges the multifaceted nature of identity and the importance of inclusivity in activism.

Expanding the Narrative of Gender in Sykarin

Ray's fearless exploration of his own gender identity serves as a beacon for others. He challenges the binary understanding of gender by advocating for a spectrum that recognizes non-binary and genderqueer identities. This shift is crucial in a society where rigid definitions often lead to exclusion and violence against those who do not conform.

For example, Ray initiates community workshops aimed at educating the public about gender diversity. These workshops employ interactive methods, such as role-playing and storytelling, to foster empathy and understanding. Participants are encouraged to share their experiences, creating a safe space for dialogue. The impact of these initiatives is profound, as they not only educate but also empower individuals to embrace their authentic selves.

The Impact of Ray's Gender Revolution

The ripple effects of Ray's gender revolution are felt throughout Sykarin. Schools begin to implement inclusive policies that recognize and support gender diversity, paving the way for safer environments for LGBTQ youth. The local government, influenced by Ray's advocacy, introduces legislation that prohibits discrimination based on gender identity, marking a significant step towards equality.

However, resistance remains. Conservative factions within Sykarin vehemently oppose these changes, arguing that they undermine traditional values. Ray counters this opposition by emphasizing the importance of human rights and dignity for all individuals, regardless of their gender identity. He articulates his vision through powerful speeches that resonate with both supporters and skeptics, urging them to reconsider their perspectives.

Ongoing Battle for Gender Inclusivity

Despite the progress, the battle for gender inclusivity is ongoing. Ray understands that activism is not a destination but a journey. He continues to advocate for comprehensive sex education that includes discussions on gender identity and sexual orientation, aiming to equip the next generation with the knowledge and understanding necessary to foster acceptance and respect.

Ray's activism also extends beyond the borders of Sykarin. He collaborates with international organizations to share best practices and strategies for promoting gender inclusivity. By participating in global forums, Ray amplifies the voices of marginalized communities, ensuring that their struggles are recognized on the world stage.

Ray's Impact on Gender Discussions in Sykarin

As Ray's revolution continues, he remains a central figure in redefining gender discussions within Sykarin. His influence extends to various sectors, including arts and media, where he champions representation of diverse gender identities. Through partnerships with local artists, Ray produces multimedia campaigns that highlight the stories of individuals from all walks of life, showcasing the beauty of diversity.

The cultural shift initiated by Ray's efforts is palpable. More individuals feel empowered to express their identities openly, leading to a flourishing LGBTQ community that celebrates its differences. Events such as Pride parades and gender-diverse art exhibitions become commonplace, symbolizing the progress made and the work that lies ahead.

In conclusion, Ray Ilan's revolution is a testament to the power of resilience and the importance of challenging societal norms. By redefining "normal" and advocating for inclusivity, Ray not only transforms the landscape of Sykarin but also inspires a global movement towards acceptance and understanding. His journey continues, fueled by the unwavering belief that every individual deserves the right to live authentically and without fear.

Redefining "Normal"

Ray's efforts in challenging societal norms and expectations

Ray Ilan's journey as a prominent LGBTQ activist in Sykarin is a testament to his unwavering commitment to challenging societal norms and expectations. From a young age, Ray recognized that the rigid structures of gender and sexuality imposed by society stifled individuality and marginalized those who dared to defy them. His efforts to dismantle these norms can be understood through various theoretical frameworks, including Judith Butler's theory of gender performativity and Michel Foucault's ideas on power and social constructs.

Theoretical Foundations

Judith Butler, in her seminal work *Gender Trouble*, posits that gender is not a fixed identity but rather a performance, shaped by societal expectations. According to Butler, the repetition of gendered behaviors creates the illusion of a stable identity. Ray embraced this concept, using his own life as a platform to showcase the fluidity of gender and the artificiality of traditional gender roles. He famously stated, "I am not just one thing; I am a spectrum of identities, and I refuse to be boxed in."

In parallel, Michel Foucault's theories on power dynamics provide a framework for understanding how societal norms are enforced and perpetuated. Foucault argued that power is not merely repressive but also productive, creating norms that individuals internalize and reproduce. Ray's activism sought to disrupt these power structures by encouraging individuals to question the norms that dictate their lives. His mantra, "Power is only as strong as our silence," became a rallying cry for many in Sykarin.

Challenging Gender Norms

One of Ray's most significant efforts in challenging societal norms was his outspoken critique of traditional gender roles. He organized workshops and community discussions that encouraged participants to explore their gender identities and express themselves authentically. In these sessions, Ray often employed creative methods, such as role-playing and artistic expression, to illustrate the absurdity of rigid gender binaries.

For example, during a particularly impactful workshop titled *Beyond the Binary*, Ray invited participants to share their experiences of gender identity. The event culminated in a theatrical performance where attendees donned costumes that represented various gender expressions, from hyper-masculine to ultra-feminine, as well as androgynous and non-binary representations. This performance not only entertained but also educated the audience about the diverse spectrum of gender identities, fostering a sense of community and acceptance.

Promoting Inclusivity

Ray's activism extended beyond personal expression; he sought to create a more inclusive society. He launched campaigns advocating for the inclusion of diverse gender identities in local policies and practices. One notable initiative was the *Sykarin Equality Act*, which aimed to protect individuals from discrimination based on gender identity and expression. Ray collaborated with local lawmakers to draft legislation that incorporated gender-neutral language and provisions for non-binary individuals.

Despite facing significant opposition, Ray's persistence paid off when the act was passed, marking a significant victory for the LGBTQ community in Sykarin. This legislation not only challenged existing societal norms but also set a precedent for other municipalities to follow. Ray's efforts demonstrated that challenging norms could lead to tangible change, empowering others to advocate for their rights.

Creating Safe Spaces

Understanding the importance of safe spaces, Ray established support groups and community centers that catered to LGBTQ individuals. These spaces provided a refuge where individuals could explore their identities without fear of judgment or discrimination. Ray emphasized the importance of intersectionality, recognizing that different identities—such as race, class, and ability—intersect with gender and sexuality, creating unique challenges for individuals.

In these safe spaces, Ray facilitated discussions on topics such as mental health, self-acceptance, and the impact of societal expectations on personal well-being. He often shared his own struggles with acceptance, illustrating that vulnerability could foster connection and healing. His approach encouraged participants to embrace their identities and challenge the societal norms that sought to diminish them.

Media Representation

Ray also recognized the power of media in shaping societal perceptions of gender and sexuality. He actively campaigned for more inclusive representation in local media, arguing that visibility was crucial in challenging stereotypes and misconceptions. Ray collaborated with filmmakers and artists to produce content that showcased diverse stories and experiences within the LGBTQ community.

One of his most notable projects was the documentary *Sykarin Unfiltered*, which highlighted the lives of LGBTQ individuals in the town. The film challenged prevailing narratives by presenting authentic stories of joy, struggle, and resilience. Ray's involvement in this project underscored his belief that representation matters, and that media has the power to challenge societal norms by amplifying marginalized voices.

Conclusion

In conclusion, Ray Ilan's efforts to challenge societal norms and expectations were multifaceted, encompassing theoretical critique, community engagement, legislative advocacy, and media representation. His work not only transformed the landscape of LGBTQ activism in Sykarin but also inspired a generation to question and redefine what it means to be true to oneself. Ray's legacy serves as a reminder that challenging societal norms is not just a personal endeavor but a collective movement towards a more inclusive and accepting world.

Expanding the narrative of gender in Sykarin

In the vibrant town of Sykarin, the narrative of gender has long been confined to rigid binaries, where traditional expectations dictated the roles individuals were expected to play. However, Ray Ilan, with his revolutionary spirit, sought to expand this narrative, challenging the status quo and advocating for a more inclusive understanding of gender. This endeavor was not merely a personal journey for Ray; it was a movement aimed at reshaping societal perceptions and fostering acceptance for all gender identities.

Theoretical Framework

To understand Ray's impact on gender narratives in Sykarin, we must first delve into the relevant theories that underpin gender identity and expression. Judith Butler's theory of gender performativity posits that gender is not an inherent quality but rather a series of actions and performances that individuals enact based on societal expectations [?]. This perspective encourages the idea that gender can be fluid and dynamic, allowing for a spectrum of identities beyond the binary classification of male and female.

Ray embraced this theory, advocating for a redefinition of gender that acknowledged its multifaceted nature. He often quoted Butler, stating, "Gender is not something we are, but something we do." This mantra resonated deeply with the youth in Sykarin, who began to see their own experiences reflected in Ray's activism.

Challenges Faced

Despite the theoretical groundwork laid by thinkers like Butler, expanding the narrative of gender in Sykarin was fraught with challenges. Many residents were steeped in traditional views that equated gender with biological sex, leading to widespread misconceptions and discrimination against those who deviated from these norms. The local government, influenced by conservative ideologies, often resisted any attempts to acknowledge non-binary and genderqueer identities, resulting in a lack of representation and support for these individuals.

Ray faced significant backlash from conservative factions, who viewed his activism as a threat to the fabric of Sykarin's society. They argued that expanding the narrative of gender would lead to confusion among youth and destabilize traditional family structures. However, Ray countered this argument by emphasizing the importance of education and awareness in fostering understanding and acceptance.

Community Engagement and Education

To combat these challenges, Ray initiated community engagement programs aimed at educating the public about gender diversity. He organized workshops and panel discussions featuring local LGBTQ activists, educators, and mental health professionals. These events focused on dismantling stereotypes and promoting empathy, allowing individuals to share their personal experiences with gender identity.

One notable event was the "Gender Spectrum Symposium," which brought together individuals from various backgrounds to discuss their journeys and the importance of recognizing diverse gender identities. Attendees participated in interactive activities that highlighted the fluidity of gender, such as role-playing scenarios where individuals could express themselves outside of societal norms. The symposium was a resounding success, drawing in over 300 participants and fostering discussions that continued long after the event concluded.

Cultural Representation

Ray also recognized the power of cultural representation in expanding the narrative of gender. He collaborated with local artists to create a series of murals throughout Sykarin that depicted individuals of diverse gender identities. These murals served as a visual reminder of the community's commitment to inclusivity and sparked conversations among residents about the importance of representation in public spaces.

In addition, Ray worked with local filmmakers to produce a documentary titled "Beyond the Binary," which explored the lives of non-binary individuals in Sykarin. The film showcased their struggles and triumphs, providing a platform for voices that had long been marginalized. Screenings of the documentary were held at community centers and schools, furthering the dialogue around gender identity and encouraging viewers to reflect on their own perceptions.

Impact on the Community

The impact of Ray's efforts in expanding the narrative of gender in Sykarin was profound. As awareness grew, so did the acceptance of diverse gender identities. Schools began to implement inclusive policies, such as gender-neutral bathrooms and anti-bullying initiatives that specifically addressed gender-based discrimination. Local businesses also adopted more inclusive practices, providing training for staff on gender sensitivity and creating environments where all customers felt welcome.

Ray's activism not only transformed the discourse around gender in Sykarin but also inspired a new generation of activists. Young individuals began to embrace their identities and advocate for their rights, leading to the formation of youth-led organizations focused on gender inclusivity. These groups organized their own events, such as pride marches and awareness campaigns, further solidifying the community's commitment to embracing diversity.

Conclusion

Ray Ilan's efforts to expand the narrative of gender in Sykarin exemplified the power of activism in challenging societal norms. By grounding his work in established theories, engaging the community, and promoting representation, Ray was able to foster a more inclusive environment for individuals of all gender identities. His legacy serves as a reminder that the fight for gender inclusivity is ongoing, and that every individual has the power to contribute to this transformative movement.

Ray's fearless exploration of his own gender identity

Ray Ilan's journey into the depths of his own gender identity was not just a personal struggle; it was a revolution that resonated throughout Sykarin and beyond. In a society where traditional gender norms were not just prevalent but enforced, Ray emerged as a beacon of hope and authenticity. His exploration was characterized by a series of revelations that challenged the binary understanding of gender and sought to redefine what it meant to exist outside of societal expectations.

Challenging Binary Constructs

The concept of gender has historically been viewed through a binary lens—male and female—often neglecting the spectrum that exists between and beyond these categories. Judith Butler's theory of gender performativity posits that gender is not an inherent quality but rather a series of performances dictated by societal norms. Ray's journey echoed Butler's ideas as he began to understand that his gender identity was not confined to the traditional roles assigned at birth.

$$G = P_1 + P_2 + P_3 + \ldots + P_n \tag{59}$$

Where G represents gender, and P_n represents the various performances that contribute to an individual's gender identity. Ray's realization that he could curate his own performances allowed him to embrace a fluidity that defied societal norms.

Personal Experiences and Public Reactions

Ray's exploration was not without challenges. He faced backlash from those who were uncomfortable with his non-conformity. For instance, during a local pride event, Ray chose to express his identity through an outfit that blended traditionally masculine and feminine elements. This bold choice elicited mixed reactions, from cheers of support to harsh criticisms. Ray's experience highlighted the societal discomfort surrounding non-binary identities, as many struggled to reconcile their understanding of gender with Ray's fearless expression.

The Impact of Intersectionality

Ray's exploration of his gender identity was also deeply intertwined with the concept of intersectionality, as articulated by Kimberlé Crenshaw. His identity as a queer individual in Sykarin was compounded by the cultural and social dynamics of his community. The intersection of his race, class, and sexual orientation influenced how he navigated his gender identity. Ray often spoke about the unique challenges faced by individuals who exist at multiple intersections, emphasizing the need for a more inclusive dialogue within the LGBTQ community.

Creating Safe Spaces for Exploration

In his quest for self-discovery, Ray recognized the importance of creating safe spaces for others to explore their gender identities. He initiated workshops and discussion groups that encouraged open dialogue about gender fluidity and expression. These gatherings provided a platform for individuals to share their experiences, fostering a sense of community and belonging. Ray's efforts were instrumental in normalizing conversations around gender and dismantling the stigma associated with non-binary identities.

Art as a Medium of Expression

Art became a crucial vehicle for Ray's exploration of gender identity. He collaborated with local artists to produce a series of installations that challenged conventional gender norms. One notable project involved a visual representation of the gender spectrum, using colors and shapes to symbolize the fluidity of identity. This artistic expression not only resonated with many in the LGBTQ community but also sparked conversations among those outside of it, broadening the understanding of gender.

Ray's Influence on Policy and Education

Ray's fearless exploration of his gender identity extended beyond personal boundaries; it influenced policy and educational reform in Sykarin. He advocated for inclusive curricula that addressed gender diversity, pushing for the integration of LGBTQ topics in schools. His efforts culminated in a landmark initiative that mandated gender sensitivity training for educators, ensuring that future generations would have a more nuanced understanding of gender identity.

Conclusion: A Legacy of Fearlessness

Ray Ilan's exploration of his gender identity was a courageous journey that challenged societal norms and inspired countless individuals. His commitment to authenticity and inclusivity paved the way for a broader understanding of gender in Sykarin. By embracing his identity fearlessly, Ray not only liberated himself but also empowered others to embark on their own journeys of self-discovery. His legacy serves as a reminder that the exploration of gender identity is not merely a personal endeavor but a collective movement towards acceptance and understanding in a world that often clings to binary definitions.

The impact of Ray's gender revolution on Sykarin's LGBTQ community

Ray Ilan's gender revolution in Sykarin was not merely a movement; it was a seismic shift that reverberated through the very fabric of the LGBTQ community. This transformation was characterized by a multifaceted approach that challenged traditional gender norms, advocated for inclusivity, and promoted a deeper understanding of gender identity among the populace.

Challenging Traditional Gender Norms

At the heart of Ray's gender revolution was the challenge to the entrenched binary view of gender that had long dominated societal discourse in Sykarin. Ray's public persona and activism emphasized the fluidity of gender, encouraging individuals to express their identities authentically. This was exemplified during the annual Sykarin Pride Parade, where Ray led a contingent of non-binary and genderqueer individuals, showcasing the spectrum of gender identities.

The impact of this visibility was profound. According to a survey conducted by the Sykarin LGBTQ Alliance, 78% of respondents reported feeling more comfortable expressing their gender identity after witnessing Ray's activism. This shift was not just anecdotal; it indicated a larger cultural acceptance of diverse gender expressions.

Educational Initiatives

Ray's gender revolution also emphasized the importance of education in dismantling prejudices. He spearheaded initiatives to integrate gender studies into local schools, aiming to educate both students and faculty about the complexities of gender identity. Workshops and seminars facilitated by Ray and his team provided safe spaces for discussions, enabling young people to explore their identities without fear of judgment.

For instance, one notable program, "Gender Spectrum Awareness," was implemented in Sykarin's middle schools. The curriculum included lessons on the history of gender identity, the significance of pronouns, and the importance of respecting individuals' self-identifications. Feedback from educators indicated a marked improvement in student interactions, with reports of reduced bullying incidents related to gender identity by over 40% in participating schools.

Creating Safe Spaces

Ray's activism extended beyond education; he recognized the necessity of safe spaces for individuals exploring their gender identity. He advocated for the establishment of community centers in Sykarin that catered specifically to the needs of gender-diverse individuals. These centers provided resources such as counseling, support groups, and social events, fostering a sense of belonging among LGBTQ individuals.

One such center, the "Ilan Haven," became a beacon of hope for many. It hosted weekly meetings where individuals could share their experiences and challenges in a supportive environment. Testimonials from attendees highlighted the center's role in helping them navigate their identities. One participant noted, "Before Ray's initiatives, I felt isolated. Now, I have a community that understands me."

Intersectionality in Ray's Activism

Ray understood that gender identity does not exist in a vacuum; it intersects with other aspects of identity, including race, class, and sexuality. His activism emphasized an intersectional approach, advocating for the rights of marginalized groups within the LGBTQ community. By collaborating with local organizations that focused on racial and economic justice, Ray ensured that the voices of all individuals were heard.

This intersectional framework was evident during the "Unity in Diversity" rally, where speakers from various backgrounds shared their stories, emphasizing the unique challenges faced by LGBTQ individuals of color. Ray's ability to unite diverse communities under a common cause was instrumental in fostering solidarity and understanding.

Challenges and Backlash

Despite the progress made, Ray's gender revolution was not without its challenges. Resistance from conservative factions in Sykarin manifested in various forms, including protests and attempts to undermine educational initiatives. For instance, a group opposing the integration of gender studies into schools launched a campaign claiming that such education was "indoctrination."

In response, Ray organized counter-protests and used social media platforms to amplify voices in support of gender inclusivity. His strategic use of public forums and media appearances helped to counteract misinformation and rally support for his initiatives. A significant moment came when Ray delivered a powerful speech at a town hall meeting, asserting, "Gender is not a limitation; it is a spectrum that enriches our community."

Legacy and Continuing Impact

The legacy of Ray's gender revolution continues to shape the LGBTQ community in Sykarin. His efforts have laid the groundwork for future generations of activists who advocate for gender inclusivity. The establishment of annual events such as the "Gender Identity Awareness Month" has kept the conversation alive and has encouraged ongoing education and advocacy.

In conclusion, Ray Ilan's gender revolution profoundly impacted Sykarin's LGBTQ community by challenging traditional norms, promoting education, creating safe spaces, and embracing intersectionality. Despite facing significant challenges, Ray's unwavering commitment to inclusivity has fostered a more accepting and understanding environment for all individuals, regardless of their gender identity. The ripple effects of his activism will undoubtedly continue to resonate, inspiring future generations to break barriers and advocate for a world where everyone can express their true selves without fear.

Ray's ongoing battle for gender inclusivity

Ray Ilan's journey towards gender inclusivity is a testament to the resilience and determination of an activist who refuses to back down in the face of societal resistance. The battle for gender inclusivity is not merely a personal struggle for Ray; it is a broader movement aimed at dismantling the rigid binary notions of gender that have long pervaded society. This section delves into Ray's ongoing efforts, the challenges he faces, and the theoretical frameworks that underpin his activism.

Understanding Gender Inclusivity

To grasp the significance of Ray's battle, it is essential to define what gender inclusivity entails. Gender inclusivity refers to the recognition and acceptance of a spectrum of gender identities beyond the traditional male-female binary. This inclusivity acknowledges the existence of non-binary, genderqueer, genderfluid, and other identities that challenge conventional gender norms. According to Judith Butler's theory of gender performativity, gender is not a fixed attribute but rather a series of performances shaped by societal expectations [?]. Ray's activism aligns with Butler's assertion that by subverting these performances, individuals can create new spaces for diverse gender expressions.

Challenges in Sykarin

In the small town of Sykarin, Ray encounters numerous challenges in his quest for gender inclusivity. The societal norms entrenched in the community often manifest as discrimination and misunderstanding towards those who do not conform to traditional gender roles. For instance, Ray frequently confronts instances of misgendering, where individuals are referred to by incorrect pronouns, leading to feelings of invalidation and exclusion. This issue is compounded by the lack of comprehensive education surrounding gender diversity in local schools, perpetuating ignorance and reinforcing harmful stereotypes.

The resistance Ray faces is not limited to interpersonal interactions; it also extends to institutional frameworks. Policies in Sykarin often lack the necessary provisions to protect individuals who identify outside the gender binary. For example, public restrooms are typically designated as male or female, creating significant barriers for non-binary individuals who may not feel comfortable using either facility. This structural exclusion highlights the urgent need for policy reform and advocacy to create more inclusive environments.

Ray's Strategies for Advocacy

To combat these challenges, Ray employs a multifaceted approach to advocacy. He organizes workshops and community forums aimed at educating the public about gender diversity. These events provide a platform for individuals to share their experiences and foster understanding among community members. Ray believes that education is a powerful tool in dismantling prejudices and fostering empathy.

Moreover, Ray collaborates with local schools to integrate gender inclusivity into the curriculum. He advocates for the inclusion of comprehensive sex education that addresses gender identity and expression, aiming to equip young people with the knowledge and understanding necessary to navigate a diverse world. By empowering the next generation with this knowledge, Ray hopes to cultivate a more accepting and inclusive society.

Ray also utilizes social media as a means of outreach and activism. By sharing personal stories and highlighting the experiences of marginalized individuals, he amplifies voices that are often silenced. This digital platform allows him to reach a broader audience, fostering conversations about gender inclusivity that transcend the boundaries of Sykarin.

Real-World Impact and Examples

One notable example of Ray's impact can be seen in the establishment of the "Gender Inclusivity Initiative" in Sykarin, a program designed to promote awareness and support for individuals of all gender identities. This initiative has successfully partnered with local businesses to create gender-neutral spaces, such as restrooms and changing facilities, ensuring that everyone feels safe and respected. The initiative has also led to the implementation of sensitivity training for employees, fostering a more inclusive atmosphere within the community.

Furthermore, Ray's activism has garnered attention beyond Sykarin, inspiring similar movements in neighboring towns. By sharing his strategies and successes, Ray has become a beacon of hope for activists facing similar challenges across the region. His commitment to collaboration and solidarity exemplifies the interconnected nature of the fight for gender inclusivity.

Conclusion

Ray Ilan's ongoing battle for gender inclusivity is a vital component of his broader activism. By challenging societal norms, advocating for policy reform, and fostering education and awareness, Ray is paving the way for a more inclusive future. His efforts not only impact the lives of individuals in Sykarin but also contribute to a global movement for gender equality and acceptance. As Ray continues to break barriers, he embodies the spirit of resilience and determination necessary to create lasting change in the fight for gender inclusivity.

Ray's impact on gender discussions in Sykarin

Ray Ilan's journey through the complexities of gender identity has not only transformed his own life but also catalyzed a significant shift in gender discussions throughout Sykarin. By bravely embracing and expressing his own gender identity, Ray has illuminated the pathways for others to explore their own identities, challenging deeply rooted societal norms and expectations.

Theoretical Frameworks

To understand Ray's impact, we can draw upon Judith Butler's theory of gender performativity, which posits that gender is not an inherent quality but rather an identity constituted through repeated performances. Ray's public persona and activism exemplify this theory, as he navigates and reshapes the narrative surrounding gender in Sykarin. By openly challenging the binary conception of gender, Ray has encouraged individuals to express their identities in ways that feel authentic to them, thereby expanding the discourse around gender fluidity and non-binary identities.

Challenges Faced

Despite his significant contributions, Ray has encountered numerous challenges in addressing gender discussions. Sykarin, like many communities, has a history of rigid gender norms that often marginalize those who do not conform. Issues such as discrimination, lack of representation, and societal stigma have made it difficult for many individuals to express their gender identities freely. Ray has faced backlash from conservative factions within the community who view his activism as a threat to traditional values.

Examples of Impact

One of the most notable examples of Ray's impact is the establishment of the "Gender Spectrum Initiative," a series of workshops and discussions aimed at educating the public about gender diversity. These events have fostered dialogue among community members, parents, and educators, creating a safe space for individuals to share their experiences and learn from one another. The initiative has successfully attracted diverse participants, including those who identify as transgender, non-binary, and genderqueer, thereby broadening the understanding of gender in Sykarin.

In addition, Ray's engagement with local schools has led to the integration of gender studies into the curriculum.   By advocating for inclusive educational practices, he has empowered young people to explore their identities in a supportive environment.   The program includes discussions about gender stereotypes, historical perspectives on gender, and the importance of representation in media. As a result, students have reported feeling more accepted and understood, contributing to a more inclusive school culture.

Cultural Shifts

Ray's influence extends beyond formal education; he has also played a pivotal role in reshaping cultural perceptions of gender in Sykarin. Through collaborations with local artists, performers, and activists, Ray has spearheaded initiatives that celebrate gender diversity in the arts. Events such as the "Sykarin Gender Festival" showcase performances and artworks that challenge traditional gender roles, providing a platform for marginalized voices. These cultural expressions not only validate individual experiences but also educate the broader community about the richness of gender diversity.

Conclusion

In summary, Ray Ilan's impact on gender discussions in Sykarin is profound and multifaceted. By leveraging theoretical frameworks, addressing challenges, and implementing practical initiatives, he has fostered a more inclusive dialogue around gender identity. Ray's work has not only empowered individuals to embrace their true selves but has also contributed to a cultural shift that recognizes and celebrates the complexity of gender. As Sykarin continues to evolve, the foundations laid by Ray's activism will undoubtedly influence future generations, ensuring that the conversation around gender remains dynamic and inclusive.

$$Gender\ Identity = f(Cultural\ Context, Personal\ Experience, Social\ Interaction)$$
$$(60)$$

This equation symbolizes the interplay between various factors that shape an individual's gender identity, highlighting the importance of both personal and societal influences in the ongoing discussions of gender in Sykarin.

Revolutionizing LGBTQ Education

Ray's mission to integrate LGBTQ education into schools

Ray Ilan recognized that education is the cornerstone of societal change. His mission to integrate LGBTQ education into schools was not merely a personal crusade; it was a strategic initiative aimed at dismantling the systemic ignorance and prejudice that often permeated educational environments. By advocating for comprehensive LGBTQ curricula, Ray sought to foster a culture of acceptance, understanding, and respect among students of all backgrounds.

Theoretical Framework

Ray's approach to LGBTQ education was grounded in several key theoretical frameworks, including Critical Pedagogy and Queer Theory. Critical Pedagogy, as articulated by Paulo Freire, emphasizes the importance of dialogue and critical reflection in the learning process. It encourages students to question societal norms and injustices, fostering a sense of agency and empowerment. By integrating LGBTQ topics into the curriculum, Ray aimed to challenge the heteronormative narratives that often dominate educational discourse.

Queer Theory, on the other hand, provided a lens through which to examine the fluidity of gender and sexuality. This theoretical perspective posits that identities are not fixed but are instead shaped by cultural, social, and historical contexts. By incorporating Queer Theory into educational settings, Ray aimed to create a more inclusive environment that acknowledged and celebrated diverse identities.

Identifying Problems

Despite the compelling theoretical underpinnings of LGBTQ education, Ray faced significant challenges in his mission. Many educators and administrators were resistant to change, often citing concerns about parental backlash or the belief that LGBTQ topics were inappropriate for young students. Additionally, existing curricula frequently omitted LGBTQ history and contributions, perpetuating a cycle of invisibility and erasure.

Moreover, the lack of training and resources for educators posed a substantial barrier. Many teachers felt ill-equipped to address LGBTQ topics, fearing they might inadvertently propagate stereotypes or misinformation. This gap in knowledge highlighted the urgent need for professional development programs focused on LGBTQ inclusivity.

Practical Examples

To address these challenges, Ray implemented a series of practical initiatives aimed at integrating LGBTQ education into schools. One of the cornerstone programs was the "Safe Schools Initiative," which provided comprehensive training for educators on LGBTQ issues, inclusive teaching strategies, and the importance of creating safe spaces for all students.

For instance, during workshops, educators engaged in role-playing scenarios that allowed them to practice responding to homophobic remarks or bullying. They learned how to facilitate discussions on LGBTQ history, such as the Stonewall Riots and the contributions of figures like Marsha P. Johnson and Harvey Milk. By equipping teachers with the tools they needed, Ray aimed to empower them to become advocates for inclusivity within their classrooms.

Ray also championed the development of LGBTQ-inclusive curricula that spanned various subjects. In history classes, students learned about the civil rights movements that intersected with LGBTQ activism, while literature classes explored works by LGBTQ authors. This interdisciplinary approach not only enriched students' understanding of LGBTQ issues but also highlighted the interconnectedness of social justice movements.

Measuring Impact

To assess the effectiveness of these initiatives, Ray collaborated with educational researchers to conduct surveys and focus groups with students and teachers. Preliminary findings indicated a marked increase in students' understanding of LGBTQ issues and a decrease in instances of bullying and discrimination.

The data revealed that schools implementing LGBTQ-inclusive curricula reported a more positive school climate, with students expressing greater feelings of safety and belonging. Furthermore, teachers noted an increase in student engagement and participation during discussions related to diversity and inclusion.

Conclusion

Ray Ilan's mission to integrate LGBTQ education into schools was a transformative endeavor that sought to challenge societal norms and foster a culture of acceptance. By grounding his efforts in critical pedagogy and queer theory, addressing practical challenges, and implementing inclusive curricula, Ray paved the way for a more equitable educational landscape. His work not only benefited LGBTQ students but also enriched the educational experiences of all students, fostering a generation committed to understanding and respecting diversity in all its forms.

The legacy of Ray's mission continues to inspire educators and activists alike, reminding us that education is not just about imparting knowledge but about shaping the hearts and minds of future generations.

Overcoming resistance and ignorance in the educational system

In the journey of integrating LGBTQ education into the school curriculum, Ray Ilan faced substantial resistance and ignorance from various stakeholders within the educational system. This resistance stemmed from deeply ingrained societal norms, fear of change, and a lack of understanding regarding LGBTQ issues. To effectively address these challenges, Ray employed a multifaceted approach that not only sought to educate but also to transform the very fabric of the educational environment.

Understanding the Resistance

Resistance to LGBTQ education can be attributed to several factors:

- **Cultural Norms:** Many educators and parents held traditional views that often marginalized LGBTQ identities. These cultural norms created an atmosphere of discomfort surrounding discussions about sexual orientation and gender identity.

- **Fear of Backlash:** Teachers feared potential backlash from parents and community members, which could jeopardize their careers and the stability of their schools. This fear often led to self-censorship and avoidance of LGBTQ topics.

- **Lack of Training:** A significant number of educators lacked proper training on LGBTQ issues, leaving them ill-equipped to handle discussions or address questions from students. This lack of training perpetuated ignorance and misunderstanding.

To combat these challenges, Ray recognized the necessity of creating an informed and supportive environment for both educators and students.

Strategies for Overcoming Ignorance

Ray's approach involved several key strategies aimed at dismantling resistance and fostering understanding:

1. **Professional Development Workshops:** Ray organized workshops for educators that focused on LGBTQ history, rights, and the importance of inclusivity in the classroom. These workshops provided teachers with the knowledge and tools necessary to engage with LGBTQ topics confidently. For instance, workshops included sessions on the significance of using inclusive language and understanding the spectrum of gender identities.

2. **Parent and Community Engagement:** Ray initiated open forums and informational sessions for parents and community members to discuss LGBTQ issues.   These sessions aimed to dispel myths and misunderstandings, fostering a dialogue that encouraged empathy and support. One notable success was the "Family Night" event, where families could learn about LGBTQ history and hear personal stories from community members, bridging the gap between fear and understanding.

3. **Curriculum Development:** Collaborating with educators, Ray played a pivotal role in developing a comprehensive LGBTQ-inclusive curriculum that highlighted the contributions of LGBTQ individuals throughout history. This curriculum was designed to be age-appropriate and relevant, aiming to normalize discussions about diversity in sexual orientation and gender identity.

Theoretical Framework

The theoretical underpinning of Ray's strategies can be linked to the **Social Learning Theory**, which posits that people learn from one another through observation, imitation, and modeling. By providing educators with positive role models and resources, Ray aimed to create an environment where inclusive practices could be observed and adopted.

$$\text{Learning} = \text{Observational Learning} + \text{Reinforcement} \qquad (61)$$

In this equation, learning is enhanced when educators observe successful implementations of LGBTQ-inclusive practices and receive positive reinforcement from their peers and community.

Examples of Success

Ray's efforts yielded tangible results. In one instance, a local high school implemented an LGBTQ history month, which included presentations, art exhibits, and discussions led by students. This initiative not only educated the student body but also fostered a sense of pride and belonging among LGBTQ students.

Moreover, Ray's work led to the establishment of Gay-Straight Alliances (GSAs) in several schools, providing safe spaces for LGBTQ students to connect and advocate for their rights. These GSAs became instrumental in promoting understanding and acceptance within the broader school community.

Conclusion

Overcoming resistance and ignorance in the educational system is an ongoing challenge that requires persistent effort and strategic engagement. Ray Ilan's multifaceted approach not only educated educators and students but also transformed the discourse surrounding LGBTQ issues within Sykarin's schools. By fostering an environment of understanding and inclusivity, Ray laid the groundwork for future generations to thrive in an educational landscape that embraces diversity and promotes equality.

The journey is far from over, but the seeds of change planted by Ray's efforts continue to grow, inspiring a new wave of educators and activists committed to breaking down barriers and creating a more inclusive world.

Ray's innovative approaches to LGBTQ education

Ray Ilan recognized early on that the key to fostering a more inclusive society lay in education. He understood that to combat ignorance and prejudice, it was essential to start with the younger generation. Thus, Ray embarked on a mission to integrate LGBTQ education into the school curriculum across Sykarin. His innovative approaches were multifaceted, aiming not only to inform but also to empower students to embrace diversity.

Inclusive Curriculum Development

One of Ray's first initiatives was the development of an inclusive curriculum that accurately represented LGBTQ history and contributions. This involved collaborating with educators, LGBTQ activists, and historians to create comprehensive lesson plans that highlighted significant events, figures, and movements within the LGBTQ community. Ray advocated for the inclusion of texts and resources that featured LGBTQ authors and perspectives, ensuring that students could see themselves reflected in their studies.

$$\text{Diversity Index} = \frac{\text{Number of LGBTQ Authors}}{\text{Total Number of Authors}} \times 100 \qquad (62)$$

This equation served as a metric for assessing the representation of LGBTQ authors in educational materials. Ray's goal was to achieve a Diversity Index of at least 30%, reflecting a commitment to inclusivity.

Workshops and Training Programs

Understanding that knowledge alone was not enough, Ray implemented workshops and training programs for teachers and school staff. These sessions focused on LGBTQ sensitivity, anti-bullying strategies, and the importance of creating safe spaces for all students. By equipping educators with the tools to address LGBTQ issues, Ray aimed to foster an environment where students felt valued and understood.

Ray's workshops included role-playing scenarios where teachers could practice responding to homophobic remarks or bullying incidents. This hands-on approach ensured that educators were not only aware of LGBTQ issues but also prepared to take action when necessary.

Peer Education Initiatives

In addition to training teachers, Ray launched peer education initiatives that empowered students to become advocates for LGBTQ inclusion within their schools. He established student-led organizations that focused on raising awareness about LGBTQ issues through campaigns, events, and discussions. These organizations provided a platform for students to share their experiences and educate their peers about the importance of acceptance and understanding.

An example of this initiative was the "Pride Ambassadors" program, where selected students received training in LGBTQ advocacy and leadership. These ambassadors organized events such as "Pride Days" and "Diversity Week," creating opportunities for students to engage in discussions about identity, love, and acceptance.

Utilizing Technology and Social Media

Ray also recognized the power of technology and social media in reaching a wider audience. He encouraged schools to incorporate digital resources into their LGBTQ education efforts. This included creating online platforms where students could access educational materials, share their stories, and connect with LGBTQ role models.

For instance, Ray collaborated with tech-savvy students to develop a mobile app called "Sykarin Pride," which featured educational resources, event calendars, and a forum for students to discuss LGBTQ topics anonymously. This innovative approach not only made information more accessible but also provided a safe space for students to express themselves.

Engaging Parents and the Community

Ray understood that for LGBTQ education to be effective, it needed the support of the entire community. He organized community forums and workshops aimed at educating parents about LGBTQ issues and the importance of inclusivity in schools. These events provided a platform for open dialogue, allowing parents to ask questions, share concerns, and learn how to support their LGBTQ children.

Ray's commitment to community engagement was evident in the "Family Acceptance Project," which aimed to reduce the stigma surrounding LGBTQ identities within families. This initiative provided resources for parents on how to create a supportive home environment, emphasizing that acceptance could significantly impact their children's mental health and well-being.

Measuring Impact and Success

To assess the effectiveness of his educational initiatives, Ray implemented feedback mechanisms and surveys within schools. By gathering data on students' attitudes towards LGBTQ individuals before and after the introduction of LGBTQ education, Ray could measure changes in perceptions and behaviors.

An example of this evaluation process involved a pre- and post-survey conducted among students participating in the "Pride Ambassadors" program. The survey included questions designed to gauge students' understanding of LGBTQ issues, their comfort level discussing these topics, and their willingness to stand up against discrimination.

$$\text{Change in Awareness} = \frac{\text{Post-Survey Score} - \text{Pre-Survey Score}}{\text{Pre-Survey Score}} \times 100 \quad (63)$$

By employing this equation, Ray could quantify the impact of his initiatives, demonstrating the importance of LGBTQ education in shaping a more inclusive society.

Conclusion

Ray Ilan's innovative approaches to LGBTQ education not only transformed the educational landscape in Sykarin but also laid the groundwork for future generations to embrace diversity and inclusion. By advocating for an inclusive curriculum, providing training for educators, empowering students, leveraging technology, and engaging the community, Ray created a comprehensive framework for LGBTQ education that continues to inspire and empower individuals today. His legacy serves as a reminder that education is a powerful tool for change, capable of breaking down barriers and fostering understanding in even the most challenging environments.

Empowering LGBTQ youth through education and representation

Empowering LGBTQ youth is a crucial aspect of Ray Ilan's activism, and it begins with education and representation. In Sykarin, where traditional values often overshadow the realities of diverse sexual orientations and gender identities, Ray recognized that education could serve as both a shield and a sword for young individuals navigating their identities.

The Importance of Education

Education is a powerful tool for social change. According to the *Social Learning Theory* proposed by Albert Bandura, individuals learn from one another through observation, imitation, and modeling. This theory underscores the need for LGBTQ representation in educational curricula, as it allows youth to see themselves reflected in the materials they study. When LGBTQ identities are included in discussions about history, literature, and health, students gain a sense of belonging and validation.

Challenges in the Educational System

Despite the potential for education to empower LGBTQ youth, significant challenges persist. Many schools in Sykarin lack comprehensive sex education that includes LGBTQ topics, often leaving students uninformed about their identities and rights. This gap can lead to feelings of isolation and confusion among LGBTQ youth. Additionally, the prevalence of bullying and discrimination within schools creates an unsafe environment for many students, further exacerbating the problem.

The *Youth Risk Behavior Surveillance System* (YRBSS) indicates that LGBTQ youth are more likely to experience bullying and harassment compared to their heterosexual peers. According to the YRBSS data from 2019, 29.4% of LGBTQ students reported being bullied on school property, compared to 18.5% of non-LGBTQ students. This stark contrast highlights the urgent need for educational reform that prioritizes inclusivity and safety.

Innovative Approaches to LGBTQ Education

Ray Ilan championed innovative educational programs designed to empower LGBTQ youth. One such initiative was the establishment of *Safe Spaces* in schools, where students could engage in open discussions about their identities without fear of judgment. These spaces provided resources, support groups, and mentorship programs tailored to the unique challenges faced by LGBTQ youth.

Furthermore, Ray advocated for the incorporation of LGBTQ history and literature into the standard curriculum. By introducing works from authors such as James Baldwin and Audre Lorde, students could explore diverse narratives that resonate with their own experiences. This not only fosters empathy among non-LGBTQ students but also helps LGBTQ youth feel seen and understood.

Empowerment Through Representation

Representation extends beyond the classroom; it is vital in extracurricular activities and leadership roles as well. Ray encouraged schools to promote LGBTQ representation in student government and clubs. By creating platforms for LGBTQ youth to voice their opinions and advocate for their rights, they develop leadership skills and confidence.

For example, the establishment of the *Sykarin Pride Club* allowed LGBTQ students to organize events, educate their peers, and engage with the broader community. This initiative empowered students to take ownership of their identities and advocate for change, demonstrating the profound impact of representation in fostering a sense of agency.

Long-lasting Impact of Educational Initiatives

The long-term effects of empowering LGBTQ youth through education are profound. Studies have shown that inclusive educational environments lead to better mental health outcomes for LGBTQ students. According to a report by the *Gay, Lesbian and Straight Education Network* (GLSEN), schools with comprehensive LGBTQ-inclusive curricula reported lower rates of bullying and higher levels of acceptance among peers.

Ray's initiatives not only provided immediate support for LGBTQ youth but also laid the groundwork for future generations. By equipping young people with knowledge, confidence, and a sense of community, Ray fostered a culture of acceptance and resilience that continues to thrive in Sykarin.

Conclusion

In conclusion, Ray Ilan's commitment to empowering LGBTQ youth through education and representation has transformed the landscape of Sykarin's educational system. By addressing the challenges faced by LGBTQ students and implementing innovative solutions, Ray has created a legacy of inclusivity that will inspire and uplift future generations. The ongoing work in this area is vital, as it ensures that every young person, regardless of their identity, has the opportunity to thrive and contribute to society.

The long-lasting impact of Ray's LGBTQ educational initiatives

Ray Ilan's commitment to integrating LGBTQ education into schools was not merely a campaign; it was a revolutionary movement that aimed to reshape the educational landscape in Sykarin and beyond. By fostering an environment of inclusivity and understanding, Ray's initiatives have had a profound and lasting impact on students, educators, and the broader community. This section explores the theoretical frameworks, challenges, and significant outcomes associated with Ray's educational initiatives.

Theoretical Frameworks

The impact of Ray's initiatives can be understood through several educational theories that emphasize inclusivity and social justice. One such theory is *Critical Pedagogy*, which advocates for an educational approach that encourages students to question and challenge domination, and the beliefs and practices that sustain it. Ray applied this theory by promoting critical discussions about gender and sexuality, encouraging students to engage with these topics in a meaningful way.

Another relevant framework is *Social Constructivism*, which posits that knowledge is constructed through social interactions and experiences. Ray's programs facilitated peer-to-peer learning and discussions, allowing students to share their experiences and perspectives, thereby fostering a deeper understanding of LGBTQ issues.

Challenges Faced

Despite the positive vision of LGBTQ education, Ray faced significant challenges in implementing these initiatives. Resistance from conservative factions within the community often manifested in protests and public outcry. For instance, during a proposed curriculum change to include LGBTQ history, Ray encountered backlash from parents and community leaders who believed such content was inappropriate for young students.

Moreover, the lack of training for educators on how to address LGBTQ topics presented a barrier. Many teachers felt unprepared to discuss these issues, which could lead to misinformation or perpetuation of stereotypes. Ray recognized this gap and initiated professional development workshops designed to equip educators with the necessary tools and confidence to handle LGBTQ discussions sensitively and effectively.

Significant Outcomes

The long-lasting impact of Ray's LGBTQ educational initiatives can be observed through various outcomes:

+ **Increased Awareness and Acceptance:** Schools that adopted LGBTQ-inclusive curricula reported a significant increase in awareness and acceptance among students. Surveys conducted post-implementation indicated a 40% rise in students' understanding of LGBTQ issues and a 30% decrease in reported instances of bullying related to sexual orientation and gender identity.

+ **Empowerment of LGBTQ Youth:** By providing a platform for LGBTQ voices within the educational system, Ray's initiatives empowered students to embrace their identities. Many students reported feeling safer and more supported in their schools, leading to improved mental health outcomes.

+ **Community Engagement:** Ray's initiatives fostered greater community engagement and dialogue surrounding LGBTQ issues. Parents and community members were invited to participate in workshops and discussions, bridging gaps between different societal segments. This engagement helped to cultivate allies and advocates within the community, furthering the reach of LGBTQ education beyond school walls.

+ **Policy Changes:** The ripple effect of Ray's initiatives led to policy changes at the district and state levels. Educational boards began to recognize the importance of inclusive education, resulting in the adoption of policies that mandated LGBTQ education as part of the standard curriculum. This shift not only legitimized the importance of LGBTQ issues in education but also set a precedent for other regions to follow suit.

Examples of Implementation

Ray's initiatives were not just theoretical; they were implemented through various programs and partnerships. One notable example was the *LGBTQ Ally Program*, which trained students to become allies and advocates within their schools. This program included workshops on empathy, active listening, and the importance of representation.

Another successful initiative was the *Inclusive History Month*, where schools dedicated an entire month to exploring LGBTQ contributions to history, literature, and culture. This event included guest speakers, art projects, and performances that celebrated LGBTQ figures and their impact on society.

In addition, Ray collaborated with local organizations to create resource centers within schools, providing students with access to literature, counseling, and support groups tailored to LGBTQ issues. These centers became safe havens for students, fostering a sense of belonging and community.

Conclusion

Ray Ilan's LGBTQ educational initiatives have left an indelible mark on Sykarin's educational landscape. By challenging societal norms, equipping educators, and empowering students, Ray created a legacy that continues to inspire future generations. The long-lasting impact of these initiatives is evident in the growing acceptance and understanding of LGBTQ issues within schools and the community at large. As Ray often stated, "Education is the key to breaking barriers," and through his relentless pursuit of inclusive education, he has opened doors that were once firmly shut, paving the way for a more equitable future for all.

Ray's influence on LGBTQ education in Sykarin

Ray Ilan's impact on LGBTQ education in Sykarin has been nothing short of revolutionary. His commitment to integrating LGBTQ topics into the educational curriculum not only challenged existing norms but also empowered a generation of students to embrace diversity and inclusivity. This section explores the theoretical frameworks, challenges, and specific examples of Ray's influence on LGBTQ education in Sykarin.

Theoretical Frameworks

Ray's approach to LGBTQ education can be understood through several theoretical lenses, including Critical Pedagogy and Queer Theory. Critical Pedagogy, as proposed by Paulo Freire, emphasizes the importance of dialogue and critical reflection in education. Ray adopted this approach by encouraging open discussions about sexual orientation and gender identity, fostering a safe environment for students to explore these topics.

$$\text{Critical Consciousness} = \text{Reflection} + \text{Action} \qquad (64)$$

This equation illustrates the core principle of Critical Pedagogy, where reflection leads to action, ultimately empowering students to challenge societal injustices, including homophobia and transphobia.

Queer Theory, on the other hand, critiques the binary understanding of gender and sexuality, advocating for a fluid interpretation of identity. Ray's initiatives aimed to dismantle these binaries within educational settings, promoting a more inclusive understanding of gender and sexuality that resonates with the diverse experiences of students in Sykarin.

Challenges in Implementation

Despite Ray's visionary leadership, the integration of LGBTQ education in Sykarin faced significant challenges. Resistance from conservative factions within the community, including parents and local political leaders, posed substantial obstacles. Many argued that LGBTQ topics were inappropriate for school settings, fearing they would corrupt the youth's moral values.

Moreover, the lack of training for educators in LGBTQ issues further complicated the implementation process. Many teachers felt ill-equipped to address these topics, leading to a gap in effective education. Ray recognized these challenges and worked tirelessly to provide resources and training for educators, ensuring they could approach LGBTQ topics with confidence and sensitivity.

Innovative Approaches to Education

To overcome these challenges, Ray introduced several innovative approaches. One of his flagship initiatives was the establishment of the "Safe Spaces Program," which aimed to create inclusive environments within schools. This program provided training sessions for teachers and staff, focusing on LGBTQ awareness, sensitivity, and inclusive teaching practices.

Additionally, Ray spearheaded the development of a comprehensive LGBTQ curriculum, which included historical perspectives, contemporary issues, and the contributions of LGBTQ individuals to society. This curriculum was designed to be age-appropriate and was implemented across various grade levels, ensuring that students received a well-rounded education on LGBTQ matters.

$$\text{Inclusivity Index} = \frac{\text{Number of Inclusive Policies}}{\text{Total Policies}} \times 100 \qquad (65)$$

This equation represents the Inclusivity Index, a metric Ray proposed to evaluate the effectiveness of educational policies in promoting LGBTQ inclusivity. By tracking this index, schools could measure their progress and identify areas for improvement.

Empowering LGBTQ Youth

Ray's influence extended beyond policy changes; he actively sought to empower LGBTQ youth in Sykarin. By organizing workshops and support groups, he provided safe spaces for students to share their experiences and challenges. These initiatives not only fostered a sense of community but also encouraged students to embrace their identities.

For instance, Ray launched the "Pride in Education" campaign, which celebrated LGBTQ History Month in schools. This campaign included guest speakers, educational materials, and events that highlighted the achievements of LGBTQ individuals. The campaign successfully raised awareness and provided students with positive role models.

Long-Lasting Impact

The long-lasting impact of Ray's initiatives is evident in the changing attitudes towards LGBTQ education in Sykarin. Schools that once resisted LGBTQ topics began to adopt inclusive practices, and students reported feeling safer and more accepted in their educational environments.

Surveys conducted post-implementation of Ray's programs indicated a significant increase in students' understanding of LGBTQ issues. Over 75% of students expressed a greater acceptance of their peers' diverse identities, illustrating the effectiveness of Ray's educational initiatives.

$$\text{Acceptance Rate} = \frac{\text{Number of Accepting Students}}{\text{Total Students}} \times 100 \qquad (66)$$

This formula highlights the importance of measuring acceptance within the student body, showcasing the positive shift in attitudes resulting from Ray's efforts.

In conclusion, Ray Ilan's influence on LGBTQ education in Sykarin has been transformative. Through innovative approaches, critical engagement with theoretical frameworks, and a commitment to empowering youth, Ray has laid the groundwork for a more inclusive and accepting educational landscape. His legacy continues to inspire educators and students alike, ensuring that the fight for LGBTQ rights and representation in education remains a priority in Sykarin and beyond.

Beyond Borders: Ray's Global Vision

Ray's efforts in fostering international LGBTQ alliances

Ray Ilan's commitment to fostering international LGBTQ alliances is a testament to his belief in the power of solidarity and collaboration across borders. Recognizing that the struggle for LGBTQ rights is a global issue, Ray sought to build bridges between diverse communities, amplifying voices that often go unheard. His approach was rooted in the understanding that LGBTQ individuals face unique challenges in different cultural contexts, and that a unified front could lead to more effective advocacy and change.

Theoretical Framework

Ray's efforts can be understood through the lens of *intersectionality*, a theory coined by Kimberlé Crenshaw, which emphasizes the interconnected nature of social categorizations such as race, class, and gender. Intersectionality posits that individuals experience overlapping systems of discrimination, and thus, a one-size-fits-all approach to activism is insufficient. By acknowledging the diverse backgrounds of LGBTQ individuals worldwide, Ray aimed to create alliances that were not only inclusive but also reflective of the varied experiences within the community.

Challenges Faced

Despite his noble intentions, Ray encountered several challenges in fostering these international alliances. One significant issue was the *cultural relativism* that often arose when discussing LGBTQ rights. In some regions, cultural norms and values starkly oppose LGBTQ acceptance, leading to resistance against what is perceived as "Western imposition." Ray had to navigate these sensitive terrains carefully, advocating for LGBTQ rights while respecting cultural differences.

Moreover, the issue of *funding* posed a significant barrier. Many LGBTQ organizations in developing countries struggle with limited resources, which hampers their ability to engage in international dialogues. Ray recognized that for alliances to thrive, there needed to be an equitable distribution of resources and support.

Initiatives and Collaborations

To overcome these challenges, Ray initiated several key projects aimed at fostering international LGBTQ alliances. One notable initiative was the *Global LGBTQ Summit*, an annual event that brought together activists, policymakers, and allies from around the world. The summit served as a platform for sharing best practices, strategizing on common goals, and creating a network of support. Participants engaged in workshops that focused on topics such as legal advocacy, mental health resources, and community-building strategies.

In addition to the summit, Ray collaborated with various international organizations, such as *ILGA World* (International Lesbian, Gay, Bisexual, Trans and Intersex Association) and *OutRight Action International*. These partnerships enabled the sharing of knowledge and resources, allowing for a more coordinated global response to LGBTQ issues. For instance, through a joint campaign with ILGA World, Ray was instrumental in advocating for the inclusion of LGBTQ rights in the United Nations' Sustainable Development Goals.

Impact and Outcomes

The impact of Ray's efforts in fostering international LGBTQ alliances was profound. One significant outcome was the establishment of the *Sykarin Network for LGBTQ Advocacy*, a coalition of LGBTQ organizations from various countries that aimed to promote mutual support and resource sharing. This network not only provided a platform for collaboration but also empowered local activists to amplify their voices on the global stage.

Ray's initiatives also led to increased visibility for LGBTQ issues in international forums. For example, his participation in the *UN Human Rights Council* allowed him to advocate for the inclusion of LGBTQ rights in discussions about human rights violations. By bringing attention to the plight of LGBTQ individuals in countries where they face persecution, Ray was able to garner international support and pressure governments to enact change.

Conclusion

In conclusion, Ray Ilan's efforts in fostering international LGBTQ alliances highlight the importance of collaboration and solidarity in the fight for equality. By embracing intersectionality and addressing the unique challenges faced by LGBTQ individuals worldwide, Ray not only strengthened the global LGBTQ movement but also paved the way for future generations of activists. His legacy serves as a reminder that the struggle for LGBTQ rights transcends borders and that unity is essential for creating a more inclusive world.

$$\text{Global LGBTQ Alliance} = \sum_{i=1}^{n} \text{Local Advocacy} \times \text{International Collaboration}$$

$$(67)$$

The global impact of Ray's activism

Ray Ilan's activism transcended the boundaries of Sykarin, resonating across continents and inspiring a global movement for LGBTQ rights. His unique approach, marked by charisma and an unwavering commitment to equality, ignited a fire that spread far beyond his small town. The impact of Ray's activism can be understood through various lenses, including the theoretical frameworks of social movements, intersectionality, and global citizenship.

At the core of Ray's global influence is the theory of *social movements*, which posits that collective efforts can lead to significant social change. Ray's ability to mobilize individuals, both locally and internationally, exemplifies this theory in action. His speeches and campaigns not only galvanized support within Sykarin but also captured the attention of LGBTQ activists worldwide. For instance, during an international LGBTQ conference in Berlin, Ray delivered a powerful keynote address that highlighted the struggles faced by LGBTQ individuals in less progressive regions. This speech resonated with activists from various countries, leading to the formation of global coalitions aimed at promoting LGBTQ rights.

One of the significant problems that Ray addressed through his activism was the pervasive issue of *discrimination and violence* against LGBTQ individuals globally. In many countries, LGBTQ individuals face legal and social repercussions for their identities. Ray's advocacy brought attention to these injustices, prompting international organizations such as Amnesty International and Human Rights Watch to include LGBTQ rights in their broader human rights agendas. His efforts contributed to the establishment of global campaigns, such as the

"#LoveIsLove" movement, which sought to unite individuals across borders in the fight against discrimination.

Furthermore, Ray's activism was deeply rooted in the concept of *intersectionality*, which recognizes that individuals experience overlapping forms of discrimination based on race, gender, class, and sexual orientation. Ray emphasized the importance of addressing these intersecting identities in his activism. By collaborating with other marginalized groups, he was able to create a more inclusive narrative that resonated with a diverse audience. For example, during Pride Month, Ray organized events that highlighted the voices of LGBTQ people of color, ensuring their stories were heard and celebrated. This approach not only strengthened the LGBTQ movement but also fostered solidarity among various social justice movements worldwide.

Ray's global impact is further illustrated through specific examples of his initiatives. One notable project was the establishment of the *Ray Ilan Global Scholarship Fund*, which aimed to support LGBTQ youth from underprivileged backgrounds in accessing education. This initiative garnered international attention, leading to partnerships with educational institutions in countries like Canada, Brazil, and South Africa. The scholarship program provided not only financial assistance but also mentorship opportunities, enabling recipients to become advocates for LGBTQ rights in their communities.

Moreover, Ray's participation in international forums, such as the United Nations Human Rights Council, allowed him to advocate for global policy changes. He was instrumental in pushing for the inclusion of LGBTQ rights in international human rights frameworks. His efforts culminated in a historic resolution that recognized the rights of LGBTQ individuals as fundamental human rights, a milestone that reverberated across nations and influenced local policies in various countries.

In conclusion, the global impact of Ray Ilan's activism is a testament to the power of one individual's voice in effecting change on a worldwide scale. Through his commitment to social justice, intersectionality, and global collaboration, Ray not only transformed the landscape of LGBTQ rights in Sykarin but also inspired a generation of activists around the globe. His legacy serves as a reminder that the fight for equality knows no borders and that the spirit of activism can unite individuals in the pursuit of a more inclusive world.

Ray's vision for a world without LGBTQ discrimination

Ray Ilan's vision for a world devoid of LGBTQ discrimination is rooted in the fundamental principles of equality, respect, and dignity for all individuals, regardless of their sexual orientation or gender identity. This vision is not merely aspirational; it is a call to action that challenges the status quo and seeks to dismantle the systemic barriers that perpetuate discrimination.

At the core of Ray's philosophy lies the belief that every person deserves to live authentically without fear of persecution or prejudice. He often cites the influential work of Judith Butler, who posits that gender is performative, suggesting that societal norms surrounding gender and sexuality are socially constructed rather than biologically predetermined. This perspective encourages individuals to embrace their identities and reject the rigid binaries that often confine them.

Ray's vision encompasses several critical components aimed at fostering a more inclusive society:

1. **Education as a Tool for Change:** Ray emphasizes the importance of comprehensive education that includes LGBTQ history, rights, and issues. By integrating LGBTQ topics into school curricula, students can develop a better understanding of diversity, which can reduce stigma and foster empathy. Research indicates that inclusive education significantly lowers rates of bullying and discrimination in schools, creating safer environments for LGBTQ youth.

2. **Policy Reform:** Ray advocates for legislative changes that protect LGBTQ rights at local, national, and international levels. He draws attention to the need for anti-discrimination laws that cover employment, housing, healthcare, and public accommodations. For example, the Equality Act in the United States aims to extend civil rights protections to LGBTQ individuals, showcasing how legal frameworks can be reformed to ensure equality.

3. **Intersectionality:** Recognizing that discrimination does not occur in isolation, Ray's vision incorporates an intersectional approach that considers how various identities—such as race, class, and disability—intersect with sexual orientation and gender identity. This approach is informed by the work of Kimberlé Crenshaw, who argues that understanding the interconnected nature of social categorizations is essential for addressing systemic inequalities.

4. **Community Empowerment:** Ray believes in empowering LGBTQ communities by fostering spaces where individuals can express themselves freely and connect with others. He highlights the importance of grassroots organizations that provide support, advocacy, and resources. By building

strong community networks, LGBTQ individuals can collectively challenge discrimination and advocate for their rights.

5. **Global Solidarity:** Ray's vision extends beyond the borders of Sykarin, recognizing that LGBTQ discrimination is a global issue. He actively collaborates with international organizations to promote LGBTQ rights worldwide. For instance, participation in global events like Pride Month helps raise awareness and solidarity among diverse communities, emphasizing that the fight for equality is universal.

6. **Cultural Representation:** Ray advocates for increased representation of LGBTQ individuals in media and the arts. By showcasing diverse narratives, he believes society can challenge harmful stereotypes and foster understanding. He often cites the impact of films like "Moonlight" and shows like "Pose," which highlight the complexities of LGBTQ lives and contribute to changing perceptions.

7. **Mental Health Support:** Recognizing the toll that discrimination can take on mental health, Ray emphasizes the need for accessible mental health resources tailored to the LGBTQ community. Studies indicate that LGBTQ individuals face higher rates of mental health issues due to societal stigma. By providing targeted support services, communities can help individuals navigate the challenges they face.

Ray's vision for a world without LGBTQ discrimination is ambitious yet attainable. He believes that by combining education, policy reform, community empowerment, and cultural representation, society can cultivate an environment where diversity is celebrated, and every individual can thrive.

In conclusion, Ray Ilan's vision is not just a dream; it is a roadmap for action. He challenges everyone—activists, policymakers, educators, and allies—to join him in this quest for equality. As he often states, "We are all in this together, and together we can break the barriers that divide us." Through collective effort and unwavering commitment, a world free from LGBTQ discrimination is within reach.

Challenges faced by Ray in spreading his message globally

As Ray Ilan embarked on his journey to spread his message of LGBTQ rights and inclusivity on a global scale, he encountered a multitude of challenges that tested his resolve and adaptability. These obstacles were not merely logistical; they were deeply rooted in cultural, political, and societal frameworks that often resisted change.

Cultural Resistance

One of the foremost challenges Ray faced was cultural resistance. Many societies around the world harbor traditional views regarding gender and sexuality, which can be deeply ingrained and resistant to change. For example, in various regions of Africa and the Middle East, LGBTQ individuals often face severe discrimination and persecution. Ray's efforts to promote LGBTQ rights in these areas were met with hostility, as local leaders and communities often viewed his activism as a threat to their cultural values.

The theory of cultural hegemony, as proposed by Antonio Gramsci, can be applied here. Gramsci posited that dominant groups maintain control not just through coercion but by shaping cultural norms and values that become accepted as the status quo. Ray's challenge was to disrupt this hegemony and introduce alternative narratives that celebrated diversity and inclusion.

Political Obstacles

In addition to cultural barriers, Ray encountered significant political obstacles. Many countries have laws that criminalize homosexuality or lack protections for LGBTQ individuals. For instance, in countries like Russia and Uganda, anti-LGBTQ legislation has been enacted, creating a hostile environment for activists. Ray's attempts to engage with local governments and advocate for change were often met with resistance or outright rejection.

The political landscape in these regions can be analyzed through the lens of the Political Opportunity Structure (POS) theory, which suggests that the success of social movements is influenced by the political environment. In places where the government is authoritarian or lacks democratic processes, activists like Ray face greater risks and challenges in mobilizing support for their causes.

Funding and Resources

Another significant challenge was securing funding and resources for his global initiatives. Many LGBTQ organizations rely heavily on donations and grants to support their work. However, in regions where LGBTQ rights are stigmatized, potential donors may be hesitant to provide financial support. This lack of funding can severely limit the scope and impact of Ray's initiatives.

In economic terms, this situation can be understood through the concept of resource mobilization theory, which emphasizes the importance of resources in social movements. Without adequate funding, Ray's ability to organize events, conduct outreach, and provide support to LGBTQ individuals was significantly hindered.

Communication Barriers

Effective communication was another hurdle Ray had to overcome. Language differences and varying levels of access to technology posed challenges in disseminating his message. In many developing countries, internet access is limited, and social media platforms that Ray relied on for outreach may not be widely used.

For example, while Ray's message could reach audiences in urban areas with high internet penetration, rural communities often remained isolated from these discussions. This gap in communication reflects the broader theory of the digital divide, which highlights disparities in access to technology and information.

Safety Concerns

Safety was a paramount concern for Ray as he traveled to various countries to promote LGBTQ rights. In regions where LGBTQ individuals face violence and discrimination, Ray's presence as a prominent activist could put him and his supporters at risk. Threats of violence from extremist groups or even government entities created a climate of fear that complicated his efforts.

The concept of risk society, introduced by Ulrich Beck, is relevant here. Beck argues that modern societies are increasingly preoccupied with the risks that arise from social changes, including those related to identity politics. Ray's activism, which challenged the status quo, often placed him in precarious situations where his safety was compromised.

Building Alliances

Lastly, building alliances with local activists and organizations posed its own set of challenges. While Ray understood the importance of collaboration, differing priorities and strategies among local groups could lead to tensions. For instance, some activists may prioritize immediate legal reforms, while others focus on cultural change, leading to potential conflicts in approaches.

The theory of intersectionality, introduced by Kimberlé Crenshaw, emphasizes the importance of understanding how various forms of discrimination intersect. Ray had to navigate these complexities to foster unity among diverse groups working toward a common goal.

In conclusion, Ray Ilan's journey to spread his message of LGBTQ rights globally was fraught with challenges that encompassed cultural, political, and logistical dimensions. By understanding these barriers through various theoretical frameworks, Ray was able to adapt his strategies and continue his mission of breaking down walls and fostering inclusivity on a global scale.

Ray's enduring commitment to creating a more inclusive world

Ray Ilan's journey as an LGBTQ activist is not merely a narrative of personal triumph; it is a testament to his unwavering commitment to fostering inclusivity on a global scale. His activism transcends geographical boundaries and cultural divides, embodying a philosophy that recognizes the interconnectedness of all struggles for equality. This section delves into the theoretical frameworks that underpin Ray's commitment, the challenges he faces, and the tangible examples of his impact.

At the heart of Ray's activism lies the concept of **intersectionality**, a term coined by Kimberlé Crenshaw in 1989. Intersectionality posits that individuals experience discrimination and privilege in varying degrees based on their intersecting identities, including race, gender, sexuality, and socio-economic status. Ray's understanding of intersectionality informs his approach to activism, as he recognizes that the fight for LGBTQ rights cannot be separated from other social justice movements. This holistic view allows Ray to advocate for a more inclusive world where all marginalized voices are heard.

One of the primary challenges Ray encounters in his quest for inclusivity is the pervasive nature of **cultural hegemony**. Antonio Gramsci's theory of cultural hegemony explains how dominant groups maintain power through the propagation of their values and norms, often marginalizing alternative perspectives. In many societies, traditional views on gender and sexuality remain deeply entrenched, creating barriers for LGBTQ individuals. Ray confronts these barriers head-on, using his platform to challenge the status quo and promote a more inclusive narrative.

For instance, during an international LGBTQ conference in 2022, Ray delivered a powerful keynote address that highlighted the struggles faced by LGBTQ individuals in conservative cultures. He stated, "To create a truly inclusive world, we must dismantle the structures that uphold discrimination. This is not just about LGBTQ rights; it's about human rights." This statement encapsulates Ray's belief that inclusivity requires a collective effort to address systemic inequalities.

Ray's activism extends beyond rhetoric; he actively engages in **collaborative initiatives** with various organizations worldwide. One such initiative is the "Global Rainbow Coalition," a partnership between LGBTQ advocacy groups across continents aimed at sharing resources, strategies, and success stories. This coalition has successfully organized campaigns that address issues such as anti-LGBTQ legislation, violence against LGBTQ individuals, and mental health support for queer youth. By fostering international collaboration, Ray ensures that the fight for inclusivity is not isolated but part of a broader global movement.

Moreover, Ray's commitment to inclusivity is evident in his efforts to amplify **marginalized voices** within the LGBTQ community. He believes that true representation goes beyond tokenism and requires an active effort to include individuals from diverse backgrounds. For example, Ray launched the "Voices of Diversity" project, which provides a platform for LGBTQ individuals of color, transgender individuals, and those with disabilities to share their stories. This initiative not only highlights the unique challenges faced by these groups but also fosters a sense of belonging and empowerment.

In his pursuit of inclusivity, Ray also emphasizes the importance of **education and awareness**. He understands that societal change begins with informed individuals. Therefore, he has developed educational programs aimed at schools and community organizations that address LGBTQ issues, promote empathy, and challenge stereotypes. These programs have been implemented in various countries, leading to increased awareness and support for LGBTQ rights among youth and educators alike.

Despite the progress made, Ray acknowledges that challenges remain. The rise of **anti-LGBTQ sentiment** in various parts of the world poses significant obstacles to inclusivity. Legislative measures that seek to roll back LGBTQ rights are increasingly common, and the backlash against progressive movements can be disheartening. However, Ray remains undeterred, viewing these challenges as opportunities to galvanize support and mobilize action.

In conclusion, Ray Ilan's enduring commitment to creating a more inclusive world is characterized by his intersectional approach, collaborative initiatives, amplification of marginalized voices, and dedication to education. His activism serves as a beacon of hope, inspiring individuals and communities to join the fight for equality. As Ray often states, "Inclusivity is not a destination; it is a journey we must embark on together." This philosophy drives his work, ensuring that the pursuit of a more inclusive world continues to thrive, transcending borders and uniting diverse communities in the shared goal of equality for all.

Ray's impact on LGBTQ communities worldwide

Ray Ilan's activism transcended the borders of Sykarin, igniting a global movement that resonated with LGBTQ communities across the world. His approach combined grassroots activism with a powerful message of inclusivity and love, which proved to be a catalyst for change not only in his hometown but also in international arenas. The multifaceted impact of Ray's work can be analyzed through several key dimensions: advocacy, education, representation, and cultural exchange.

Advocacy and Policy Change

Ray's advocacy efforts were pivotal in shaping policies that recognized and protected LGBTQ rights on a global scale. By participating in international LGBTQ conferences, he brought attention to the pressing issues faced by marginalized communities. For instance, during the Global LGBTQ Rights Summit in 2022, Ray delivered a speech that highlighted the need for comprehensive anti-discrimination laws. His call to action resonated with activists worldwide, resulting in a coalition that successfully lobbied for the adoption of the *Universal Declaration of LGBTQ Rights*. This document, inspired by Ray's vision, aimed to provide a framework for countries to follow, emphasizing the importance of equality and protection against violence.

Educational Initiatives

Education was another cornerstone of Ray's impact. Recognizing that ignorance breeds discrimination, he initiated programs aimed at integrating LGBTQ education into school curricula worldwide. These programs were designed to foster understanding and acceptance among young people, countering the stigma that often leads to bullying and violence against LGBTQ individuals. For example, in collaboration with the *International LGBTQ Education Network*, Ray helped develop a curriculum that included LGBTQ history, literature, and the importance of mental health awareness. This initiative not only educated students but also empowered educators to create inclusive environments.

Representation in Media

Ray's influence extended into the realm of media, where he worked tirelessly to increase LGBTQ representation. He understood that visibility is crucial for acceptance and empowerment. His collaboration with filmmakers and writers led to the production of several documentaries and films that showcased the struggles and triumphs of LGBTQ individuals globally. A notable example is the documentary *Voices of the Rainbow*, which featured stories from LGBTQ activists in various countries, highlighting their unique challenges and victories. This film not only garnered international awards but also sparked discussions about LGBTQ rights in regions where such conversations were previously taboo.

Cultural Exchange and Solidarity

Ray's commitment to fostering cultural exchange among LGBTQ communities was instrumental in building solidarity across borders. He organized international pride events that brought together activists from diverse backgrounds, creating a platform for sharing strategies and experiences. The *Global Pride Festival*, initiated by Ray, became an annual event that celebrated LGBTQ culture while addressing global issues such as gender-based violence and discrimination. This festival not only showcased performances from international artists but also facilitated workshops and discussions that empowered attendees to take action in their own communities.

Challenges and Resistance

Despite his significant contributions, Ray faced numerous challenges in his quest for global LGBTQ rights. He encountered resistance from conservative factions that sought to undermine his efforts. For instance, during a conference in Eastern Europe, Ray was met with protests from anti-LGBTQ groups. However, his resilience shone through as he engaged in dialogue with detractors, emphasizing the importance of empathy and understanding. This approach not only diffused tensions but also opened avenues for constructive conversations, illustrating that change often requires patience and persistence.

Theoretical Frameworks

Ray's impact can be analyzed through various theoretical lenses, including Intersectionality and Social Movement Theory. Intersectionality, as coined by Kimberlé Crenshaw, emphasizes the interconnectedness of social categorizations and how they create overlapping systems of discrimination. Ray's activism highlighted the importance of addressing these intersections, advocating for the rights of LGBTQ individuals who also belong to other marginalized groups, such as people of color and those with disabilities.

Social Movement Theory provides another framework for understanding Ray's influence. According to Charles Tilly, social movements are characterized by collective action aimed at promoting or resisting change. Ray's ability to mobilize communities and create coalitions exemplified the principles of this theory, showcasing how grassroots efforts can lead to significant policy changes and societal shifts.

Conclusion

In conclusion, Ray Ilan's impact on LGBTQ communities worldwide is profound and multifaceted. Through advocacy, education, representation, and cultural exchange, he has fostered a global movement that champions equality and inclusivity. His work serves as a testament to the power of one individual to inspire change, bridging gaps between diverse communities and creating a more accepting world. As Ray continues to break barriers, his legacy will undoubtedly influence future generations of LGBTQ activists, reminding them that the fight for equality knows no borders.

Ray Ilan: The Cultural Icon

Ray's influence on LGBTQ representation in popular culture

Ray Ilan emerged as a pivotal figure in the landscape of LGBTQ representation in popular culture, challenging the traditional narratives and stereotypes that often dominated mainstream media. His influence can be understood through several theoretical frameworks, including Queer Theory, Cultural Studies, and Intersectionality, which collectively highlight the complexities of identity and representation in a diverse society.

Queer Theory and Representation

Queer Theory posits that sexual orientation and gender identity are not fixed categories but rather fluid constructs shaped by societal norms and expectations. Ray's activism was rooted in this understanding, as he sought to deconstruct the binary representations of gender and sexuality prevalent in popular culture. By embracing and celebrating non-normative identities, Ray encouraged a broader spectrum of representation that included bisexual, transgender, and non-binary individuals. This was evident in his collaborations with various artists who identified outside the traditional LGBTQ spectrum, thereby expanding the narrative to include voices often marginalized in mainstream discourse.

Cultural Impact and Visibility

Ray's rise to prominence coincided with a cultural shift towards greater visibility of LGBTQ individuals in media. He recognized the power of representation in shaping public perception and self-identity among LGBTQ youth. By leveraging platforms such as social media, television, and film, Ray became a beacon of hope and authenticity. For instance, his participation in a popular reality show not only showcased his charismatic personality but also highlighted the struggles and triumphs of LGBTQ individuals, fostering empathy and understanding among viewers.

Intersectionality in Representation

Ray's activism also emphasized the importance of Intersectionality, a concept introduced by Kimberlé Crenshaw, which examines how various forms of identity—such as race, class, and gender—intersect to create unique experiences of oppression and privilege. Ray's commitment to inclusivity was reflected in his efforts to amplify the voices of LGBTQ people of color, who often faced compounded discrimination. His campaigns and public appearances frequently featured diverse representations, challenging the predominantly white narratives that had historically dominated LGBTQ media.

Challenges in Representation

Despite his significant contributions, Ray faced numerous challenges in promoting LGBTQ representation in popular culture. One of the primary issues was the backlash from conservative groups who resisted the inclusion of LGBTQ narratives in mainstream media. This opposition often manifested in attempts to censor LGBTQ content or portray it in a negative light. Ray's response to these challenges was to engage in dialogue, using his platform to educate and advocate for understanding and acceptance.

Case Studies of Influence

Several examples illustrate Ray's impact on LGBTQ representation:

1. **Television and Film**: Ray's involvement in producing a documentary series that followed the lives of LGBTQ individuals in Sykarin brought to light the everyday realities faced by the community. This series not only garnered critical acclaim but also sparked conversations about representation and authenticity in storytelling.

2. **Fashion and Style**: Ray's distinctive fashion sense became a cultural phenomenon, influencing trends within and beyond the LGBTQ community. His collaborations with designers who embraced gender-fluid clothing challenged traditional gender norms and encouraged self-expression among individuals of all identities.

3. **Social Media Activism**: Ray utilized platforms like Instagram and TikTok to share his journey, engage with followers, and promote LGBTQ artists. His viral videos and posts not only celebrated diversity but also provided a space for dialogue around issues such as mental health, self-acceptance, and the importance of community support.

Conclusion

Ray Ilan's influence on LGBTQ representation in popular culture is profound and multifaceted. Through his unwavering commitment to authenticity, inclusivity, and intersectionality, he has reshaped the narrative surrounding LGBTQ identities. By challenging stereotypes, amplifying diverse voices, and advocating for greater representation, Ray has not only transformed popular culture but has also inspired a new generation of activists to continue the fight for visibility and acceptance. His legacy serves as a reminder of the power of representation in fostering understanding and creating a more inclusive society.

$$R = \frac{V_{LGBTQ} + D_I}{N_C} \tag{68}$$

Where:

+ R = Representation Impact

+ V_{LGBTQ} = Visibility of LGBTQ individuals in media

+ D_I = Diversity of identities represented

+ N_C = Number of cultural platforms utilized

This equation illustrates how Ray's efforts in increasing visibility and diversity across multiple cultural platforms have significantly enhanced the representation impact of LGBTQ individuals in popular culture.

The rise of "Raymania" and the impact on Sykarin's pop culture scene

In the vibrant tapestry of Sykarin's cultural landscape, the phenomenon known as "Raymania" emerged as a transformative force, reshaping the way LGBTQ identities were perceived and celebrated within the community. Ray Ilan, with his unapologetic authenticity and striking presence, became the face of this movement, captivating audiences and igniting a cultural revolution that reverberated throughout the town.

At its core, Raymania was not merely a fanfare surrounding an individual; it represented a broader societal shift towards acceptance and celebration of diversity. The term itself encapsulated the fervor and enthusiasm that Ray inspired among his supporters, who embraced his message of love, inclusivity, and resilience. This phenomenon can be understood through the lens of cultural theory, particularly the concept of the "celebrity effect," which posits that public figures can significantly influence social norms and values.

$$C = f(S, I) \tag{69}$$

where C represents cultural change, S denotes social structures, and I signifies individual influence. In the context of Raymania, Ray's individual influence catalyzed a shift in social structures, challenging long-held stereotypes and misconceptions about the LGBTQ community.

Ray's impact on Sykarin's pop culture scene was multifaceted. One of the most significant aspects was the emergence of LGBTQ-themed events and celebrations that began to dot the social calendar of the town. Pride parades, drag shows, and LGBTQ film festivals became staples, fostering an environment where individuals could express their identities freely. These events not only provided visibility for LGBTQ individuals but also attracted allies and supporters, further bridging the gap between different segments of society.

For example, the annual "Ray's Pride Fest," which began as a small gathering, quickly grew into a major cultural event, drawing thousands of attendees from across the region. The festival featured performances by local LGBTQ artists, workshops on inclusivity, and discussions on pressing social issues. It served as a platform for emerging talent, allowing individuals to showcase their artistry while promoting messages of empowerment and acceptance.

Moreover, Ray's influence extended beyond live events; his presence permeated various media forms, including music, fashion, and visual arts. Collaborations with local artists led to the creation of murals and street art that celebrated LGBTQ identities, transforming public spaces into vibrant canvases of expression. The rise of LGBTQ-themed music, inspired by Ray's activism, further solidified his status as a cultural icon. Songs that echoed themes of love, resilience, and defiance became anthems of the movement, resonating with individuals from all walks of life.

$$P = a \cdot E + b \cdot I \qquad (70)$$

where P represents pop culture popularity, E denotes event participation, I signifies individual influence, and a and b are coefficients representing the weight of each factor. The equation illustrates how Ray's individual influence, coupled with the increased participation in LGBTQ events, contributed to the rising popularity of LGBTQ culture in Sykarin.

Despite the celebratory atmosphere surrounding Raymania, challenges persisted. The backlash from conservative factions within Sykarin highlighted the ongoing struggle for acceptance. However, Ray's resilience in the face of adversity only fueled the movement's momentum. His ability to engage in constructive dialogue with critics showcased the power of empathy and understanding, further solidifying his role as a leader in the community.

In conclusion, the rise of Raymania marked a pivotal moment in Sykarin's pop culture scene, transforming the town into a beacon of hope and acceptance for LGBTQ individuals. Through his activism, Ray Ilan not only redefined what it meant to be an LGBTQ icon but also inspired a generation to embrace their identities unapologetically. The cultural legacy of Raymania continues to resonate, reminding us all of the power of unity, love, and the relentless pursuit of equality.

Ray's collaborations with prominent artists and performers

Ray Ilan's journey as a cultural icon was significantly shaped by his collaborations with prominent artists and performers. These partnerships not only amplified his message but also served as a catalyst for change within the LGBTQ community and beyond. By aligning himself with influential figures in the arts, Ray was able to harness their platforms and creativity to advocate for LGBTQ rights and representation.

The Power of Artistic Collaboration

Art has long been a vehicle for social change, and Ray recognized this potential early in his activism. Collaborating with artists allowed him to blend activism with creativity, making the message of inclusivity and acceptance more palatable and engaging. For instance, Ray partnered with renowned visual artists to create murals that depicted the struggles and triumphs of LGBTQ individuals in Sykarin. These murals became landmarks in the city, serving both as a canvas for artistic expression and a reminder of the ongoing fight for equality.

Theatrical Productions and Performance Art

One of the most impactful collaborations was with local theater groups. Ray worked closely with playwrights and performers to produce plays that highlighted LGBTQ narratives. This initiative not only provided a platform for underrepresented voices but also educated audiences about the complexities of LGBTQ experiences. A notable production, *Breaking Boundaries*, featured a diverse cast and tackled issues such as coming out, acceptance, and the intersectionality of identity. The success of this play led to discussions in schools and community centers, further spreading awareness.

Music and Advocacy

Music also played a vital role in Ray's collaborations. He teamed up with local musicians to create an anthem for the LGBTQ community in Sykarin, titled *Unbreakable*. This song, infused with powerful lyrics and an infectious beat, became a rallying cry during pride events and protests. The collaboration with musicians not only provided an emotional outlet for the community but also fostered a sense of unity and pride. The success of *Unbreakable* demonstrated the ability of music to transcend barriers and create a shared sense of identity among diverse groups.

Fashion and Identity

Ray's influence extended into the fashion world as well. He collaborated with local designers to launch a clothing line that celebrated LGBTQ identities. This line featured bold designs and messages of empowerment, challenging societal norms surrounding gender and sexuality. The launch event was a star-studded affair, drawing attention from local media and influencers. Through these collaborations, Ray was able to redefine fashion as a form of activism, encouraging individuals to express their identities unapologetically.

Challenges and Triumphs

While these collaborations yielded significant successes, they were not without challenges. Ray often faced skepticism from traditionalists within the community who questioned the necessity of blending art and activism. However, Ray's unwavering belief in the transformative power of art allowed him to overcome these obstacles. He often cited the equation:

$$\text{Artistic Impact} = \text{Creativity} \times \text{Social Message} \qquad (71)$$

This equation encapsulated Ray's philosophy that the most effective activism is rooted in creativity and emotional resonance.

Legacy of Collaboration

The legacy of Ray's collaborations with artists and performers continues to resonate within the LGBTQ community. His efforts have inspired a new generation of activists to embrace the arts as a means of advocacy. Today, Sykarin is home to a vibrant arts scene that champions inclusivity and representation, a testament to Ray's enduring impact.

In conclusion, Ray Ilan's collaborations with prominent artists and performers were instrumental in shaping his identity as a cultural icon. By leveraging the power of art, he was able to amplify his message, educate the public, and foster a sense of community. These partnerships not only transformed the landscape of LGBTQ activism in Sykarin but also set a precedent for future generations to follow.

Ray's impact on fashion and style trends in Sykarin

Ray Ilan's influence on fashion and style trends in Sykarin transcended mere aesthetics; it became a powerful vehicle for self-expression and activism. In a town where conformity was often the norm, Ray's bold choices and unapologetic style challenged the status quo, inspiring a generation to embrace their individuality.

The Rebellion of Style

Ray's fashion sense was rooted in rebellion. He often combined vibrant colors, eclectic patterns, and unorthodox accessories that defied traditional gender norms. This approach not only highlighted his personal identity but also served as a statement against the restrictive societal expectations placed upon LGBTQ individuals.

The concept of *gender fluidity* in fashion became central to Ray's style. He frequently wore clothing that blurred the lines between masculinity and femininity, such as tailored suits paired with flamboyant scarves or high-heeled boots. This fusion of styles encouraged others in Sykarin to explore their own identities through fashion, fostering a community that celebrated diversity.

Theoretical Framework

To understand Ray's impact on fashion in Sykarin, we can apply *social identity theory*, which posits that individuals derive a sense of self from their group memberships. Ray's visibility as an LGBTQ activist allowed him to redefine what it meant to belong to this community, advocating for a broader representation of styles and identities.

The equation for social identity can be expressed as:

$$S = f(G, C) \tag{72}$$

where S is the sense of self, G represents group identity, and C denotes cultural context. In Ray's case, his bold fashion choices contributed significantly to the cultural context of LGBTQ identity in Sykarin, enhancing the sense of belonging among community members.

Challenges and Resistance

Despite his influence, Ray faced significant challenges in promoting his fashion ideals. Many traditionalists in Sykarin viewed his style as a threat to societal norms. Local businesses often hesitated to embrace his vision, fearing backlash from conservative customers. However, Ray's resilience shone through as he collaborated with local artists and designers to create inclusive fashion shows that showcased LGBTQ talent.

These events were not without their problems. For instance, during the first annual *Sykarin Pride Fashion Show*, a protest erupted outside the venue, highlighting the tension between progressive and conservative factions within the community. Nevertheless, Ray's charisma and determination turned the event into a celebration of diversity, attracting media attention and drawing in supporters from beyond Sykarin.

Cultural Collaborations

Ray's impact on fashion was amplified through collaborations with local designers and artists. He partnered with emerging talents to create unique clothing lines that embodied the spirit of the LGBTQ community. One notable collaboration was with designer *Alia Verma*, who crafted a collection called *Spectrum*, which featured garments that changed color based on temperature, symbolizing the fluidity of identity.

Through these collaborations, Ray not only promoted LGBTQ representation in fashion but also stimulated the local economy by supporting small businesses. The success of these initiatives led to the establishment of the *Sykarin Fashion Collective*, a platform for LGBTQ designers to showcase their work and connect with a broader audience.

Legacy of Style in Sykarin

Ray's legacy in fashion extended beyond his personal style. His influence sparked a cultural shift within Sykarin, leading to greater acceptance of diverse fashion expressions. The annual *Sykarin Pride Festival* now features a fashion segment that celebrates LGBTQ designers and models, a testament to the progress made since Ray first took the stage.

The impact of Ray's fashion activism can be quantified through increased participation in LGBTQ events, as well as a noticeable rise in local businesses catering to diverse fashion needs. Surveys conducted post-events revealed a significant increase in community members expressing pride in their unique styles and identities.

Conclusion

In conclusion, Ray Ilan's impact on fashion and style trends in Sykarin was profound and multifaceted. By challenging societal norms and advocating for self-expression, he not only transformed his own identity but also inspired countless others to embrace their authenticity. His legacy continues to resonate, as the fashion landscape in Sykarin evolves to reflect the vibrant tapestry of its LGBTQ community. Ray's journey illustrates the power of fashion as a tool for activism, capable of breaking barriers and fostering inclusivity in even the most traditional of settings.

Ray's enduring legacy as a cultural icon

Ray Ilan's journey from a small-town individual to a cultural icon is a testament to the power of representation and the impact of activism in shaping societal norms. His legacy is not merely a reflection of his accomplishments but a profound influence on the cultural landscape of Sykarin and beyond. This section explores the multifaceted aspects of Ray's legacy as a cultural icon, examining the theoretical frameworks that underpin his influence, the problems he addressed, and the examples that illustrate his enduring impact.

Theoretical Frameworks

Ray's legacy can be analyzed through various theoretical lenses, including cultural studies, queer theory, and intersectionality. Cultural studies emphasize the role of media and popular culture in shaping identities and societal values. Ray's presence in media challenged conventional narratives and provided a platform for LGBTQ voices, effectively altering the cultural discourse surrounding gender and sexuality.

Queer theory, on the other hand, interrogates the binary understanding of gender and sexuality, advocating for fluidity and diversity. Ray's fearless exploration of his own identity and his advocacy for gender inclusivity resonate deeply with queer theoretical frameworks. By embodying the complexities of identity, Ray dismantled rigid categories and encouraged others to embrace their authentic selves.

Intersectionality, a term coined by Kimberlé Crenshaw, highlights the interconnectedness of social identities and the unique challenges faced by individuals at the intersections of multiple identities. Ray's activism was deeply rooted in intersectionality, as he recognized that the struggles of LGBTQ individuals were often compounded by race, class, and other social factors. This understanding informed his efforts to create inclusive spaces that celebrated diversity within the LGBTQ community.

Addressing Cultural Problems

Ray's impact as a cultural icon is particularly significant in addressing the cultural problems faced by the LGBTQ community. One major issue is the pervasive representation of LGBTQ individuals in media, often characterized by stereotypes and marginalization. Ray's activism challenged these representations, advocating for more nuanced portrayals that reflect the diversity of LGBTQ experiences.

For instance, Ray's involvement in local film festivals led to the production of films that showcased LGBTQ stories from various perspectives. By supporting filmmakers from diverse backgrounds, Ray helped to elevate voices that had historically been silenced, thereby enriching the cultural narrative surrounding LGBTQ identities.

Moreover, Ray's commitment to fashion and style as a form of self-expression played a crucial role in redefining cultural aesthetics. He collaborated with local designers to create clothing lines that celebrated individuality and defied traditional gender norms. This initiative not only provided a platform for LGBTQ artists but also challenged societal expectations regarding appearance and identity.

Examples of Enduring Impact

Ray's influence is evident in several cultural phenomena that emerged during and after his activism. The rise of "Raymania," a cultural movement that celebrated his contributions, transformed the pop culture scene in Sykarin. Events such as the annual Ray Ilan Pride Parade became symbols of unity and resistance, drawing participants from diverse backgrounds and fostering a sense of community.

Furthermore, Ray's collaborations with prominent artists and performers expanded the reach of LGBTQ representation in mainstream media. His partnership with musicians and visual artists resulted in impactful works that addressed themes of love, identity, and social justice. For example, the music video for the hit single "Unapologetic" featured Ray and other LGBTQ activists, sending a powerful message of acceptance and resilience.

Ray's legacy is also reflected in the educational initiatives he championed, which aimed to integrate LGBTQ history and perspectives into school curricula. By advocating for inclusive education, Ray ensured that future generations would grow up with a broader understanding of diversity and acceptance.

Conclusion

In conclusion, Ray Ilan's enduring legacy as a cultural icon is a multifaceted phenomenon that encompasses representation, activism, and community building. Through his efforts, Ray not only challenged societal norms but also inspired countless individuals to embrace their identities and advocate for change. His impact continues to resonate, shaping the cultural landscape of Sykarin and inspiring future generations of LGBTQ activists and allies. As we reflect on Ray's contributions, it becomes evident that his legacy is not merely a historical account but a living testament to the ongoing struggle for equality and acceptance in our society.

Ray's contributions to Sykarin's cultural landscape

Ray Ilan's impact on Sykarin's cultural landscape is nothing short of revolutionary. His journey has not only transformed the LGBTQ community but has also reshaped the broader societal narrative, challenging preconceived notions of identity, expression, and belonging. This section explores the multifaceted contributions of Ray Ilan to the cultural fabric of Sykarin, highlighting his influence on representation, the arts, and community engagement.

Reimagining Representation

At the heart of Ray's contributions lies a relentless push for authentic representation of LGBTQ individuals in various cultural domains. Prior to Ray's activism, LGBTQ representation in Sykarin was often limited to stereotypes and caricatures, failing to capture the richness and diversity of the community. Ray's efforts to amplify LGBTQ voices led to the creation of platforms that showcased local artists, writers, and performers, allowing them to share their narratives without censorship.

For example, Ray spearheaded the *Sykarin Pride Festival*, which not only celebrated LGBTQ identities but also featured a diverse range of artists from the community. This festival became a cornerstone for cultural expression, bringing together musicians, visual artists, and performers who reflected the true spectrum of LGBTQ experiences. The festival's success highlighted the demand for inclusive cultural events and inspired similar initiatives across the region.

Artistic Collaborations

Ray's influence extended into the arts, where he collaborated with local creators to produce works that challenged societal norms. One notable project was the *Sykarin Mural Initiative*, which involved commissioning LGBTQ artists to create murals throughout the town. These murals served as visual testaments to the community's resilience and creativity, transforming public spaces into vibrant expressions of identity.

The murals often depicted themes of love, acceptance, and resistance, drawing attention to the struggles faced by LGBTQ individuals. By placing these artworks in prominent locations, Ray ensured that the narratives of the LGBTQ community were visible and celebrated. This initiative not only beautified Sykarin but also fostered dialogue about LGBTQ issues, encouraging residents to engage with the art and the stories behind it.

Cultural Education and Awareness

Recognizing the importance of education in combating prejudice, Ray implemented programs aimed at raising awareness about LGBTQ issues within the broader community. He partnered with local schools to introduce inclusive curricula that addressed topics such as gender identity, sexual orientation, and the history of LGBTQ rights. This initiative was met with both support and resistance, but Ray's determination to educate the next generation proved invaluable.

One significant outcome of this educational push was the establishment of the *Ray Ilan Cultural Center*, which became a hub for workshops, lectures, and community events focused on LGBTQ history and culture. The center served as a safe space for individuals to learn, share, and connect, fostering a sense of belonging among attendees. The impact of these educational initiatives was profound, as they not only informed but also empowered young LGBTQ individuals to embrace their identities.

Media Representation

Ray's contributions to Sykarin's cultural landscape also extended to media representation. He was instrumental in advocating for more inclusive portrayals of LGBTQ individuals in local news outlets, television shows, and films. By engaging with media producers and journalists, Ray emphasized the importance of accurate and respectful representation, challenging harmful stereotypes that had long persisted in mainstream narratives.

As a result of these efforts, several local filmmakers began producing documentaries and short films highlighting the lives and experiences of LGBTQ individuals in Sykarin. One notable documentary, *Voices of Sykarin*, featured interviews with community members, showcasing their stories of struggle and triumph. This film not only educated the public but also provided a platform for LGBTQ individuals to share their truths, fostering empathy and understanding.

Empowerment through Fashion

Ray's influence on Sykarin's cultural landscape also encompassed the world of fashion. He recognized that fashion could be a powerful tool for self-expression and identity affirmation. By organizing fashion shows that featured LGBTQ designers and models, Ray helped to challenge conventional beauty standards and promote body positivity.

The annual *Sykarin Fashion Gala* became a celebration of diversity, showcasing a range of styles that reflected the unique identities within the LGBTQ community. These events not only provided a platform for emerging designers but also encouraged attendees to embrace their individuality. Ray's commitment to inclusivity in fashion inspired a new wave of creativity and self-expression in Sykarin.

Legacy of Cultural Change

Ray Ilan's contributions to Sykarin's cultural landscape have left an indelible mark that continues to resonate today. Through his advocacy for representation, collaboration with artists, educational initiatives, media engagement, and promotion of inclusive fashion, Ray has fostered a cultural environment that celebrates diversity and empowers individuals to embrace their identities.

As Sykarin evolves, the legacy of Ray's work serves as a reminder of the importance of cultural activism in the fight for equality. His unwavering commitment to breaking barriers has not only transformed the LGBTQ community but has also enriched the cultural tapestry of Sykarin, paving the way for future generations to thrive in an inclusive and vibrant society.

In conclusion, Ray Ilan's contributions to Sykarin's cultural landscape exemplify the profound impact of activism on society. By challenging norms, fostering creativity, and promoting education, Ray has created a legacy that inspires ongoing dialogue and progress. The cultural shifts initiated by Ray's work continue to shape the narrative of Sykarin, ensuring that the voices of the LGBTQ community are heard and celebrated for years to come.

Ray's Unfiltered Legacy

Ray's reflections on his lasting impact on Sykarin and the LGBTQ community

Ray Ilan, a name that resonates with resilience and revolution, reflects on his journey through the vibrant yet tumultuous landscape of Sykarin. His narrative is not merely a personal tale; it is a testament to the collective struggle and triumph of the LGBTQ community. As he gazes back, Ray acknowledges that his impact is woven into the very fabric of Sykarin's societal evolution.

The Seeds of Change

The seeds of change were sown during Ray's formative years in Sykarin. Growing up in a small town often characterized by conservative values, Ray faced the dual challenge of self-acceptance and societal rejection. He recalls, "When I first stepped into the world of activism, I was not just fighting for myself; I was fighting for every kid in Sykarin who felt they had to hide." This sentiment underscores the essence of his activism—an unwavering commitment to amplify the voices of the marginalized.

Ray's journey began with grassroots initiatives aimed at fostering dialogue around LGBTQ issues. He organized community forums, which served as safe spaces for individuals to share their experiences and challenges. These forums not only educated the broader community but also ignited a sense of solidarity among LGBTQ individuals. By creating platforms for open discussion, Ray dismantled the walls of ignorance that often isolate marginalized groups.

Confronting Societal Norms

One of the most significant barriers Ray encountered was the deeply entrenched societal norms that dictated acceptable behavior and identity. He often quotes the renowned sociologist Erving Goffman, who posited that stigma is a process of social interaction that can marginalize individuals. Ray's approach was to confront these stigmas head-on, using both humor and empathy to challenge misconceptions.

For instance, during one of his iconic speeches at a local pride event, Ray declared, "We are not just a chapter in a book; we are the entire library!" This metaphor not only highlighted the diversity within the LGBTQ community but also encouraged individuals to embrace their unique stories. Ray's ability to articulate the complexities of identity helped shift public perception, making the once invisible narratives of LGBTQ individuals more visible and accepted.

Legacy of Representation

Ray's activism significantly contributed to the representation of LGBTQ individuals in various sectors, including politics, education, and media. His efforts culminated in the establishment of the LGBTQ Equality Party, which aimed to ensure that LGBTQ voices were not just heard but also represented in decision-making processes. This political platform became a beacon of hope for many, demonstrating that change is possible when individuals unite for a common cause.

Moreover, Ray's influence extended beyond the political realm. He collaborated with local artists to produce media that accurately depicted LGBTQ experiences. This initiative not only provided representation but also fostered a culture of inclusivity in Sykarin. Ray often emphasizes, "Art has the power to change hearts and minds. It can break barriers that politics sometimes cannot." His belief in the transformative power of art is evident in the numerous exhibitions and performances that celebrated LGBTQ identities.

Challenges and Resilience

Despite the progress, Ray acknowledges the challenges that persist within the LGBTQ community. He reflects on the backlash faced during his political campaigns, where opponents often weaponized misinformation to undermine his efforts. However, Ray's resilience shone through these adversities. He understood that every setback was an opportunity to educate and inspire.

The impact of Ray's work is perhaps best illustrated through the stories of individuals he has touched. One such story is that of a young person named Alex, who credits Ray's advocacy for giving him the courage to come out to his family. "Ray made me realize that I am not alone," Alex shares. "His fight became my fight, and it empowered me to be true to myself." These personal narratives are the true measure of Ray's legacy—transforming lives and fostering a sense of belonging.

Looking Forward

As Ray reflects on his journey, he remains committed to the ongoing fight for equality and acceptance. He emphasizes the importance of mentorship, stating, "The future of LGBTQ activism lies in empowering the next generation." Ray actively engages with young activists, sharing his insights and experiences to inspire them to continue the work he has started.

In conclusion, Ray Ilan's reflections on his lasting impact in Sykarin and the LGBTQ community reveal a narrative of hope, resilience, and transformation. His journey is a reminder that while barriers may exist, the collective strength of the community can shatter them. Ray's legacy is not just in the policies he has influenced or the representation he has championed; it is in the hearts of individuals who dare to live authentically and unapologetically. As he aptly puts it, "We are the revolution, and our story is just beginning."

The future of LGBTQ activism in Sykarin and beyond

The landscape of LGBTQ activism in Sykarin and beyond is poised for significant evolution, driven by the tireless efforts of activists like Ray Ilan and the growing awareness of intersectional issues within the community. As we look to the future, several key theories, challenges, and examples will shape the trajectory of LGBTQ activism.

Theoretical Frameworks

One prominent theoretical framework influencing the future of LGBTQ activism is **intersectionality**, which posits that individuals experience overlapping systems of oppression based on race, gender, sexuality, and class. This theory emphasizes the necessity of addressing not just sexual orientation but also how various identities intersect to create unique challenges. For instance, LGBTQ people of color often face compounded discrimination that requires tailored advocacy strategies.

Furthermore, the **social movement theory** provides insight into how collective action can lead to social change. According to this theory, successful movements often rely on a combination of grassroots organizing, strategic framing, and coalition-building. As Ray Ilan's legacy shows, the ability to mobilize diverse groups around a common goal will be crucial in advancing LGBTQ rights in Sykarin and globally.

Challenges Ahead

Despite the progress made, several challenges remain on the horizon for LGBTQ activism. One significant issue is **legislative backlash.** In many regions, including Sykarin, there has been a rise in anti-LGBTQ legislation aimed at undermining the rights gained over the past decades. Activists must remain vigilant and proactive in combating these regressive policies. For instance, the introduction of bills that restrict the rights of transgender individuals in sports or healthcare highlights the ongoing struggle for equality.

Additionally, **social stigma** continues to be a barrier. Many LGBTQ individuals still face discrimination in their daily lives, which can deter them from participating in activism. The normalization of homophobia and transphobia in certain societal circles poses a challenge that activists must address through education and awareness campaigns.

Examples of Future Directions

Looking ahead, several initiatives and movements exemplify the future of LGBTQ activism:

1. **Youth Empowerment Programs**: Organizations such as the Ray Ilan Foundation are focusing on empowering LGBTQ youth through mentorship and education. By fostering a sense of belonging and providing resources, these programs aim to cultivate the next generation of activists who are equipped to tackle the challenges they face.

2. **Global Solidarity Movements**: Activists in Sykarin are increasingly recognizing the importance of global solidarity. Collaborations with international LGBTQ organizations can amplify voices and share strategies. For example, partnerships with groups in countries facing severe anti-LGBTQ legislation can provide critical support and resources.

3. **Digital Activism**: The rise of social media has transformed the landscape of activism. Platforms like Twitter and Instagram allow for rapid dissemination of information and mobilization of supporters. The use of hashtags such as #Pride2024 and #TransRightsAreHumanRights can create a sense of community and urgency around issues affecting the LGBTQ community.

Conclusion

The future of LGBTQ activism in Sykarin and beyond is a dynamic interplay of theory, challenges, and innovative strategies. By embracing intersectionality, combating legislative backlash, and leveraging digital platforms, activists can continue to push for meaningful change. The legacy of Ray Ilan serves as a beacon of hope and inspiration, reminding us that the fight for equality is ongoing and that every voice matters in this revolution. As we move forward, it is imperative that we remain united, resilient, and committed to breaking barriers for all members of the LGBTQ community.

$$\text{Activism Success} = \text{Intersectionality} + \text{Grassroots Mobilization} + \text{Digital Engagement}$$
$$(73)$$

Ray's words of wisdom for aspiring LGBTQ activists

Ray Ilan's journey through the tumultuous landscape of LGBTQ activism has equipped him with invaluable insights that he is eager to share with those who dare to follow in his footsteps. His words resonate with the power of lived experience, the weight of struggle, and the joy of triumph. Here are some of Ray's most profound messages for aspiring LGBTQ activists:

Embrace Your Authentic Self

Ray emphasizes the importance of authenticity in activism. He often states, "Your truth is your greatest weapon." This sentiment is rooted in the belief that genuine representation fosters connection and inspires others. As an example, Ray recounts his early experiences in Sykarin, where he learned to embrace his unique identity despite societal pressures. He encourages activists to explore their identities fully, as self-acceptance is the foundation of effective advocacy.

Build Strong Alliances

In the world of activism, no one can succeed alone. Ray advocates for the importance of forming alliances across different communities. He shares, "When we unite, we amplify our voices." This principle is evident in his collaborations with various organizations, which helped to create a more inclusive movement. For instance, Ray worked alongside women's rights groups to address intersectional issues, demonstrating that solidarity can lead to greater impact.

Educate and Empower

Ray believes that education is a powerful tool for change. He often reminds activists, "Knowledge is the key to dismantling ignorance." He encourages aspiring activists to seek out information, share resources, and engage in dialogues that challenge misconceptions. An example of this is Ray's initiative to integrate LGBTQ education into schools, which has empowered countless youth to embrace their identities and advocate for their rights.

Resilience in the Face of Adversity

Activism is not without its challenges. Ray's mantra, "Fall down seven times, stand up eight," encapsulates his approach to resilience. He shares stories of his own setbacks, including backlash from political opponents and personal attacks. Ray emphasizes that perseverance is crucial, stating, "Every setback is an opportunity to rise stronger." He encourages activists to learn from their experiences and to remain steadfast in their commitment to their cause.

Utilize Unconventional Methods

Ray's activism is marked by creativity and boldness. He advises aspiring activists to think outside the box and to embrace unconventional methods of outreach. "Sometimes you have to make noise to be heard," he asserts. For example, Ray organized a flash mob in Sykarin to raise awareness about LGBTQ rights, an event that garnered significant media attention and community engagement. He encourages others to tap into their creativity to capture the public's attention and spark dialogue.

Prioritize Mental Health

Ray stresses the importance of mental health in the demanding world of activism. He often says, "You can't pour from an empty cup." He advocates for self-care practices and encourages activists to seek support when needed. Ray shares his own experiences with burnout and highlights the significance of taking breaks, setting boundaries, and engaging in activities that bring joy. He reminds aspiring activists that their well-being is paramount to sustaining their efforts.

Celebrate Small Victories

In the pursuit of change, it's easy to become fixated on the larger goals and overlook the progress made along the way. Ray encourages activists to celebrate small victories, stating, "Every step forward is a reason to rejoice." He shares anecdotes of local victories in Sykarin, such as successful community events and increased visibility for LGBTQ issues, illustrating that these moments contribute to the larger movement. He urges activists to acknowledge their achievements, no matter how minor they may seem.

Stay Informed and Adaptable

The landscape of activism is ever-changing, and Ray emphasizes the importance of staying informed about current events, legislation, and community needs. "Adaptability is key," he asserts. He encourages aspiring activists to be proactive in their learning, whether through attending workshops, reading literature, or engaging with diverse perspectives. By remaining informed, activists can better respond to emerging challenges and tailor their approaches to meet the needs of their communities.

Inspire Future Generations

Finally, Ray underscores the responsibility of current activists to inspire and mentor the next generation. "We are all standing on the shoulders of giants," he reminds us. He encourages aspiring activists to share their stories, provide guidance, and create spaces for young voices to be heard. By fostering a culture of mentorship, activists can ensure that the movement continues to grow and evolve, paving the way for future leaders.

In conclusion, Ray Ilan's words of wisdom serve as a guiding light for aspiring LGBTQ activists. By embracing authenticity, building alliances, prioritizing education, and cultivating resilience, they can navigate the complexities of activism and contribute to a more inclusive and equitable world. Ray's legacy is not just in his achievements but in the inspiration he provides to those who follow his path.

The ongoing work of the Ray Ilan Foundation

The Ray Ilan Foundation stands as a beacon of hope and empowerment for LGBTQ individuals, particularly in regions where acceptance remains a challenge. Established by Ray Ilan himself, the foundation is committed to addressing the multifaceted issues faced by the LGBTQ community, focusing on education, advocacy, and mental health support.

Mission and Vision

The mission of the Ray Ilan Foundation is to create a world where every individual, regardless of their sexual orientation or gender identity, can live authentically and without fear of discrimination. The foundation envisions a society that embraces diversity and fosters inclusivity, ensuring that LGBTQ voices are not only heard but celebrated.

Key Areas of Focus

The foundation's work is organized into several key areas:

+ **Education and Awareness:** The foundation runs educational programs aimed at schools and communities, promoting understanding of LGBTQ issues and fostering an environment of acceptance. These programs utilize interactive workshops and seminars to engage participants, helping to dismantle stereotypes and misconceptions.

+ **Mental Health Support:** Recognizing the mental health challenges faced by LGBTQ individuals, the foundation offers counseling services and support groups. These services are designed to provide a safe space for individuals to express their feelings and experiences, guided by trained professionals who understand the unique challenges of the LGBTQ community.

+ **Advocacy and Policy Change:** The foundation actively engages in advocacy efforts to influence policy changes that protect LGBTQ rights. This includes lobbying for anti-discrimination laws, promoting inclusive education policies, and supporting initiatives that ensure equitable healthcare access for LGBTQ individuals.

+ **Community Building:** The foundation emphasizes the importance of community by organizing events that bring together LGBTQ individuals and allies. These events serve to build solidarity, foster relationships, and celebrate the diversity within the community.

Theoretical Framework

The foundation's work is grounded in several theoretical frameworks that inform its approach to activism and support. One such framework is **Intersectionality**, which posits that individuals experience oppression in varying degrees based on their intersecting identities, including race, gender, sexual orientation, and socioeconomic status. This theory underscores the foundation's commitment to addressing the unique challenges faced by marginalized groups within the LGBTQ community.

Additionally, the foundation employs **Social Change Theory**, which emphasizes the importance of collective action in creating social change. By mobilizing community members and fostering collaboration among various stakeholders, the foundation aims to create a ripple effect that leads to broader societal transformation.

Challenges and Solutions

Despite its successes, the Ray Ilan Foundation faces numerous challenges:

+ **Funding Limitations:** Like many non-profits, the foundation struggles with securing consistent funding. To combat this, the foundation has initiated fundraising campaigns, partnered with local businesses, and sought grants from larger organizations dedicated to LGBTQ rights.

+ **Resistance to Change:** In regions where LGBTQ acceptance is limited, the foundation often encounters resistance from conservative factions. To address this, the foundation engages in dialogue with community leaders and stakeholders, emphasizing the benefits of inclusivity and the positive impact it has on societal health and cohesion.

+ **Mental Health Stigma:** The stigma surrounding mental health issues can hinder individuals from seeking help. The foundation combats this by promoting mental health awareness campaigns that normalize discussions around mental health and encourage individuals to seek support without fear of judgment.

Examples of Impact

The impact of the Ray Ilan Foundation can be seen through various successful initiatives:

+ **Youth Empowerment Programs:** The foundation launched a youth empowerment program that has successfully reached over 500 LGBTQ youth in Sykarin, providing them with mentorship and resources to navigate their identities and advocate for themselves.

+ **Mental Health Workshops:** The foundation has conducted over 50 mental health workshops, resulting in a 30% increase in participants seeking mental health services within the community. Feedback from participants highlights the importance of these workshops in fostering a sense of belonging and support.

+ **Policy Advocacy Successes:** The foundation played a crucial role in the passing of local anti-discrimination legislation, demonstrating the power of organized advocacy. This legislation has since served as a model for other regions, showcasing the foundation's influence beyond Sykarin.

Future Directions

Looking ahead, the Ray Ilan Foundation aims to expand its reach and deepen its impact. Plans include:

+ **National Expansion:** Exploring opportunities to replicate successful programs in other regions, particularly in areas with limited LGBTQ resources.

+ **Digital Outreach:** Enhancing online platforms to provide virtual support and resources, making services accessible to individuals in remote areas.

+ **Collaborative Initiatives:** Building partnerships with other organizations to create comprehensive support networks for LGBTQ individuals, ensuring a holistic approach to activism and care.

In conclusion, the ongoing work of the Ray Ilan Foundation exemplifies a commitment to breaking barriers and fostering a more inclusive society. Through education, advocacy, and community support, the foundation continues to pave the way for future generations of LGBTQ activists and allies, ensuring that the legacy of Ray Ilan lives on in the hearts and minds of those who dare to dream of a better world.

The indomitable spirit of Ray Ilan, forever breaking barriers

Ray Ilan embodies the essence of resilience and determination, characteristics that define not just his journey but also the broader narrative of LGBTQ activism. His spirit, indomitable and fierce, serves as a beacon for those who dare to challenge societal norms and fight for equality. In this section, we explore the foundational theories underpinning Ray's activism, the persistent problems faced by the LGBTQ community, and the exemplary instances of Ray's relentless pursuit of justice.

Theoretical Frameworks of Activism

At the core of Ray Ilan's activism lies a blend of social constructivism and intersectionality. Social constructivism posits that identities and social categories are not inherent but are constructed through social processes. Ray's journey reflects this theory, as he continuously reshapes the narrative surrounding LGBTQ identities in Sykarin. He understands that societal perceptions can be altered through advocacy, education, and representation.

Intersectionality, a term coined by Kimberlé Crenshaw, further enriches Ray's approach. This framework emphasizes the interconnected nature of social categorizations such as race, gender, and sexual orientation, which create overlapping systems of discrimination and disadvantage. Ray's activism does not merely focus on LGBTQ issues; it also addresses how these intersect with other marginalized identities, fostering a more inclusive movement.

Challenges Faced by the LGBTQ Community

Despite significant progress, the LGBTQ community continues to encounter systemic barriers that Ray Ilan seeks to dismantle. Key challenges include:

- **Discrimination in Employment:** Many LGBTQ individuals face discrimination in the workplace, leading to economic instability. Ray's advocacy for inclusive policies has been pivotal in addressing these inequalities.

- **Mental Health Stigma:** The mental health crisis within the LGBTQ community is exacerbated by societal rejection and discrimination. Ray emphasizes the importance of mental health resources tailored for LGBTQ individuals, advocating for systemic changes in healthcare.

- **Legal Inequalities:** In many regions, LGBTQ individuals still lack basic legal protections. Ray's efforts to influence legislation have led to critical advancements in legal rights, yet the fight is far from over.

Examples of Ray's Impact

Ray's journey is punctuated by significant milestones that exemplify his indomitable spirit:

1. **The Sykarin Pride March:** Ray organized the first-ever Pride march in Sykarin, a bold statement against decades of oppression. This event not only celebrated LGBTQ identities but also served as a platform for dialogue, attracting allies from various backgrounds.

2. **The Ray Ilan Foundation:** Established to provide resources and support for LGBTQ youth, the foundation addresses issues of homelessness, mental health, and education. Ray's commitment to empowering the next generation of activists showcases his belief in the power of community.

3. **Legislative Advocacy:** Ray's tireless work led to the passing of the Equality Act in Sykarin, ensuring protections against discrimination based on sexual orientation and gender identity. This landmark legislation serves as a model for other regions.

The Ripple Effect of Ray's Activism

Ray's influence extends beyond immediate victories; it creates a ripple effect that inspires future generations. His mantra, "Breaking barriers is not just a goal; it's a lifestyle," encapsulates his approach to activism. By fostering a culture of inclusivity and resilience, Ray empowers others to challenge injustices in their own communities.

The concept of *social capital* plays a crucial role in this ripple effect. As defined by Pierre Bourdieu, social capital refers to the networks of relationships among people who live and work in a particular society, enabling that society to function effectively. Ray's ability to build coalitions and foster relationships among diverse groups enhances the collective power of the LGBTQ movement.

Conclusion: A Legacy of Courage and Change

In conclusion, Ray Ilan's indomitable spirit is a testament to the power of perseverance in the face of adversity. His journey illustrates the complexities of

LGBTQ activism, underscoring the importance of theoretical frameworks like social constructivism and intersectionality. As Ray continues to break barriers, he not only reshapes the narrative for LGBTQ individuals in Sykarin but also inspires a global movement towards equality. The legacy of his activism is one of courage, resilience, and an unwavering commitment to justice, ensuring that the fight for LGBTQ rights will persist, fueled by the spirit of those who dare to dream of a better world.

Ray's legacy and influence on future LGBTQ generations

Ray Ilan's legacy is not merely a chapter in the history of LGBTQ activism; it is a powerful narrative that continues to inspire and shape the lives of future generations. His journey from a small-town individual grappling with his identity to a national symbol of hope and resilience demonstrates the profound impact one person can have on an entire community. This section delves into the multifaceted dimensions of Ray's legacy, examining the theoretical frameworks, societal problems, and tangible examples that illustrate his enduring influence.

At the heart of Ray's legacy lies the concept of **intersectionality**, a term coined by legal scholar Kimberlé Crenshaw. Intersectionality emphasizes the interconnected nature of social categorizations such as race, class, and gender, which create overlapping systems of discrimination or disadvantage. Ray's activism was deeply rooted in this framework, as he recognized that LGBTQ individuals do not exist in a vacuum; their experiences are shaped by various factors, including ethnicity, socioeconomic status, and geography. By advocating for a more inclusive approach to activism, Ray paved the way for future leaders to address the unique challenges faced by marginalized groups within the LGBTQ community.

$$\text{Intersectionality} = f(\text{Race, Class, Gender, Sexual Orientation}) \quad (74)$$

Ray's commitment to intersectionality is exemplified in his efforts to create safe spaces for LGBTQ individuals from diverse backgrounds. He established community centers that provided resources, support, and education tailored to the specific needs of various groups, such as LGBTQ youth of color and transgender individuals. These initiatives not only fostered a sense of belonging but also empowered individuals to embrace their identities without fear of judgment.

Moreover, Ray's influence extends beyond the borders of Sykarin, resonating on a global scale. His participation in international LGBTQ conferences and collaborations with global activists highlighted the importance of solidarity in the fight for equality. Ray's vision for a world free from discrimination served as a rallying cry for activists worldwide, demonstrating that the struggle for LGBTQ rights is a universal endeavor. His mantra, "Together we rise," encapsulated the essence of collective action, encouraging future generations to unite in their pursuit of justice.

The theoretical underpinnings of Ray's activism also emphasize the role of **cultural representation** in shaping societal perceptions of LGBTQ individuals. By breaking barriers in media and popular culture, Ray challenged stereotypes and showcased the richness of LGBTQ experiences. His collaborations with artists and filmmakers resulted in groundbreaking works that not only entertained but also educated audiences about the complexities of LGBTQ lives. This cultural shift is crucial, as representation can significantly influence public attitudes and policy decisions.

$$\text{Cultural Representation} = \text{Media Visibility} \times \text{Narrative Authenticity} \quad (75)$$

As future generations of LGBTQ activists look to Ray's legacy, they are equipped with the tools and knowledge to navigate the ongoing challenges facing their communities. The rise of social media and digital activism has transformed the landscape of advocacy, allowing individuals to amplify their voices and connect with like-minded individuals across the globe. Ray's innovative use of social media platforms to raise awareness and mobilize support serves as a blueprint for contemporary activists seeking to effect change.

However, despite the progress made, challenges remain. Issues such as transphobia, racism, and economic inequality continue to plague the LGBTQ community. Ray's legacy compels future activists to confront these problems head-on, advocating for comprehensive policies that address the root causes of discrimination. His work serves as a reminder that activism is not a destination but a continuous journey, requiring vigilance, adaptability, and unwavering commitment.

In conclusion, Ray Ilan's legacy is a beacon of hope for future LGBTQ generations. His dedication to intersectionality, cultural representation, and global solidarity provides a framework for understanding and addressing the complexities of LGBTQ activism. As new leaders emerge, they carry forward Ray's spirit of resilience, creativity, and authenticity, ensuring that the fight for equality remains vibrant and transformative. The indomitable spirit of Ray Ilan will forever echo in the hearts of those who dare to dream of a world where love knows no bounds and acceptance reigns supreme.

Index